An Enchantment of Digital Archaeology

Digital Archaeology: Documenting the Anthropocene

Series Editor: **Andrew Reinhard** (American Numismatic Society)

The archaeology of the late 20th and 21st centuries supplements traditional landscapes, sites and artefacts with those that are digital. People increasingly inhabit digital places, investing time and money into spaces accessed only through screens. People and corporations continue to create these digital built environments and their supporting, physical architecture at an astonishing rate for a rich diversity of purposes. This series aims to answer the questions of what the heritage of digital things and places looks like and how it can be understood archaeologically.

Volume 1
An Enchantment of Digital Archaeology: Raising the Dead with Agent-Based Models, Archaeogaming and Artificial Intelligence
Shawn Graham

An Enchantment of Digital Archaeology

Raising the Dead with Agent-Based Models, Archaeogaming and Artificial Intelligence

Shawn Graham

berghahn
NEW YORK · OXFORD
www.berghahnbooks.com

First published in 2020 by

Berghahn Books

www.berghahnbooks.com

© 2020 Shawn Graham

Library of Congress Cataloging-in-Publication Data

A C.I.P. cataloging record is available from the Library of Congress
Library of Congress Cataloging in Publication Control Number: 2020937013

British Library Cataloguing in Publication Data

A catalogue record for this book is available from the British Library

ISBN 978-1-78920-786-6 hardback
ISBN 978-1-78920-871-9 paperback
ISBN 978-1-78920-787-3 ebook

https://doi.org/10.3167/gra7866

Contents

Tables

Acknowledgements

This book has been through many iterations. Thank you to Caryn Berg for taking a chance on it. At various points, conversations or interventions by Andrew Reinhard, Sara Perry, Colleen Morgan, Steve Leahy, Alex Lane, John Aycock, Erik Champion, Tara Copplestone, Meghan Dennis, Christian Rollinger, Andreas Angourakis, Angus Moll, Iza Romanowska and Tom Brughmans made this a better book than it would otherwise have been. Lea Stirling gave me the second chance from which all others flowed: thank you, Lea! Rob Blades, Nadine Feuerherm and other souls in FYSM1405a in 2010/11 got to 'enjoy' a very early attempt at fostering digital enchantment with agent-based models; I'd like to think I'm better at it now and that their work was not in vain. Thank you.

Much of this book was written at the Second Cup; I can recommend the butter tarts.

Parts of chapter 1 are a reworked version of my chapter 'Counting Bricks and Stacking Wood: Providing the Physical Fabric', in *The Cambridge Companion to Ancient Rome*, ed. Paul Erdkamp (Cambridge University Press, 2013), 278–96. Used with permission.

Chapter 2 integrates edited materials from the following: S. Graham, 'Networks, Agent-Based Modeling, and the Antonine Itineraries', *Journal of Mediterranean Archaeology* 19, no. 1 (2006): 45–64, reproduced with the kind permission of Equinox Publishing Limited; S. Graham, 'Behaviour Space: Simulating Roman Social Life and Civil Violence', *Digital Studies/le Champ Numérique* 1, no. 2 (2009), DOI: http://doi .org/10.16995/dscn.109, CC BY 4.0; chapter 3 also includes material from the latter piece.

Parts of chapter 4 contain a slightly reworked version of 'Pulling Back the Curtain: Writing History through Video Games', in *Web Writing: Why and How for Liberal Arts Teaching and Learning*, ed. Jack Dougherty and Tennyson O'Donnel (University of Michigan Press, 2014), 149–60, chapter copyright S. Graham.

Chapter 4 also contains a modified version of 'On Games That Play Themselves: Agent-Based Models, Archaeogaming, and the Useful Deaths of Digital Romans', in *The Interactive Past: Archaeology, Her-*

itage, and Video Games, ed. Angus A.A. Mol, Csilla E. Ariese-Vande-meulebroucke, Krijn H.J. Boom and Aris Politopoulos (Sidestone Press, 2017), 123–31, used with permission.

Appendices A and B reimplement and modify code developed by Tom Brughmans, reused with permission.

Introduction

This is a book about enchantment and digital archaeology. It is a book about trying to pull together the connective threads on nearly twenty years of work in simulation, agent modelling, video games and Roman economic history. These are not, on the face of it, 'enchanting' topics. But hear me out. It's about trying to remember what it was that was magical about archaeology when I first began, and why I find digital approaches to archaeology to still be magical.

This book is about, in a narrow sense, the ways in which I've reanimated Roman society using agent-based modelling and archaeogaming. But in a larger sense, it's about digital *enchantment* in the ways that scholars like Sara Perry (2018, 2019) and Russell Staiff (2014) envision. It's about responding to archaeology not as a crisis to be solved, but as a source of wonder. It is about responding to digital archaeology as if it is 'sensible' in the ways people like Yannis Hamilakis (2014) have written. It's about whether digital archaeology is fast or slow, whether it is engaging or alienating, whether or not it is sensory and sensual. My aim is for you to be enchanted and delighted by digital archaeology as I trace a line through my own history of disenchantment and the reawakening of wonder through agent modelling, archaeogaming and artificial intelligence.

What are computers *for*, in archaeology?

The question might seem absurd. What is a pencil for? A shovel? A database? Our tools are only ever appropriate to particular situations. Not every moment on an excavation requires a mattock or a pail; a dental pick and a dustpan might be called for. By the same token, maybe we don't always require a desktop computer to achieve a digital archaeology. Maybe a smartphone is all we need. Maybe an iPad. Maybe we just need what Jentery Sayers (2018, elaborating on Kirshenbaum 2009) calls 'paper computers', or the habits of thought that are themselves digital.

The point is, if we stop simply accepting the ubiquity of a computer, we can see again some of the enchantment these amazing devices possess, and we can begin to imagine again the kinds of questions to which they might be best suited. There is plenty of criticism of computing and of digital archaeology that focuses on the alienating aspects of the work. Caraher (2015, 2016, 2019), for instance, has argued that to use a computer as part of your process, whether in the field or in the lab, is to somehow be pushed away from the tacit and sensuous ways-of-knowing that characterize the doing of archaeology.

Perhaps we are asking the wrong questions of these devices. For me, the use of computation in archaeology is a kind of magic, a way of heightening my archaeological imagination to see in ways I otherwise couldn't. It lets me raise the dead (digital zombies?) with all the terror, wonder and ethical problems that that implies. Shouldn't we raise the dead? Why shouldn't we put words in their mouths, give them voices and talk with them to find out more about their (after) lives?

This is a book that shows a way to raise the dead. It is a practical digital necromancy.

I'm making an argument that a slow, reflexive, sensorial, enchanted engagement with the past is possible (even desirable) when we use digital computational approaches. That is not to say that it is not a rigorous approach. The first step in this approach is a clear formalism, a clear restatement *in code* about what I believe to be true about the past. It has to be that way because the fundamental action of the computer is to copy. Decisions we take in a computational medium are multiplied and accelerated, so those initial decisions can have unintended or unforeseen consequences when they are rendered computational.

Such formalisms also have to be rendered as relationships as well. Research on artificial neural networks demonstrates that meaning can emerge through cascades of coordinated firings of neurones through weighted channels, backwards and forwards. These weights do not need to be known beforehand, but can be learned as the network is exposed to stimuli. To my mind, this points to a way of computing the past that does not rely on higher-level equations that describe a social phenomenon, but rather a way of letting interaction precede the equation. We set up and describe the conditions for interactions, relationships and networks to emerge. Understand that I am not arguing for a naive use of computing and letting answers percolate out. That is nonsense. Rather, I am arguing for the correct level of complexity to model, to put into a simulation. In chapter 1, I consider networks as a substrate and then I revivify these networks, raising the dead through simulation in chapters 2 and 3.

These are games that play themselves, these simulations. Wouldn't it be interesting to enter the game ourselves? This is part of the enchantment. In chapters 4 and 5, I discuss what it takes to make this archaeogaming happen. In chapter 6 I look at what chatbots and other playful digital toys can offer to our research and, more importantly, for the audience for whom archaeology holds wonder. I weave throughout my engagement what makes digital work sensuous and enchanting in the ways that Perry and Staiff describe. It is unapologetically a personal engagement. In which case, the tone of this book will often be rather informal. It is not necessarily an academic book, but a book that emerges from academic thinking.

Insofar as the actual archaeological data in this book and my computational engagements with them are concerned, I have collected together and edited some of my previously published papers that employ a variety of small thought experiments and agent-based models and toys (the tone in these sections will be somewhat more formal, an artefact of their genesis and original audience). The computational parts are tools-to-think-with, rather than things that will prove a hypothesis. They are arranged in a logic that reflects the way that I have come to think about Roman society, especially cities and the social life within them. It seems to me that Roman cities and societies can be thought of as nodes of entangled systems, as biological processes that smear across boundaries and scales, and whose actions can be modelled upon those entanglements. With video game technologies, we can insert the researcher/student/public into the model for deeper learning, or engagement: a first person perspective. Not, I should hasten to add, a *Roman* perspective; rather, a deformation of our own just-so stories we tell about the past with the authority provided by a disembodied narration. If there is truth in the stories we tell, then there is truth in the embodied perspective provided by a computational rendering of that story.

I have tried to write as accessibly as I can. Forgive me my failures. I write not so much for an academic audience invested heavily in modelling and simulation, but rather for my archaeology and history students afraid to engage with digital work. It is when things break and in the cleavages that we see most clearly the problems and potentials of technology, and so failure is a necessary part of the process. We have to talk about things that do not work, as much as (if not more than) the things that do.

These particular case studies are wrapped in a larger argument about the proper role of computation in archaeology. In the end, I do not subscribe to a techno-chauvinism that sees digital responses as the obvious goal for archaeology, nor a techno-utopianism that describes what ought to be (see Broussard 2018). Rather, I see space for a creative engagement with digital tools that opens up a landscape, a taskscape, for returning some enchantment to what we do.

What This Book Is Not

This is not a typical academic book, and the tone and voice will vary from time to time. Portions of the present work republish or reproduce materials that first saw the light of day in academic articles. I have been blogging my research since 2006, a process that began when I was an unemployed/underemployed archaeologist, and I was trying to develop agent-based models at second hand from the archaeological data I found in repositories or university websites. Blogging is a platform, not a genre; a blog post can occupy any tone or style the author chooses. However, my blogging is often in the style of trying to tell the story of what I've done back to myself, to try to see what I've missed. I imagine, as I write, that I'm speaking to a person sitting across the coffee table from me. It is in many ways my 'teaching' voice. As the years have passed, the blogging has gathered a larger audience, but the discipline of telling the story has (you may disagree) improved my writing and teaching. Over the same period, my work began to be published, and I had to learn the very different style of writing that formal academic articles require. An academic article aims for economy of expression, and, while it is about furthering knowledge of a subject, it is also about signalling one's authority or positioning in various networks of academic capital. We can cast the difference here, in simplified terms, as being informal versus formal. One is not inherently better than the other, but they do have different aims. Academic books tend to not go for an informal voice, but it is important here to do so because anything with 'digital' in the title tends to frighten people off needlessly. I recently had reason to go and dig back through my early blogging, and found a post from 2007 that in many ways seems as if it is one of the kernels from which the present work springs. In that post, I wrote, 'The serious face of archaeology we present to the public is so lifeless: how can we expect government and the public to be excited about our work if we ourselves give every indication of not being excited either?' I am excited about digital archaeology. The tone of this book is chosen deliberately to convey and capture some of what it is I find exciting about doing digital archaeology, and so it deals with a lot of things I have already done and only a few of the things that I am starting to do; these latter things (including the explorations of what artificial intelligence or neural networks offer archaeology) are still coming into focus for me. I have settled on the idea of 'enchantment' as the leitmotiv that connects the various elements of my work together: playfulness, the craftwork of pulling code together and storytelling. I am speaking to students whom I wish to enthuse and who might, so inspired, seek out their own ways of enchanting archaeology for themselves.

Groundwork

My first encounter with 'real' archaeology was as an eighteen-year-old college student on his first real adventure out of the country (out of the backwoods, in truth). We were working (paying to work) on an excavation in the Peloponnesus, in the hinterland of Corinth. In the bottom of the high mountain valley of Zaraka, you will find Lake Stymphalos, where Hercules defeated the Stymphalian Birds. Not much of note happened in this valley. The Romans marched through on their way to annihilating Corinth in 146 BCE. The crusaders of the Fourth Crusade built a monastery. During the Second World War and subsequent Greek Civil War, bitter battles were fought for control of the area. Sometime in the fifteenth century, a person was buried and their head lopped off, for future archaeologists to find, and to feed stories of Balkan vampires. But that's about it.

My trench? My trench was full of bricks. The trench next to mine? *That* was the trench with the vampire in it. Every day, I cleared the bricks from my trench, slowly getting down to the doorstep of the monastery, while I watched the experienced excavators carefully record and remove the body; at night in the quiet, I could easily imagine the terror of watching someone waste away and die, not knowing what – or who – was responsible. I wondered about those lives and those people, as I trudged back to my trench full of rubble, quietly irritated that nothing in my trench afforded any sort of connection to . . . well, anything at all. They were just bricks.

Fast forward a few years, and I'm now in Rome, hot on the trail of aqueduct remains across the Roman countryside on a Vespa scooter. Thomas Ashby and Esther van Deman had done this during the interwar years (without the Vespa), but Rome and its countryside were a very different place then. Armed with copious photocopies, a dog-eared edition of Trevor Hodge's *Roman Aqueducts and Water Supply* (1989) and a military topographic map (thirty years out of date), I zoomed down the lanes and byways and industrial estates on the modern periphery of Rome. When I found some ruins, I tried to correlate what I found with the descriptions in Ashby and Van Deman. I measured, I photographed, and I drew. The point of these exertions was a massive Excel database that used my basic understanding of the geometry of solids (*is it pi-r-squared or half the width times the height or . . .*) to build a beautiful mathematical model of the finished aqueduct. I spent three months pulling this model apart to figure out the quantities of human labour and materials to make the Aqua Claudia. Then back on the road, to double check, to find the missing pieces – a glorious summer of roadside picnics, coffees in truck stops, shepherd dogs chasing me from the fields, climbing down into ravines or up onto brick-lined vaults. I wasn't much concerned with, or imagining the life of, the people who built the aqueduct. But I was proud of *my* model, *my* wrestling with data to learn something new.

A few years later, and it's just me staring at a storage shed full of bricks. Roman bricks are heavy. They are large, and they are thick. They litter the fields of Italy. When they are collected, it is sometimes to take a geochemical peek at their composition. Where might the clays come from? More often, it is because they contain very complex makers' marks, these bricks from near Rome. They tell you a year, an estate, a brickmaker, a landlord. They remind me a lot of how marks on timber floated down the Ottawa River were used by the timber barons to keep records straight, for paying for the use of timber slides, for working out who owned what. They are interesting, but I'm having a hard time imagining what I can do with them that is new. In self-defence against the teasing I receive – hey brickstamp boy! – I play up the boring bit. Hell, we're archaeologists; we can't always excavate vampires, right?

Vampires.

Raising the dead.

Hmmmm . . .

It's about this point where I first encounter the idea of 'social networks' – a full decade before Facebook – and I start to wonder what I might see if I tie these estate owners, estate names, brickmakers, makers' marks and so on together. In the blue glow of the cathode-ray monitor, the tangled hairball of connections starts to emerge, and I begin to see changing patterns over time, patterns that begin to *give life* to these long-dead workers, and they start to become *people* again, in the way I first imagined I might know the past, when I started all of this archaeology business. I learn their names and can dimly see the outlines of some of their lives.

This is a book about the practical magic – the practical necromancy? – that digital archaeology brings to the larger field. To use computers in the course of doing archaeological research does not a digital archaeology make. Digital archaeology requires enchantment. For me, enchantment as a concept captures the playfulness and craftwork and indeed magic that I have come to see as key elements in the useful employment of computers for the work of archaeology. Enchantment is not just a mode of being but also an enactment, a spell-casting, a singing-into-being (*chanter*, as Bennett 2001: 6 reminds us). Enchantment is the opposite of disenchantment, or that mode that requires a disinterested, distanced, dis-intermediated approach to the past. Enchantment works against the decoupling of the world that splits it into two halves, me and everything else. It requires an alertness to both how I affect, and am affected by, the world. It requires that we attend to emotion. R.G. Collingwood's work on folktales and magic (published in 2005 as part of a collection of previously unpublished manuscripts and titled *The Philosophy of Enchantment*) is apposite here:

> We all have a feeling – not an intellectual idea, but an emotional one – of an intimate connexion between ourselves and the things which we have made. These things are felt as parts of ourselves, in the sense that an injury to them is felt as an injury to us. If a picture I have drawn, or a letter I have written, or some trifling thing, useful or useless, which I have made, is destroyed by accident, my sense of loss bears no relation to the intrinsic value or merit of what has been destroyed; it is like a wound or blow to myself, as if the destroyed thing had been a deposit or outpost of my personality in the world around me. (Collingwood 2005: 196–97)

It is in this feeling that Collingwood located the operations of magic in a society – not 'magic' as a byword for a superstitious awe at unexplained natural forces, but rather magic as the ritualized expression of that emotion. In his discussion of ghosts and their appearance and function across multiple cultures, he identifies the role of the magician as one who banishes the emotional vulnerability (Collingwood 2005: 205). He goes on:

> If magical practices are not utilitarian activities based on scientific theories whether true or false, but spontaneous expressions of emotion whose utility, so far as they have any utility, lies in the fact that they resolve emotional conflicts in the agent and so readjust him to the practical life for which these conflicts render him unfitted; then a new problem arises about our own civilization. We pride ourselves

on always acting from utilitarian motives or scientific theories; but that very pride should warn us that this belief about ourselves may perhaps be unjustified. We may be conceiving our own civilization not as it actually is, but as, with our utilitarian obsession, we should like it to be. We think that our rationalism has done away with magic because that is what we want to think; but is it true? (Collingwood 2005: 208)

What is more rational than a computer, reducing all phenomena down to tractable ones and zeros? What is more magical than a computer, that we tie our identities to the particular hardware or software machines we use? Collingwood (2005: 279) saw modern Western society as no less magical than any other, in that it is now 'science' doing the work of resolving the 'emotional conflicts'. Archaeology, as conventionally practiced, uses computation to effect a distancing from the world; perhaps not intentionally, but practically. Its rituals (the plotting of points on a map, the carefully controlled vocabularies to encode the messiness of the world into a database and thence a report, and so on) relieves us of the task of feeling the past, of telling the tales that enable us to envision actual lives lived. The power of the computer relieves us of the burden of having to be human. An enchanted digital archaeology remembers that when we are using computers, the computer is not a passive tool. It is an active agent in its own right (in the same way that an environment can be seen to be active). The way it is built, the way the code is designed, contains so many elements of unconscious bias from all of its myriad creators (and blood: do not forget how much actual human blood is shed to obtain the rare earths and minerals upon which computing rests; see, for instance, Crawford and Jolen 2018) means that the computer is our co-creator. It uses us as much as we use it. In a video game, the experience of the player is not the result of a passive reception of representation by the game author. The player's active engagement with the emergent representation of the rules put in motion by the author but interpreted in the context of the local game environment implies that the meaning of the game is the product of at least three authors, and one of them is not human. We can see this in video games, but it's not always apparent to us that this is also true of, say, GIS or 3d photogrammetry.

In that emergent dynamic, in that co-creation with a nonhuman but active agent, we might find the enchantment, the magic, of archaeology that is currently lacking. Sara Perry (2019) identifies the lack of magic, the lack of enchantment, in the 'crisis' model of archaeology that animates our teaching, our research and our public

outreach. If archaeology is always in danger, then every act of archaeology is an act of rescue, and every act of rescue implies a morality
play, a this-is-good-for-you ethic to which the public should respond
appropriately. April Beisaw (2017), in her reflection on the role local
archaeology might play in a community, contrasts the way archaeologists talk about the past and the way ghost hunters talk about it:

> Ghost hunters don't go into a new community and explain their past
> to them – they listen to what the community has to say about a place
> and then explore their stories. Ghost hunters bring others along to
> participate at every level of that exploration. They show their meth-
> ods and their results and ask the audience to help draw conclusions.
> Ghost hunters leave questions unanswered so that wondering can
> continue. . . . Archaeologists can learn how to become more relevant
> to the wider public. . . . Find their mysteries, but don't spoil them.
> Encourage participatory exploration of the past but leave room for
> continued speculation.

Archaeology – academic archaeology – has lost its grip on wonder and
enchantment and romance. This is not a plea to sanitize the past or
to pander to tired tropes (but remember: most of those tropes were
created by archaeologists who went out of their way to communicate
their research to the public. It is not their fault that subsequent archaeologists turned their backs on the public and let those tropes fester).
It is a plea to reinscribe the magic and wonder in what they do – to
leave space for, and acknowledge, mystery: 'Archaeology has always
been where non-archaeologists turn for stories about adventure and
the unexplainable. . . . If my [local] community forgot someone or
something, or invented a tale to explain something, they did so for
a reason' (Beisaw 2017). Be scholarly, be rigorous, but leave space for
enchantment and wonder, and understand what work these stories do
(MacDougall 2019) for those who tell them.

And so I offer this book in that spirit. By pulling together the connective threads on nearly twenty years of work in simulation, agent
modelling, video games and Roman economic history, which re-en-
chanted archaeology for me, I want to map out a way for digital archaeology to connect with what Andrew Reinhard has identified as
'archaeogaming': if I take the fossils of a Roman social network and
reanimate them with autonomous software agents, just what kind of
digital archaeology have I created? What other kinds are out there?
Where does an archaeology so enchanted intersect with public archaeology, public stories, the work of archaeology in a community?

I want a digitally enchanted archaeology.

An Apologia for Simulation

In 2000, J.P. Marney and Heather Tarbert published a paper in the *Journal of Artificial Societies and Social Simulation* called, 'Why Do Simulation? Towards a Working Epistemology for Practitioners of the Dark Arts'. It was a tongue-in-cheek way of acknowledging the peripheral status of work in simulation in many of the social sciences, and the piece is a philosophical reflection on the methods of simulation and how simulation constructs knowledge.

To call something a dark art, though, is to draw on the long history of magic, ritual and religion (particularly in the West). It is a rhetorical move meant largely to cast certain practices as part of the in-group versus the out-group. To be accused of being a magician in Greco-Roman antiquity was to be accused of practicing rituals that did not have the imprimatur of 'official' sanction. The priest – the representative of the in-group, per the ancient author's experience or approval – examines the entrails, watches the flight of birds, performs the rituals correctly and is rewarded with some glimpse into divine will. The magician, on the other hand (the representative of the out-group), compels the spirits to visit her – necromancy, in fact – through spells and carefully guarded craft, and wrests the certain knowledge of what is to come by dint of her own skill (Otto 2013 provides an accessible overview of the subject).

In the humanities, when we are concerned about the human past, we read the texts closely, we follow our rituals correctly, and we are rewarded with a story about history; in simulation, our skill enables us to raise the dead, putting them through their paces, and we are rewarded with not just one history, but an entire landscape of possible histories – simulation as dark art, as the pursuit of peripheral academics, indeed; and dark arts, as Harry Potter taught us, must be defended against.

'Agent modelling might be useful for those nonliterate societies, but we've got more than enough materials to work on here, Shawn' is the gist of a conversation I have had more than once with some of my Romanist colleagues. Nevertheless, Marney and Tarbert (2000) argue that simulation is perhaps the only way of addressing situations

1. where there are complex emergent global processes and dynamics from simple local behaviour
2. where coordinated global outcomes are generated by the heterogeneous local decision rules [amongst others]

... both of which describe Rome pretty nicely. Or human culture more generally.

The next criticism that we often encounter when we do simulation is that our agent models – any computational model – are simply tautological, that we only get out what we put in. This weary chestnut fundamentally misunderstands a significant characteristic of complex systems. The dynamics of one level of organization do not lead linearly to, or necessarily imply, the dynamics of another level. Hence if we are interested in culture, we model at the level of an individual. What comes out of the model is the emergent by-product of countless individual interactions. What comes out is definitely not what went in.

A final issue is about what, exactly, we are modelling. Are we really simulating the past? Of course not. We are actually creating zombies.

Zombies?

In popular culture, a zombie can be understood as a resurrected partial human, animated by a limited set of appetites and urges, and responding to its wider environment in limited or particular ways. In the same way, the computer lets us resurrect or create similarly limited partial humans, or agents, whose aggregated actions and emergent patterns give us insight. It is an attainable necromancy.

I used to call these autonomous software agents 'zombies' partly for the reason that it is a lively metaphor for driving home what the agents in an agent-based model do – the agents are mindlessly driven by their appetites. I have to clearly specify these appetites, these motive desires for the zombies to mindlessly carry out.

I was thinking of John Romero *Day of the Dead*–type zombies, but the original 'zombie' of Haitian folklore represents compelled labour after death (e.g. McAlister 2012: 459); when we reflect on the compelled labour that goes to underpinning our digital lifestyles, to speak of 'zombies' is too glib. We might do well to explore those networks stretching from rare earth mining in Africa to factory conditions in China to retail networks in America, a fitting subject for an archaeology of the Anthropocene. For my present purpose then, a better metaphor might be 'golem', of the kind envisioned in Terry Pratchett's *Discworld* stories: creatures that have to follow the words written on paper placed in their heads. (The golem emerges in our world from Jewish folklore as an 'unfinished man' and is most famously the protector of Prague's Jewish population. Unlike in the Discworld, which implies that the words animating a golem can include quite precise instructions [see Pratchett, *Going Postal*, 2004], the golems of Jewish folklore are animated by mystical wordplay related to the name of God. Cohen 2015 points to similarities between golems and zombies in current popular understandings).

In any event, I need to clearly specify what it is I believe about some phenomenon in the past in order for these golems to perform that behaviour. They do not think: they follow instructions, my model of past behaviour at the individual level. What I end up simulating then is not the past, but the story I am telling about the past. This lets me escape nearly all of the criticisms that my colleagues in the humanities raise about this dark art of simulation.

If I am simulating in effect a historiography, then the results, the landscape of possible emergent outcomes, are the consequences of that story I am telling about the past. Simulation becomes a way for me to explore the surprising outcomes about my stories about the past. I perform the past; I deform it.

The method forces me to become clear about what it is I believe about the past in an utterly transparent way. If I cannot encode those beliefs, then clearly I need to think more deeply. I use NetLogo (Wilensky 1999) for my agent modelling for a couple of reasons. One, its near-English syntax makes it easier for me to develop simulations. It also makes it possible for my colleagues to examine the procedural rhetoric (Bogost 2007), the argument-in-code of my simulation. A simulation is not complete until somebody else opens the hood and examines the code for your mistakes, your assumptions and the rhetorics hidden therein. I often tell my students that unless they can look at the code for themselves, they have no reason to believe the results of a simulation. My students are history students, without any great affinity for computing, but, with a bit of help, they can easily flowchart a NetLogo simulation to get a sense of what is going on.

The end result, then, is that I have found that I have to keep my models as tightly focused as possible. If my model becomes too ambitious, I typically have two problems. One, it becomes difficult for me to tell the story of what is going on in my model, to tease apart the critical interactions that are producing the landscape of possibilities that have emerged. Two, there is little engagement with my code by those who could best critique it, as it becomes seemingly too complex.

Let me give you a brief example. I became interested in the social networks surrounding landholding in the immediate vicinity of Rome during the first three centuries CE. I did some network analysis of this data (stitched together from the epigraphy of stamped bricks), but I wanted to reanimate these patterns. There are many episodes in Roman history of elite self-extermination, as different factions vying for power eliminated rivals through murder, forced suicide or exile. How much disruption could these networks I observed endure? Thus, I became interested in the sources of civil violence in the Roman world (I explore this in depth in chapter 3).

I created a simulation where a population of agents were interlinked in the patterns suggested from the archaeology. Over this network would flow prestige, gifts and money as the agents vied for status, drawing on the literature connected with the Roman tradition of the *salutatio*, or morning greeting given by a client to his patron(s). No patron has to accept a client who is not suitably prestigious, and no one gains prestige without a patron, thus shutting individuals out of the networks – the source for civil violence in the Roman world, I argued.

I was able to put these agents in a world where the economy ranged from one where everything was roses to one where everything was sackcloth and ashes; I imagined that there would be no violence in the rose world and lots of violence in the sackcloth world. And yes, this is duly what I saw, but there were surprising, unpredicted bouts of violence where there should be peace, and peace where there should be violence. This is something worth exploring.

In another model, I simulated an excruciatingly simple mechanic representing the contentious process of 'Romanization'. In my model, which is based on an even simpler model of disease transmission, an agent is 'non-Romanized' until they run into an agent who has become 'Romanized'. Poof! The first agent now becomes Romanized. Romero Zombies indeed. (And of course, there are models of zombie infection too!) (I explore this model in more depth in chapter 2).

The key element here was that the agents were not wandering around in an amorphous space. Rather, they were constrained to move along the paths suggested by the third century Antonine Itineraries, the lists of towns one would use in order to figure out how to get from point A to point B. To get to Honolulu from Ottawa, go to Toronto, Winnipeg, Calgary, Vancouver, Seattle, Honolulu.

Thus, I was interested in exploring the consequences of this list-like, networked conception of geographic space. I could measure the amount of model time it took for everyone in the model to become 'Romanized' as they moved over the network of Roman Spain versus Roman Britain, versus Roman Gaul, versus Roman Italy. I graphed these results, and the shape of this diffusionist model implied something about the way ideas of Romanness could penetrate, and how deeply, in these different regions. The model then became a guide for looking at the archaeology in a new way.

This use of agent-based simulation fits into a kind of experimental archaeology mindset, of building as a way of knowing; indeed, it also puts it in the developing traditions of the digital humanities. Trevor

Owens (2012), a digital archivist with the Library of Congress, wrote about the mutual incomprehension of computer scientists and humanists: 'I don't think the issue here is different ways of knowing, incompatible paradigms, or anything big and lofty like that. I think the issue at the heart of this back and forth dialog is about two different contexts. This is about what you can do in the generative context of discovery vs. what you get can do in the context of justifying a set of claims.' What Owens argues is that, in the humanities, computational approaches are best suited for 'the generative world of discovery'. He continues:

> If you aren't using the results of a digital tool as evidence then anything goes. More specifically, if you aren't trying to attribute particular inferential value to a particular process that process is simply producing another artifact which you can then go about considering, exploring, probing and analyzing. I take this to be one of the key values of the idea of 'deformance'. The results of a particular computational or statistical tool don't need to be treated as facts, but instead can be used as part of an ongoing exploration. (Owens 2012)

Allow me to be contentious: the proper role of agent modelling in archaeology is not to try to justify stories of the past, but to generate new stories, new ways of looking at the evidence. The proper role is to deform. We are not simulating the past, but rather building what we believe to be true (or what might be true) about the past in a computer model. We are raising simulacra of the dead, we are breathing life into digital golems and putting words in their head, and we watch them so that we can tell stories that help us make sense of the past in the present. The emergent results of our simple models, our active nonhuman agents, help the past intrude on the present. We see *a* past performed in the present. And this is uncanny. This encounter with the uncanny is also part of the enchantment.

Deep History of Field and Bog

There is a field near my parents' home. In the summer, the heat shimmers off the field and the June bugs' roar gets louder the hotter it gets. In the middle of the field is a stand of trees – ancient maples, some apple trees and, on the windward side, a row of spruce trees. This is the site of my ancestor's first homestead in Western Quebec. On a summer day nearly two hundred years ago, he and his family walked up the six miles from the riverboat landing and said 'Here'. I can imagine his walk was much different than mine – in the cool of the deep forest, free of undergrowth, dappled light through the branches of the white pine, but still the June bugs' roar.

In those days, the requirement was to clear a certain amount of land every year in order to retain ownership of the one hundred acres. The results of his work are all around me – the flat open field on this ridge from which I can see the ridges and hills on the Ontario side of the Ottawa River. There is a faint depression in the ground, the filled-in cavity of his root cellar. Nothing else but the trees remain.

In my part of the country, perhaps this can count as deep time. We live every day in this constructed landscape, but seldom reflect on the labour and violence necessary to build it. But if I walked the six miles down to the river, I would encounter burial mounds and camp sites of the archaic Woodlands peoples who portaged around Chats Falls. I would encounter intrusions from this deeper time, ghosts and haunt-ings. The modern hydroelectric dam has obliterated most of these, but still, when you walk through the quiet of the bogs and flooded marshlands, you will encounter these mounds as they rise above the high-water line. The area is now mostly nature or hunting preserve. Its human history is largely forgotten or, at best, recast as the history of colonization. Recent work in the environmental humanities has dis-cussed encounters with deep time via various 'modes' – enchantment, violence and haunting: 'Deep time has an uncanny ability to telescope into and out of everyday moments. We never really encounter deep time: deep time pulls at us as it manifests through places, objects, or affective atmospheres' (Ginn et al. 2018: 5).

Enchantment, for archaeologists, is perhaps this uncanny encoun-ter with deep time. Because it *is* uncanny, we need to be aware of violence (whether effected by us or in the past) and haunting. En-chantment collapses time into the present and unsettles our relation-ship to the past (Fredengren 2016: 7). Fredengren (2016) discusses how the ways we experience enchantment are similar to the ways we experience 'authenticity' or 'aura'. She draws on the work of Jones (2010), who discusses the way 'authenticity' is constructed in mod-ern discourses. On the one hand, authenticity is a principle of matter, with measurable characteristics – the ash of the handle of this axe dates to the nineteenth century; the iron of the axe blade was smelted from the local mines in the nineteenth century. On the other, there is the experience of the axe as a node in several different networks – this was my great-great-grandfather's axe; a different branch of the family held it for many years, but now it is mine. Over the years, it has seen much use, and perhaps the handle has had to be replaced from time to time, perhaps the head has had to be refashioned, *but this is my great-great-grandfather's axe.* For Jones, authenticity resides in this tension between, on the one hand, modernity's need to delimit and define and order and purify, and, on the other, what might be called 'enchanted practices' that emerge at the entangled knots of different networks of objects and people and places (Jones 2010: 3, 19). 'However, when we look at how people experience and negotiate authenticity through objects, it is the networks of relationships between people, places and things that appear to be central, not the things in themselves' (Jones 2010: 1). These networks co-generate authenticity as they generate themselves (Fredengren 2016: 12, elaborating on Jones 2010).

When I walk in the bush and the bog by the river, I am entangled with the place through ties of family and through my training as an archaeologist. My encounters with deep time emerge as I confront the ghosts of colonization and dispossession. Enchantment is not always pleasant.

Now consider how this bog, this marshland, is often represented in archaeology. We would mark these mounds, these trackways, the campsites, the scatters of artefacts, as polygons and dots on a map in a geographic information system (GIS). The GIS as a technology emerged first in Canada as a tool of land management, often of lands from which Indigenous peoples have been dispossessed. The technology is not just about representation of the land, but also about representation about who gets to speak about the land, who gets to tell the stories of the land (see Risam 2019: 136 on which kinds of human are imagined in digital technologies). A digital archaeology should foreground this. Huggett argues that the 'New Aesthetic' – which emerges in the world of digital art and primarily was about glitching digital data in order to reveal the ways 'technology insinuates into modern life, changing perceptions and understanding' (Huggett 2015: 86) – is very much an archaeological way of looking at data, even if digital archaeologists haven't done this very much yet. He elaborates on what a 'New Aesthetic' perspective offers digital archaeology:

> Digital data containers are not neutral, nor are they an 'empty vessel' into which data can be poured: data have to be structured in order to be represented, and the choice of representation has implications for the data. What effect does the process of structuring data for a database have on the way that we think about that data, on the way we go about recording that data, the way in which we retrieve that data, and the way in which we subsequently analyze that data? . . . The theory-laden, purpose-laden, and process-laden nature of the data remains largely hidden. (Huggett, 2015: 90; see also Risam 2019: 30–35)

Bennett (2001) argued that encountering or seeking out enchantment would move one towards an ethics of generosity. Perry (2019) argues that an archaeology of enchantment would move us away from a crisis-driven mode of engagement in archaeology and make our stories about the past more compelling, more affective and effective, in the world. The first people on whom such enchantment should work should be we archaeologists ourselves. Enchantment is present in digital archaeology, and, when we detect its effects, its moral imperative should be to move us to understand also the violence and ghosts, the New Aesthetic, in our data and processes.

Sense, Sensibility and Enchantment

'Enchantment never really left the world but only changed its forms', says Jane Bennett (2001: 91). In her meditation on the sources of enchantment in the modern world, Bennett (2001: 131) argues that to be open to enchantment is to enter into productive assemblages of the type familiar from the work of Deleuze and Guattari (an idea she develops further in her 2010 *Vibrant Matter*, especially her chapter 2). The assemblages, the *agéncement* (layout) that Deleuze and Guattari (1980) describe, have entered into the archaeological literature and, to my mind, might be consonant with what Ingold (2011) has called 'meshworks' and Hodder (2012) calls 'entanglements' and Wylie (1989, 2002) calls 'cabling'.

As I read this literature, I understand these assemblages/meshworks/entanglements/cables as extended networks of people, things, moods and modes of being, where flows of energy (of whatever kind) move along the (nonlinear) relationships, allowing for emergent phenomena that exist at a higher level of complexity. To be enchanted, then, is to participate in a mood that allows us to identify and be moved by the extraordinary 'that lives amid the familiar and the everyday' (Bennett 2001: 4). The point of being attuned to enchantment is that it offers a compelling counternarrative against modernity, against alienation and disconnection. What is more alienating that the computer, the algorithm, the black box of digital archaeology?

Bennett tells many parables of enchantment, and one place where she finds enchantment is in complexity theory, far from equilibrium systems. Such systems are familiar to any archaeologist who dabbles in agent-based models. Indeed, Bennett (2001: 103) discusses one of the first models novice agent modellers encounter, the termite mound. In the termite mound model (which is bundled as one of the example models in the NetLogo modelling environment), termites wander aimlessly across a landscape. When they encounter a wood chip, they pick it up. When they encounter another wood chip, they put their wood chip down. From this simple dynamic, a complex structure – the termite mound – emerges. Is there not something extraordinary about this? That simple actions can give rise to complex results? That there exist points of bifurcation in the world where an individual moment, an individual choice, can send the system down another path entirely? She also points out that our machines, our computing devices, are also sources of enchantment because they satisfy a need for magic (Bennett 2001: 171): 'it just works', in Steve Jobs's famous formulation. To enchant: *chanter (fr)*, to sing; sing a new song or a new thing into being; to cast a spell (Bennett 2001: 6). Remember our golems who are brought to life by the words in their heads.

Enchantment drives joy, and joy moves the body into an ethic of generosity. Being alive to the possibilities of enchantment in our world, according to Bennett (2001: 156), opens us to this ethical stance:

> Enchantment is a feeling of being connected in an affirmative way to existence; it is to be under the momentary impression that the natural and cultural worlds *offer gifts*, and, in so doing, remind us that it is good to be alive. This sense of fullness . . . encourages the finite human animal, in turn, to give away some of its own time and effort on behalf of other creatures.

Generosity is part of being enchanted. What would archaeological generosity entail? An enchanted archaeology, a generous archaeology, would be attuned to the full complexity (never possible to fully map) of things and people and animals and the environment. It would be delighted in the unexpected, the pleasure of knowing and the liturgy of archaeological work (liturgy: the rites, rituals and formalisms of fieldwork). It would be motivated to share and enfold others in that enchanting moment – including the messy methods of the field and the untidy code at the computer; it would offer an invitation in: come help! It would not say 'archaeology is important!' while at the same time denigrating the work of archaeology ('digging is boring, tedious work') or the ways that people come to want to know about the past ('huh, ghost hunters'). It would not be an archaeology of crisis (as Perry 2019 argues) written from the perspective of disenchantment (a place of cold reason and control), but an archaeology that celebrates not only the subject but also the archaeologist's own process of coming to know, of coming to be enchanted.

In this way, it would also intersect with the work of people like Yannis Hamilakis (2014) on sense and sensibility in archaeology, or

Cornelius Holtorf (2009), who discusses archaeology's brand, or Mc-Kinney (2018), who opens up the possibilities of empathy, the most important of which is to tell compelling stories. I have already told some of my own personal stories about how I come to the past, of how I am enchanted by the powerful work of deformance that the computer permits me to do. In this volume, I will tell more: how digital archaeology moved me from a profound *disenchantment* with the discipline to a point where I find something akin to magic every day. I am unapologetic about this. In the current political moment, with the resurgence of white nationalism and the abuse of Greco-Roman antiquity as a source of authority for these narratives of white supremacy, we are losing the battle. We lose the battle when we undermine our own powerful narratives about the past by appealing to a crisis mode. We lose the battle when we tell people that 'archaeology is actually very boring; we don't have adventures'. We lose the battle when we try to inject a spurious objectivity into archaeology. Understand me clearly: I am not saying that we should not practice archaeology properly. I am not arguing against fieldwork, stratigraphy, archaeometry, or careful statistical analysis. I am not saying we should use antiquity in the same ways the white supremacists do. I am saying that we made a mistake when we stopped admitting the wonder in what we do, the affective nature of our work, our practice. We made a mistake when we removed ourselves from the stories we tell to other people.

As an archaeologist, I exist in a complex assemblage at the intersection of computing power, computing networks, technological history, Roman history, the Italian countryside, the histories of resource extraction in Italy and Canada, the networks of ancient and modern imperialism, of migrations and economic upheavals, of the academy and of publishing. Enchantment lets me participate in the great stories, the great adventures, and it makes great adventures of my own small archaeological contributions: and if I tell the stories to you of what I do such that I provide moments of enchantment for you, perhaps we can change the world a bit.

Let me put it this way: what's the point of an unenchanted archaeology?

Enchantment and Seduction

A powerful critique of 'datafication' is provided by Gavin Smith (2018: 2–3), who is interested in exploring how repeated encounters with data (through everything from the ad trackers, to health monitors, to the increasing normalization of facial recognition) normalize and legitimize the transfers of power and capital that surveillance capitalism profits from. He argues that there are three types of relationships with data that allow this to happen, *fetishisation*, *habit* and *enchantment*: 'Each of these relations come to mediate public understandings of digital devices and data, obscuring the multifaceted nature and hidden depths of data and their propensity to double up as technologies of exposure and discipline' (Smith 2018: 2).

It is this last one I want to explore: if I am arguing for an enchanted digital archaeology, am I unwittingly arguing for the exploitation at scale that currently enables the power and wealth of Google, of Facebook? Am I participating in the sensibility that Smith (2018: 5) calls 'data doxa', 'a sensibility that limits critical engagement with data beyond the immediate ends they serve'? Smith goes on to gloss his three 'doxa', where to fetishize data is to inflate its explanatory power; to make data is to forget about the ways data are constructed; and to be enchanted by data is to be seduced, to slip into the easy flow that modern digital media technologies promote (while hiding how they shape and promote habit and fetish).

Jeremy Hugget (2018) has wrestled with these issues in public on his *Introspective Digital Archaeology* blog. Discussing Smith in a reflection on meanings of the word 'data', he writes,

> A digital environment which increasingly facilitates the aggregation of datasets into meta-analyses or large-scale synthetic analyses, based on the availability of large quantities of variable-quality data held in open repositories and used for purposes for which they were not originally intended, can inadvertently heighten the risks of fetishisation, habituation, and seduction of our digital data. (Hugget 2018)

I think in these discussions we are getting away from the idea of 'enchantment' as framed in the work of Bennett and elaborated in the work of Perry. Seduction and enchantment are not equivalent. As I understand 'enchantment', it is precisely in the ruptures and things that break when doing digital work, delighting in the inefficiencies of digital work, that we become enchanted. As I will show later, 'more data' actually gets in the way of doing effective digital work, of understanding what's happening.

On the other hand, Smith and Hugget are definitely right to warn against fetishization, habit and seduction when we see digital as a synecdoche for 'efficient'. This, I think, is where Caraher's (2019) formulation of 'slow' archaeology intersects with Hugget and Smith. Caraher (2019: 4–6) locates his concern in the evolution of twentieth-century archaeology as an industrial practice, its atomization and the use of digital tools to accelerate practice in the service of efficiency. Efficiency requires logistics, and logistics 'fragment data so that it can be rearranged and redeployed globally for an increasingly seamless system . . . each generation of digital tools makes it possible to shatter the integrity of the site, the link between the individual, work, and knowledge, and to redefine the organization of archaeological knowledge-making' (Caraher 2019: 10).

But . . . what if digital work is *not* efficient? I think Caraher here has been seduced by the digital in the way that Smith warns, seeing in the easy flow of certain digital technologies an equivalence with 'faster'. Digital archaeology understood in this way might well accelerate some tasks, but if the acceleration leads to poor archaeology, that's a bad outcome. If digital archaeology is about a creative engagement, where the computing device is a prosthesis for thought, where 'you try things out and see what happens', to create an 'art of inquiry', to explore 'correspondence with the world' (as per Ingold 2013: 5–7), it is necessarily not 'efficient'. An enchanted digital archaeology is not efficient in the logistics sense that worries Caraher.

In which case, what *does* digital archaeology enable? In my mind, it is the ability to iterate, to recombine, to remix, remesh, replay, replicate, reuse. If the use of computation does accelerate some aspects of practice, in this acceleration it creates spaces of possibility for other aspects. This means that digital archaeology is not an 'industrial' mode of knowledge production, but a 'craft' mode. It requires that you engage with the particularities of each situation to make 'good' archaeology. Responding to Caraher's (2016) thought on my blog, I wrote,

> To get digital stuff to work involves a constant cycle of feedback and productive failure. 'Digital archaeology' is sometimes the slowest archaeology around. There's nothing inherent in the *craft* aspect of 'slow' archaeology that isn't also true of digital work. Digital work **is inefficient** in my view – it never works the first time. That's its strength. It allows us to fail faster, and that's where the illusion of 'efficiency' comes from. Let's consider 3d photogrammetry. It is not the case that one clicks the button and *poof* a 3d model is born and we are absolved of having to *know* the artifact, the context, any less deeply than if we were drawing it. Indeed, this is something that my own students have commented on: that it is remarkably hard to produce a decent 3d photogrammetry model and in the *process* of taking the photos over and over again, building and rebuilding the model, they come to know the object very well indeed. It is because these steps are the ones that are intuitive when one puts pen to paper: the digital

forces the students to think these normally unexamined steps out in full. (Graham 2017b)

As I imagine digital archaeology, it guards against the 'data doxa' that Smith warns us about. In fact, it resembles what Caraher (2019: 2), in his response to critiques of his developing ideas of 'slow' archaeology, terms an 'archaeology of care', where we consider how various digital technologies 'shape the structure of the discipline, social conditions in field practice, and obscure the place of individuals in producing knowledge of the past', noting that there are 'social responsibilities inherent in archaeological knowledge-making, both to the discipline itself and to the communities where we work'.

This is precisely what an enchanted digital archaeology pushes us towards.

A Concluding Thought

Enchantment can be magical. But it can be terrifying too – not just in what it unleashes, but in how it makes visible the violence and hauntings that generate the past in the present. Digital archaeology exists at this knot of entangled networks – of new media technologies and their networks of capital, labour and power, and of networks of extraction and colonialism that allow these magical devices to exist, and the tension between perceived efficiencies and productive failures. Narratives of disenchantment, of modernity, serve to create a crisis mode whose subtext is 'things can't change for the better; everything is destruction'. Enchantment, then, is necessary to envision a better world, to enable engagements with deep time, to create affective and effective archaeologies. Enchantment requires a focus on process and making that is open and reflective, which would guard against the data doxa. An enchanted digital archaeology folds its audience into itself.

This book is a spell book. This book is an autobiography. This book is a book about how to be an archaeologist when you can't get your hands in the dirt and have to make do with second-hand data. It's a book about how to generate the compelling stories, the enchanting stories, to re-run the past for yourself, to put words in the heads of digital golems and to see what happens next.

CHAPTER 1

Imagine a Network

An enchanted digital archaeology has to begin with a serious engagement with a methodology that emphasizes relationships. In recent years, network analysis (as borrowed from sociology's social network analysis) has emerged as one approach to dealing with archaeological relationships at scale. My intention here is to show that even the metaphor of a network can become a vector for enchantment. Once we are in the habit of thought to look for networks, we will then move to how we can represent networks as dynamic environments to explore what emerges.

Bricks I Have Known

There's a word to describe the smell of the earth after the rains have fallen – petrichor. I don't know what the word to describe the exact opposite of that smell is, but that afternoon at the Cistercian monastery of Zaraka in the hinterland of Corinth, anti-petrichor permeated everything. I was eighteen and on my first excavation. My task? To clear away the rubble of a collapsed wall to find the floor level. Hot, back-breaking work, tasting the dust with every breath. And then I broke a roof tile. I did not know it was diagnostic, that is to say I did not know that it mattered, or that it connected one part of the puzzle with another. I did spend some time looking at the break, looking at the colours of the fabric, the minerals, the inclusions, the way they sparkled in the sun. But, having demonstrated that I could not be trusted to handle the job in front of me, I found myself reassigned to clearing back the spoil heaps that had grown so large. Such was my introduction to archaeology.

Archaeology is a small world, and I mean that in the network-theoretic sense of the word. We all know each other, or we know of each other, in only a few short steps. An excavation is a tangled node of relationships, of ties across scholarly communities, universities and colleges, cliques of friendships, long standing feuds and arguments. People move from project to project; experts appear briefly in one publication, then another. These connections are not ephemeral: money, prestige, political power and social power slosh backwards and forwards across these connections, and everyone has stories of power abused, connections severed, connections leveraged. Connections are made; connections wither away or are snapped.

I was dimly aware of these things as an eighteen-year-old kid, listening to the others talking over beers in the evening. But I never really appreciated the role that networks and bricks – simple, dusty, heavy, boring bricks – would play in everything that was to come in my own career. Advice over beers one night – which school to go to? whom to study with? – led eventually to another confrontation with that hot, anti-petrichor smell of ancient building material sitting in the sun. This time, it was an entire shed full of Roman brick and tile kept at the British School at Rome, collected under the auspices of the South Etruria Project in the 1950s and '60s.

My god. Bricks. Hundreds of bricks. Rome famously was a city of bricks turned into marble – or, at least, so Augustus boasted. The reality was more prosaic. Rome remained a city of brick, and of concrete, and, yes, marble cladding. It was a city of wood, a city of plaster.

What do I do with these things?

The answer, it would turn out, would be, network them.

Networks and Entanglements

'Ah, you're the brickstamp fellow.' It was more of a sneer than an acknowledgement. On the one hand, I suppose I should have been gratified that the Famous Important Person had deigned to recognize me, the lowly archaeological assistant in the archaeology lab upstairs from the dining room. On the other hand, it was clear that what I was studying didn't matter. And what's more, I didn't have a good response. Could I make an impassioned argument about why it was so important that I should have moved from Canada to work on these crates of stamped bricks collected forty years ago and sitting in the back shed ever since? Could I say, 'These are the bricks that changed the Roman world'; could I say, 'Agrippa himself chose these bricks to build the Pantheon'; could I say anything that would wipe that sneer off his face?

Of course not. I was up against class, accent and family ties. The only way forward was self-mockery and quiet loathing, in order to fit in, to be accepted. This was the price of trying to be part of the fish bowl. 'Of course I'm only doing this so I can live in Rome. I pay less tuition if I'm not at the university. Of course these bricks don't really matter but they were collected and somebody must study them so here I am, willing to do the dirty work. No rational person would really be interested in these things, ha ha!'

And I learned to loathe these bricks, these stamps, the scholarship that seemed so much to be the result of the worst excesses of the collecting impulse. I really didn't have a very healthy frame of mind towards the subject: imposter syndrome's bastard. I'm still dealing with the damage I mostly inflicted upon myself. Why shouldn't I have been excited to study these things? Someone nearly two thousand years ago made this mark, thought it important, and used it to do something in the world. Of course it matters! But I didn't know how, because I was too much aware of the pecking order, the quiet insults. I tried though. For two years I tried to catalogue and study bricks and brick stamps the way they were supposed to be studied. I measured; I photographed; I tried to develop expertise in mineralogy and petrology. I wasn't much good at it because I couldn't let myself enjoy it. To show myself enjoying what others openly mocked required a scholarly maturity I didn't have.

One day I read John Urry's *Sociology beyond Society* (2000) – each page a revelation, each page an invitation to read more, read faster, to scribble in the margins, to tear up to the computer room and try to find his references in the library catalogue. The relief I felt! Here was permission, here was an example, of a different way of thinking about things. Reading Urry led me to networks as a metaphor and a method. It wasn't just about connecting things up. Things moved. Things flowed over networks. Paths could become blocked. Nodes could control the flow. I began to see that there are several dimensions of connectivity within a single stamped Roman brick. There are the obvious connections of brickmaker to landowner. Of brickmaker to other brickmakers. Of signa (quasi-heraldic devices) to estates. Of clay fabrics to people and places, sites of production, sites of consumption. Roman bricks, and the stamps sometimes found on them, are the fossilized traces of power, of social obligations, of control. Others of course had seen this before but I now had a formal method for mapping these connections out and for seeing changes over time in flows of information and power over the landscape. Bricks didn't litter the landscape. They were intrusions from the deep past into the present.

It was heady stuff. And it made the PhD I had a path forward. I didn't know it at the time, but that was the start for me of a digital archaeology, of an enchanted archaeology. Not everyone was sold, of course. Whenever I begin to push on these more speculative aspects to digital archaeology, I am reminded of the evergreen comment by one of my PhD examiners during my viva voce examination (the defence), as he turned to my chapter on networks: 'This is the point where I wanted to fall on my pencil and die.' To which I responded, 'That's unfortunate, because this is the most interesting bit.'

No more self-loathing. No more apologies. To watch these networks emerge, dilate, contract, expand, to read these on the ground, to see them in the fabric of a building, to know that these are the maps of human lives: this is a source of enchantment.

Nowadays, network approaches to archaeology are firmly established, especially by the work of scholars such as Tom Brughmans or Fiona Coward (see Peeples 2019 for an overview of the field). We can talk about meshworks and taskscapes (Ingold 2011, 1993), entanglements (Hodder 2012) and intertwining, and bring these formal approaches to bear on a wide variety of materials. Archaeological networks are particularly interesting in that they intertwine not just the spaces of the past, but also of the present through time. Fredengren (2016) shows these entanglements in the context of Irish crannogs (artificial islands in lakes and bogs), which bind people today to their deep past and provide an affective, meaningful and enchanted connection. I should like to see more writing like this. It is a beautiful piece.

The 'network' is the foundation for creating an enchanted digital archaeology. It provides the armature, the underlying skeleton, for the digital life that we are going to create. Let's explore 'networks' from the perspective of flow and control, the things that animate the skeleton. In this chapter, I have fused together some previous publications and edited them to highlight what we might know about the past using 'networks' first as a metaphor, then in the next chapter as a structure for simulating past interconnectivity of sites and towns at local and larger scales with agent-based models. These previous publications deal with materials drawn from the Roman world, and mostly the Roman world of the Early Empire; this is a function of the original collection of materials I was working with, the stamped bricks from South Etruria. It is also one of the richest periods for both historical and literary materials that help to fill in some of the blanks suggested by the archaeological materials.

The discussion concludes in the following chapter with a consideration of an archaeological 'network' as a fossilized social network that becomes the point of departure for a simulation of social activity in the past. It is not necessary here to reproduce the complete original articles, because I want to draw your attention here to particular elements of the way the idea of the 'network' can become operationalized. That is to say, the observation of relationships in the past, the weighting and interconnections of those relationships, can become something that the computer computes with. This is, after all, how the artificial neural networks that power the latest artificial intelligences work. If you are familiar with how networks and agent-based simulations are employed in archaeology, you may wish to skip these recaps, but do take a moment to read the 'interludes'. In the appendices, you will find a walk-through and code examples for building your own agent-based models that are based on these earlier published models but updated to take into account the most recent versions of the NetLogo language.

The City as Network[1]

Imagine the whole history of the city of Rome played out as a time-lapsed film. One sees it emerge, amoeba-like, from the landscape. Over time, the rhythms and flows of the city pulse with life, growing ever bigger. Towards the latter stages of the film, the city grows hard, and buildings are transformed to concrete and brick and marble. Enormous monuments emerge. The humans scuttle about. The pulse, the flow, the energy, the vitality of the city is constant, constantly renewing its exoskeleton: its built fabric.

This is the city of Rome. Viewed on this time scale, the city is clearly a living thing. I could have described it in terms of a giant machine, which would have focussed the subsequent discussion in terms of interchangeable parts, closed-loop systems, and the people of Rome would be only so much background noise to the systems in which they are embedded. The metaphors we use to describe the city condition our thinking about it. By saying that 'the city is alive', I want to focus the attention on how the city is an emergent feature of the way its citizens interact. The city is a complex system.

Cities are more than simple conglomerations of people. If cities were merely complicated (as a machine is complicated), then it would be true to say that a city is simply a very big village. A city is a place where, over the course of a single day, an individual might move into and out of many different worlds, depending on with whom (and where) they interact. The client meeting a patron in the Forum lives, for a time, in the world of high politics, but returns to a very different world when dealing with the bailiff of his fullery. Another way of thinking about these worlds is to consider them as different kinds of networks. The same individual can play different roles in different networks of social or economic ties. What makes each city unique in its own way is the way these networks play across space, and how they become intensified in specific locations. Cities represent the intensification in a particular geographical location of multiple intersecting and overlapping networks (Massey et al. 1999: 49, 100–36). When we played the movie of Rome's history, what we observed was the intensification, collision and evolution of complex networks in one single place.

We have to consider what flows through these networks. Some of those things will be intangible, like the exercise of power or social obligation, but they will leave traces for us to recover, in the brick, concrete, marble and timbers of the city. In this section, I want to explore and examine some of these networks and the energy flows in them as they precipitate to form the exoskeleton of Rome. We need to remember always, though, that networks do not exist independently of the people within them. It is not enough that mere interconnections exist. Individuals matter, and individuals must make something of these interconnections for the networks to work (for example, see Laurence's 2001 discussion of the Antonine Itineraries and the transformation of Britain into a Roman province. For Laurence, the Itineraries are evidence of the purposeful reconfiguration of existing networks, over which people, goods and capital flowed, into a distinctly Roman pattern).

Consider the question of scale first. How much energy was flowing through these networks? Take the networks at the heart of Rome, coalesced around the figure of the emperor. The emperor (in this case, Caracalla) wishes to construct the most magnificent baths. This idea in his head, this act of will, is communicated to his underlings, and, within a few short years, his baths are constructed. In the resultant mobilization of men and resources, the networks called into being, repurposed or otherwise employed, extend to the furthest reaches of the empire. The networks that formed around the emperor are not, however, the only ones that existed in Rome. Others, less formal and more ad hoc, existed as well.

How do networks organize and structure an entity such as Rome? Some of the networks that provided material for Rome seem to have been self-organizing – like the Tiber Valley brick industry (Graham 2006a). Others required a certain amount of top-down organization (Fant 1993). Yet it is extremely difficult to disentangle each kind from the other. The building industry of Rome is one area of ancient activity where these different networks leave traces for us to find.

Janet DeLaine (1997) has pioneered the study of ancient buildings in terms of the raw energy involved in constructing them by reverse-engineering from the standing ruins to quantities of labour and materials. In this she works from labour constants developed over the nineteenth century in the context of railroad construction. She turned her method to the Baths of Caracalla (DeLaine, 1997) to study the economic impact of this singular imperial building project. Painstakingly measuring every wall, every elevation, Delaine worked out that the average minimum workforce over the four main years of construction employed

7,200 men directly on the production of materials and in construction;
1,800 men and pairs of oxen for transport around Rome itself.

These numbers rose to 10,400 and 3,200 respectively during the peak periods, to a high of 13,100 during the year 213 CE, when the project was at its highest. A sense of the sheer mass of materials used are provided by DeLaine: over 70,000 m³ of pozzolana for instance, nearly 3 million bessales bricks, more than 12,000 m³ of quicklime, 118,000 m³ of tufa, 3,200 m³ of timber. For comparison, a cubic metre of water at 4 Celsius at sea-level has a mass of 1,000 kg. Think of the things that have to be in place for quicklime to be made, or tufa to be quarried, or timber to be harvested.

DeLaine's work offers us the most detailed investigation of the social and economic impact of the Roman construction industry to date. By the logic of critical path analysis (i.e. before event Y can happen, event X absolutely must take place; before event X, W; and so on), she also worked out the scheduling of provisioning of all these men and materials (DeLaine 1997: 190). What she was doing was mapping out the numerous flows of energy and material arriving at a single point in space and time (cf. Davies 2005: 140 on mapping flows).

Picture the scene on a Roman road outside the city – all those men, all those wagons. How many wagons? A Roman road is only so wide, and the amount of material an ox-drawn cart may pull, only so much. DeLaine (1997: 200) worked out nose-to-tail the implications of all that traffic. Cleary, for this enormous bath-building project to work, for it to be feasible, it must have been organized somehow.

It was formally organized, yet at the same time, it was not. An enormous imperial building project created a deformation in the natural economic gravity of Rome, creating incentives for the smart operator to respond to. At the same time, without pre-existing structures – dynamic networks – in place, it would not have been possible (or would have been a great deal more difficult) for the project to take place.

An imperial building project is a discordant note against the normal background hum of Rome. It is a distortion for us now because it survives (and so attracts our attention), and it was a distortion then because it warped the natural economic networks of the city. Back-of-the-envelope calculations (which I detail in Graham 2013b) are predicated on underestimating the private building stock in Rome, the brick-faced concrete structures. Brick-faced concrete was the major construction style from the mid-first century CE until the Middle Ages (in reality, Rome, of course, was a mixture of all kinds of buildings stock – timber-framed, *opus incertum*, *opus reticulatum*, brick-faced concrete and so on). But I leave out all public buildings, all temples, all precincts and so on, as well as not accounting for staircases, embankments or other kinds of urban furniture. By underestimating, I should end up with figures on the right order of magnitude. In another sense, though, we are over-emphasizing the importance of brick and concrete and under-emphasizing the role of timber. Much of Rome's housing and other building stock would have been more akin to timber-framed, wattle-and-daub construction prior to the first century CE; indeed, well into the Imperial era, many upper floors and interior partition walls would also have been timber-framed (Adam 1994: 122–24). I do attempt to account somewhat for timber requirements, though this is the area where our knowledge is most uncertain.

The next problem is one of coming up with an estimate of how many buildings stood in Rome, on average, over the period that we are concerned with, and how big they were, on average. Roman Ostia plays an important role here. G.R. Storey (2001) uses the evidence of Ostia and the Regionary catalogues for Rome to test various hypotheses concerning the meaning of the term 'insulae'. He decides that 'insulae' most likely refers to 'enclosed unitary units within the fabric of a single city street block . . . basically, but not necessarily exclusively, apartments within a structure' (Storey 2001: 390–1, and n8). For the purposes of his analysis, Storey (2001: 393) calls these 'architectural/residential units' (ARUs). He then looks at the average number of these

ARUs per building per hectare, comparing them with the ratio of insulae to domus recorded in the Regionaries; calculating from the Regionaries for Rome using the Ostian figure of 6.84 units per hectare gives a resultant 9.9 buildings per hectare (Storey 2001: 397).

In part 2 of his study, Storey (2002: 421–29) then uses a geographic information system to work out how many such 'architectural/residential units' might fit into one of Rome's Augustan regions. He estimates that there were approximately ten to fifteen buildings per hectare (Storey 2002: 429) that could be considered 'apartment buildings' of the style we know from Ostia. The size of the city at its height was on the order of 1,400 to 1,800 hectares (Storey 2001: 398, n36). Assuming 1,400 hectares for the size of Rome, with ten buildings per hectare, we end up with 14,000 buildings.

The caveats to this exercise are numerous and obvious. There is no accounting for bricks used in arches, for instance, and there were, of course, many other kinds of buildings and structures in Rome (not to mention the aqueducts stretching into the hinterland). It is important to remember that we are not trying to produce the correct figure here; rather, we want to illustrate the magnitude of Rome's appetite for resources and energy. In this way, we can describe the shape, texture and relative size of some of these different flows and delineate something of the shape of the networks that carried them. We can extract and highlight the self-organizing versus the top-down dynamics at play and contrast the distortions of the Imperial programs with the general background hum.

Suffice to say, I end up calculating fifteen million days of work. However, if we imagine that all of this building stock was erected over about 350 years (first to fourth centuries CE), and we further imagine that the construction season lasted 220 days each year (following DeLaine 1997), that gives us seventy-seven thousand possible working days. How many oxen would be necessary to do this much work? Divide the amount of work done (remembering that each trip uses a pair of oxen) by the available amount of days, and we get just under four hundred pairs of oxen. However, it is unreasonable to imagine that construction happened every day for every one of those years. The record shows that construction was much more punctuated. Construction would peak in the years after major fires, earthquakes or other such events. If we imagine that flat-out construction took place over one hundred not-necessarily-consecutive years, the number of pairs of oxen rises to 1,400. DeLaine (1997: 193,199) estimated for the Baths of Caracalla – an extremely intense project – that within Rome 1,800 to 3,200 pairs of oxen were used, and somewhere between 4,000 and 5,000 pairs of oxen were in use for the building industry as a whole.

The background noise of the Roman building industry brought an enormous amount of material into the city of Rome, but, contrary to what we might have imagined, it was not an unmanageable amount. At least, that is, until an Imperial project began, at which point the amount of activity could triple or more!

Interlude

The network is a beguiling metaphor. It excuses all manner of ills. Used loosely, *everything* can be connected up as a network. Used tightly, only certain things count, under certain conditions, and the implications of how and when those connections came to be can be useful for us as ancient historians (or archaeologists or sociologists or whatever).

Counting bricks and working out the on-the-ground implications of the fact of a network existing tends to give one a concrete perspective on theories of network/meshwork/entangled formation. Once, I was sent from Rome to Pompeii to pick up tools and materials at the end of the field season. The Ducato was a rust-bucket death-trap of a vehicle – just a large volume of empty space on wheels. Sufficiently large, in fact, that as I navigated the back streets of ancient Pompeii, I found that I couldn't make that left-hand turn and managed to get myself almost hung up on top of an ancient fountain basin. It was rather like that scene from the first Austin Powers movie where he has the cart stuck perpendicular inside the tunnel. Soon, the *custodes* appeared, and while my Italian wasn't sufficient to catch the nuance in the local dialect, I had no illusions about just what they thought of the situation. Five men, several dogs, shouting, gears grinding, me standing on the side of the street wringing my hat in worry while my co-pilot split his sides laughing. I'm sure the streets of Pompeii hadn't seen such traffic since the rebuilding effort after the earthquake in 62 CE. A whole series of networks existed to bring the seven of us together at that one node in time and space. A whole slew of information, power and money traversed those networks to facilitate my transportation of ancient materials and modern tools out of the site. How can we hope to map all of these intersecting networks? How can we even begin to think, to have the audacity to imagine, that we can measure the flows of so many things through, over, across and intertwined?

For perspective, let us consider the viewpoints of two of fiction's greatest detectives, Sherlock Holmes and Samuel Vimes:

Sherlock Holmes (Conan Doyle 1890, *The Sign of the Four*): 'How often have I said to you that when you have eliminated the impossible, whatever remains, however improbable, must be the truth?'

Sam Vimes (Pratchett 1996, *Feet of Clay*): 'The real world was far too real to leave neat little hints. It was full of too many things. It wasn't by eliminating the impossible that you got at the truth, however improbable; it was by the much harder process of eliminating the possibilities.'

For my money, Sam Vimes is the better detective. Here he has nailed the concept of equifinality, the idea that many different paths could lead to the evidence that we find. Vimes would make a good archaeologist. The problem, though, for archaeology (or history or anthropology or . . . or . . . or . . .) is that we don't really grapple with the idea of equifinality in our writing. This is why history, archaeology, digital humanities, needs an experimental mindset. Through experimentation, we can whittle down the possibilities. Scott Weingart (2014) has an excellent blog post on this very issue, through analogy with astronomy:

> Astronomers and historians both view their subjects from great distances; too far to send instruments for direct measurement and experimentation. . . . Historians are still stuck looking at the past in the same way we looked at the stars for so many thousands of years: through a glass, darkly. Like astronomers, we face countless observational distortions, twisting the evidence that appears before us until we're left with an echo of a shadow of the past. We recreate the past through narratives, combining what we know of human nature with the evidence we've gathered, eventually (hopefully) painting ever-clearer pictures of a time we could never touch with our fingers.

In which case, what we need is a laboratory for running different micro might-have-beens. I distrust do-everything social models, because with so many moving parts, how do you know what's going on? I said earlier that networks provide the armature, the skeleton, for building a digital enchantment. In the next section, I show some attempts at putting flesh on these skeletons. Like all mad scientists, we need a laboratory.

Note

1. A version of this was published in 'Counting Bricks and Stacking Wood: Providing the Physical Fabric', in *The Cambridge Companion to Ancient Rome*, ed. Paul Erdkamp (Cambridge University Press, 2013), 278–96. This version has been edited in some regards.

CHAPTER 2

Reanimating Networks

Agent-based models provide the laboratory we need for running different micro might-have-beens.[1] Years ago, in an article in the *Atlantic*, Jeffrey Rauch (2002) called it 'seeing around corners'. In keeping with the theme of this book, I like to think of it instead as a kind of digital necromancy, where we are able to interrogate not the dead, but rather simulacra of the dead, and ask them the questions about their lives that we otherwise can't. These simulacra, of course, are our digital golems, activated by the words in their heads. They are ersatz humans, stand-ins, puppets. The words that we put there are based on the archaeological materials that we have observed, put into dialogue according to those networks – that skeleton – of interactions we observed in the archaeology.

I'm mixing metaphors freely here, because I'm reaching for language to describe the systematic investigation of things that don't/ didn't exist: in literature we read of Cicero's decision to help his friend with a gift of money. What is the importance of the decision that Cicero did not make to not help his friend? (See Brughmans 2012.) How can we bridge the gap between the archaeological traces of an individual's decision and the option he or she chose not to pursue in order to understand the society that emerged from countless instances of individual decision-making?

It depends on levels. Are levels about control? Do we imagine levels where there are chains of command, privates to corporals and all the way up? Or do we imagine levels as being like Russian dolls, where each level is contained within the next one? Are levels like time, where seconds add up to minutes that add up to . . . years? Wilensky and Resnick (1999: 4) regard levels as being defined by the patterning of their interactions. Traffic jams exist independently of the cars that, entering and exiting the jam, interact to make up the jam itself. If you can describe different levels as individual actors in themselves (traffic jams move backwards down highways despite the forward movement of the cars) then you're dealing with a complex system. Agent-based models are entirely appropriate to use to study such phenomena.

Agent-based models (ABMs) do not specify the macro-scale behaviour of the systems they model. Research in archaeology at one time described society much like a machine. Cultures were comprised of different systems and subsystems, all operating in balance (Aldenderfer 1998: 91–120). However, chaos and complexity theories indicate that most natural and social phenomena do not exist in a state of equilibrium. The consequence of this realization is that the inter-relationships between the components are unstable, nonlinear and often cannot be discovered (Aldenderfer 1998: 104; cf. Cilliers 1998; Lewin 1993). Further, complexity theorists argue that the large-scale structures we identify with 'society' emerge because of individual interactions on the ground (Barrett 2001: 155). What ABMs do – and do well – is model the interactions of individuals so that emergent phenomenon may be studied. It is a generative, rather than reductionist, approach. (Epstein 2006: 41–42; 2008). It builds from the ground up, rather than reducing from the top down.

An ABM works by modelling phenomena in a computer using 'self-contained programs [agents] that can control their own actions based on their perceptions of their operating environment' (Huhns and Singh 1998 quoted in Gilbert and Troitzsch 2005: 172). It is explicitly built on the premise of individual actions, not systems. The agents in the model are usually autonomous: they have social ability; they can perceive and react to their environment; and they can engage in goal-oriented behaviour (Gilbert and Troitzsch 2005: 73). They have basic operating instructions (rule-sets) to govern their decision-making.

A certain anthropomorphism is hard to avoid when speaking of 'agents', but I do not know whether this is a strength or a failing, for it is a source of enchantment and of wonder, provided we do not transfer the anthropomorphism of talking about our agents onto the actual humans whose traces were extracted to give these agents digital life.

It is more correct to say that the agents represent simulated individuals, where the simulacra are autonomous pieces of software that are allowed to interact with each other and their environment. Each agent is its own bounded heterogeneous object. While every agent may have the same suite of variables, the combination of values for each agent is unique. The agents are given simple rules of behaviour drawn from whatever phenomenon we wish to study. How each individual agent implements the rules depends on its combination of characteristics and its situation vis-à-vis its local environment and neighbouring agents. The focus is on the particular. From these interactions, an artificial society begins to emerge. Creating an ABM requires clarity. We have to specify exactly what we think, and why, in order to translate our understanding of a phenomenon into code.

Joshua Epstein (1999) argues that this, in fact, is the principal strength of agent-based modelling: it requires modellers to make explicit their assumptions about how the world operates. This is the same argument made by Bogost (2007) for the video game: it is an argument in code, a rhetoric for a particular view of the world. As scholars, we make our own models every day when we conceive how a particular event occurred. The key difference is that the assumptions underlying our descriptions are often implicit.

Of Black Boxes

For those of us who have not built such models, it is worrisome to put so much faith in an approach where we cannot see what is happening and where we cannot even understand the language used. This is an entirely reasonable concern! If the rule-sets are not carefully defined and cannot be examined or verified by a knowledgeable outsider, it might be that we do indeed have an interesting artificial society, but one without relevance to the original society from which the model is ostensibly drawn. Even worse would be a scenario in which a relevant model, one with important things to teach us, is rejected by the academic community because its workings are murky and not susceptible to critical evaluation.

Most of us do not have the computer science or mathematics background to program our own models from scratch. Even if you did have access to a sympathetic computer science department at a university to assist in the development of a model, it would still be difficult. As a PhD student, I persuaded a mathematics graduate student I knew to implement a model I had found published in the literature (Rihll and Wilson 1987). He duly completed the code, building the model as a series of differential equations; I could run it, and I was presented with a list of outputs. I included it in my thesis, praying that during the viva voce I would not be asked the penetrating questions about whether or not the code actually did what we said it did. (Much later, when I had some programming ability, I tried to implement the model as an ABM.)

What I needed was a 'for dummies' environment where I myself could do the building, could show how the code worked, and why, and could set up a model as a kind of experiment. Just as I finished my PhD, I came across a platform tailor-made for exactly that: NetLogo.

The ABM authoring environment NetLogo is designed for the precise purpose of supporting researchers who do not have a computer science background (Wilensky 1999). NetLogo is a descendent of the Logo programming language. Models created with NetLogo are written in a syntax that is easily understandable and adaptable. It is an object-oriented approach. Each of the particular behaviours is modelled as its own object. Then the various objects are arranged in a specified order for the agents to perform. When the simulations run, each individual agent performs the rule-sets, the strategies for behaviour listed in the objects, at the same time as every other agent. Mastering NetLogo is simple enough that complicated models can be created by the user after working with a day-long tutorial, yet it's powerful enough to create simulations devoted to crowd dynamics and the emergence of cities in the third millennium BCE (Heinen and White 2004; Ourednik and Dessemontet 2007). A number of tutorials and sample models come bundled with the program.

For instance, one might create a model where agents are supposed to negotiate a best price for a product. The main routines of the model might look like this:

```
to go ;;; 'go' is a procedure that sets the model running
    am-I-a-buyer-or-a-seller
    search-for-a-partner
    set-my-price
    negotiate-the-sale
    do-my-accounting
end

to am-I-a-buyer-or-a-seller ;;; this is the 1st procedure
    if resource < 0 [set status 'buyer']
    if resource > 0 [set status 'seller']
end
```

Then, to run the model, the user simply types 'go'. Each line in the model refers to an 'object' or, in NetLogo-speak, a procedure. Each agent in the model simultaneously follows the instructions in each procedure. And since events in the model are historically contingent, agents, depending on the given circumstances of the given run, may select different roles. In one round, an agent might be a buyer; in another, it might be a seller if it has the required 'resource'. This resource could be 'harvested' from the environment where the agent operates, or it could be assigned at random depending on the objectives of the model. The entire model can be monitored for emergent properties. In our buyer-seller model described here, we might include a graph to monitor the flow of money – one that would indicate important developments such as a price-crash.

NetLogo militates against black-box syndrome because every part of a model is put on display, and the programming language associated with the application is simple to learn. Indeed, NetLogo was first developed as a teaching tool for secondary-level students to learn about complex phenomena (Wilensky 1999). In the intervening decades, it has attracted a large community of researchers. Its ease of use and power make it a feasible option for investigators with an average level of computer literacy.

Acts of Translation

Scholars who use NetLogo face the problem of developing appropriate rule-sets to govern social behaviour and then encoding them. That is, it is extremely hard to translate what we know about the past – or what we surmise – into an operationalized expression. One important guideline to remember here is not to become fixated on the process of assigning a numerical value. The numbers themselves are significant only because they allow a certain range of behaviours. In a model devoted to assessing the prestige of an individual Roman, and its impact on the economy, we might develop a scale of 'prestige importance' with a range of 1 to 100. The importance of the numbers is simply that '100' signifies 'very' and '1' signifies 'not much at all'. Once the model was constructed, it would then be possible to run the simulation multiple times, with each run altering the 'prestige importance' parameter in increments of ten in order to see if there is a point where some new behaviour of interest emerges (Agar 2003: 4.16–4.18).

With agent-based models, it is possible to run an artificial society – such as the model of Rome described in chapter 3 – through a series of artificial histories. After the set of simulations has been completed, the historian's next task is to select the runs that best correspond with history as it actually occurred. Here the primary task is to determine the parameter settings for the best runs. If the model has been carefully designed and validated, the historian will have learned something new about the original society, namely the parameter settings and the agent behaviours indicated by the parameter settings. That is the power and promise of agent-based modelling.

It is worth repeating that agent-based modelling forces us to formalize our thoughts about the phenomenon under consideration. There is no room for fuzzy thinking. We make the argument in code. Doing so allows us to experiment with past and present human agents in ways that could never be done in the real world. Some ABMs, for example, infect agents with a 'disease' to determine how fast it spreads. An ABM allows us to connect individual interactions with globally emergent behaviours. It allows us to create data for statistical study that would be impossible to obtain from real-world phenomena. It lets us raise the dead – or a version thereof – and if we know the pattern of their interactions because we have drawn out a network from the archaeological materials we've recovered, we can say something new about the past.

'We didn't understand a word of what you wrote in your application', was more or less what my potential postdoc supervisor said to me on the phone, '. . . but let's find out!' I had applied for a postdoctoral position in Roman archaeology, and it was my Hail Mary pass. In all of my applications for tenure-track jobs, sessional positions, short contracts and postdoctoral spots, I had been trying to read the entrails to work out what kind of person they wanted, and to fit what I had done into the boxes I thought I saw. It had been several years of disappointment: in leaving the academic scene in the United Kingdom and in Italy by returning to Canada, I had severed what scholarly networks I had, and starting over from scratch was not going well. For this position I thought, to hell with it; I will write the most out-there thing I can, the one thing I would really like to do if I had the chance. If I didn't get it, well, it was always a long shot. So I wrote, 'I would like to raise the dead. I know the patterns of past social interactions; I want to build autonomous software agents who will interact on these patterns.'

Raising the dead, through a formalized statement of what I believed to have been true of the past (informed by scholarship and experience) required several acts of translation, not least of which was translating the language of agent-based modelling into something I could understand. It involved learning for myself the potentials and limitations of what agent-based modelling could do. I gave a couple of talks during that year in Manitoba that were as much me talking to myself to figure things out as it was me communicating the results of scholarship. I decided early on that trying to raise the dead straight out of the gate would probably be a step too far. I began by doing the tutorials that come bundled with the NetLogo modelling environment. There were a number, even then, that explored the dynamics of networks and how different network shapes have an impact on, for instance, disease transmission and epidemics. These simple models of disease transmission made sense to me. I was already accustomed to using 'network' as a metaphor for trying to get a handle on the background hum of construction in Rome, for understanding Rome as its own higher-level emergent phenomena from all of those low-level interactions within the building trade. What could I model, in the Roman world, that made sense to think of as an actual network, over which something travelled? What could I model that would make sense to my new colleagues as a reasonable thing to model, a model easy to digest and critique? The more complex a model, the harder to work out whether the results are just artefacts of the code. *Keep It Simple, Shawn . . .*

Sometimes, getting a van stuck in ancient Pompeii can pay off in interesting ways. I decided to look at something a good deal less complicated that the social structure of Rome. I decided to look at the road network of Rome – the most obvious network I could think of – and turn some golems loose. I would start with the least complex model of human interaction I could devise; like the termite model where the termite agents pick up or put down a wood chip when they bump into another agent, my model would feature golems that passed on a 'message' when they bumped into other golems. As with the termite model, I hoped that simple actions would give rise to complex dynamics.

Networks in Global Space[2]

Let's simulate how we find – or how the Romans may have found – their way through space. I wanted to explore wayfinding in the Roman world, and how we might represent that. The agent model, and its results, do not necessarily tell us how the Romans understood space, but it does tell us what kinds of consequences we might expect to see in the archaeology of the Roman world if this kind of representation of space I modelled holds currency.

How do we find our way in new territory? We have a particular 'mind map', which hangs on points of our own experiences and our relationships with other individuals and institutions (Gould and White 1974), with which we structure our understanding of space. Kevin Lynch's (1960) book *The Image of the City* prompted much research into how we conceptualize space. One of the main points is that the construction of space is socially mediated (cf. Urry 2000: 49–76 on the sociology of 'travellings'; Mark et al. 1999). How we represent that socially mediated understanding of geographic space in turn affects our interpretation of it (Batty 2003; Montello et al. 2003). In tests where subjects are shown scatters of points against a neutral background (something that the viewer implicitly recognizes as a map), it has been found that the subjects are more inclined to associate points together in the up-down dimension than in the left-right dimension – even though the spacing between all the points is the same (Montello et al. 2003: 316–37). In modern Western culture, we are accustomed to orienting our maps so that north is always at the top (by default, then, as viewers we are prioritizing relationships in the up-down dimension, which may not be warranted). If understanding space is so complicated in the modern world (what we understand is based on our experiences; how we represent what we understand in turn affects our understanding), it is doubly so for understanding an ancient conception of space. For antiquity, Favro (1996) connected the Roman orator's 'house of memory' to a way of reading the urban image of Augustan Rome, for understanding the interconnections and meanings between places in the city (following Lynch 1960). Using a 'stranger in town' – Pompeii – as an example, Ling (1990) wondered how visitors to a new town might find their way (they would have to use ad hoc directions based on recognizable landmarks). The volume *Travel and Geography in the Roman Empire* (Adams and Laurence 2001) explicitly considers the Roman representation of large-scale geographic space as opposed to these smaller, urban representations. For the Roman, large-scale geographical space was often viewed as a list of what-comes-next. The most famous of these lists today are the Antonine Itineraries (Salway 2001; Brodersen 2001; Arnaud 1992; Capelli and Pesando 1991). Details about the space between places could always be supplied by a knowledgeable local, but the global perception was courtesy of a list, an itinerary. The success of one's journey depended on the quality of the itinerary at hand: see, for example, Galen's misadventures on his way to Lemnos in the second century CE (discussed by Brodersen 2001: 8–9).

The Itineraries

The Antonine Itineraries are a collection of routes within the Roman Empire, with the starting and ending points and intervening stages along the routes listed, along with the appropriate mileages between stages. There are breaks in the sequence, which imply that up to ten separate smaller itinerary lists were collated to create the collection. These routes of travel do not necessarily map exactly onto the Roman road system (and sometimes they imply a certain amount of river-travel). There are, in fact, a number of maritime itineraries included, which follow the Greek tradition of mariners' coastline descriptions, the peripli, and probably have their sources in these as well. These sections measure distance in Greek stadia, although some use miles instead. Some itineraries listed seem to suggest that a real journey was recorded and incorporated, perhaps a journey of an Emperor Antoninus. The omission of places in the Agri Decumantes or in Dacia point to a compilation date sometime after the abandonment of these regions in the latter half of the third century CE (Salway 2001: 26–43). Salway (2001: 58) discusses how the lists were compiled from milestones and other public displays of stages and distances, how they are 'very much rooted in the experience of travel rather than the theory of geography'.

Who was the traveller? This question is tied up with how the itineraries were compiled from other documents: 'These instruments of public display meet the needs of the private individual forced occasionally to make journeys beyond the region with which he or she is normally familiar. Such a constituency will have changed over time' (Salway 2001: 59). Salway (2001: 60) concludes that the final compilation of these documents from different periods into the itineraries as we know them in the fourth century CE reflects the need to be able to find one's way to whatever city the Imperial Court happened to be in. They reflect the experience of local geographies stitched together for a particular purpose that may not reflect the multifarious purposes for which the original texts (inscribed in stone, erected in town centres and so on) were used. But they do, at bottom, reflect some of the realities of travelling around the lands controlled by Rome.

It is in this bottom level that I was interested. What do the surviving itineraries suggest for how geographic space was organized and experienced in the Roman world? The itineraries are not simply lists: they are records of journeys, both real and potential, across the vast landscape of the Roman Empire, and they are the static presentation of dynamic relationships between the towns listed. These relationships were the normal comings and goings associated with trade, extended families and culture between any two neighbouring settlements.

The Starting Point

I took as a starting point Laurence's (2001) work on the Romanization of Britain. He uses the evidence of the itineraries to compare different provinces' space-economies. 'Space-economy' is based on the idea that good, all-weather roads allowing easier travel between areas created a new conception of space, shortening the temporal distance between places. In Italy, the net result was its unification (Laurence 2002). Laurence (2001, 2002) was interested to see if the distances recorded in the itineraries for Britain were similar to those around the Mediterranean and if the geography of Britain was organized along similar lines. He calls this 'the infrastructure of Imperialism' (Laurence 2001: 67, 74–75). Focusing on the mileage between centres, Laurence (2001: 90–91) concludes that the 'connectivity' of Britain was not significantly different from the Mediterranean world. He argues that this is a better measure of the Romanization of Britain – its incorporation into the Roman world – than the monumentalization of urban centres.

It is worth pointing out that Laurence's 'connectivity' focuses exclusively on the distances between places – the mileages – rather than the overall patterning of the connections themselves, an important distinction (see further below). I wanted to use the itineraries to try to experience this Roman view of space. I asked, if we do this, would we find the same results as Laurence? What would be our perception of the different provinces? What would be the aggregate perception of the different provinces? Would there be something at that level different from our individual perception?

Social Networks, Town Networks and the Itineraries: Static Space

In 1931, Henry Beck invented the modern London Underground diagram that now guides millions of people's navigation of London. By ignoring 'real-world' geography, instead placing stations so that their relationships one to another were clearly evident, Beck made a 'network diagram' map that simplified the (daunting) task of getting around the metropolis (Brodersen 2001: 18) – that is, his 'map' is a topological representation of the connections between places. This is the heart of social network analysis (Hanneman and Riddle 2005), the body of methodologies used here to analyse the implications for the human geography of the Roman Empire based on the Antonine Itineraries.

Cities are the foci of multiple networks. Networks extend beyond the city, linking different cities together in different ways, but also incorporating every point in between along the continuum of settlement types, from humble rural farmsteads upwards. According to this model, it is cities themselves which are nodes of social relations in time and space (Massey et al. 1999: 100–36). At all times, however, people must be taken into account: it is not enough that interconnections should exist. Rather, people must make something of these interconnections (Massey et al. 1999: 121). That is, in studying the interrelationships of cities, we have to formulate that interrelationship at the level of individuals. This problem is resolved by considering what flows through these networks – information, commerce and culture – and the agents who carry those flows. In the agent-based model discussed below, the transmission of information is explicitly considered to be through the agency of individuals. The itineraries represent a type of social network, and they represent one instance of the various possible networks suggest by Massey et al. (1999).

To turn these itineraries into a network that we may study needs some sort of formalization of the relationships between the listed towns. In order to keep the analysis simple, we can presume that towns listed one after another in an itinerary have an implied link between them (a foundational observation for Cherry's (1977) study of the political geography of the Mycenaean kingdom of Pylos, and for Kendall's (1971, 1977) use of networks and graph theory for geographic analysis). Simple geographical proximity implies a certain amount of trade and cultural contacts. Presumably, towns listed together would be more alike socially than towns at either end of an itinerary.

This is not to say that neighbouring towns will perform the same role in a society, but rather that they will share cultural and social contacts which, in the main, are more similar than they are different. Not every possible settlement, however, was listed in the itineraries. The compiler chose which towns and which routes to include, implying that something more than simple geographic space was a factor in how the towns were listed. This is why it makes sense to consider the itineraries as a social network. We can analyse the entire network of towns in the itineraries for a global view of how the empire was connected. By formalizing the structure of the itineraries in a network, we can study the relative positioning of towns and cities vis-à-vis each other.

The argument, then, is that the structure of the itineraries is a mirror for the structure of Roman urban society (at the regional level) – at least as it was conceived by the individual who compiled the lists.

(Although beyond the scope of this section, the towns left out of the itineraries could also be considered. A study comparing the topologies of the real road network against the topology of the itineraries would go a long way toward putting the itineraries in their proper context and would allow us to judge whether the emphasis we place on the itineraries is warranted).

So What Do We See?

When the itineraries are stitched together, we begin to see in them the overall pattern of connectivity for the empire. The towns and settlements form the 'nodes' of the network, the connecting points; the links are the spaces implied by the settlements' positioning in the list. Towns listed consecutively in the itineraries are joined by single links. Before looking at individual provinces, let us examine the whole empire. There are over five hundred towns or cities listed in the Antonine Itineraries. The distance between any two settlements in the empire-wide network ranges from one link (for adjacent towns) to a maximum of sixty-nine links. The shortest average path between any two settlements in the empire-wide network is about nineteen: that is, if we select any two towns at random, on average there will be a route connecting them by way of eighteen other towns. Path length in the itineraries is significant on a number of accounts. First, there is the seeming regularity of the average path length in each region studied. This would suggest that there is a great deal of internal homogeneity in each region (the closer settlements appear on the itinerary, the more likely they shared cultural traits). This contrasts with the path length for the empire as a whole, which points to the great diversity within it. Yet to what degree is path length significant? One is cautious of coincidences: could the regularity be a by-product of the compiler's methodology? It is doubtful whether the regularity observed here was intentional, because it is only evident when viewed from a social network analysis.

A more significant statistic may be the cohesion score, since this is dependent on interlinkages in the routes themselves. 'Cohesion' in this context means the proportion of links that exist in the network compared to a network with the same number of nodes, where the nodes are all completely connected. On this score, Italy and Spain appear to be very similar, while Gaul is not very tightly knit. This perhaps reflects the importance of major rivers for the history of settlement in Gaul and the stringing out of settlements along their banks. The empire as a whole is less cohesive by almost another order of magnitude, no doubt due to the small number of itineraries that include sea travel (on which more below). Now, there are far more sophisticated representations of connectivity in the Roman world – the ORBIS model by Scheidel and Meeks (2012) not only incorporates far more sources on connectivity, but also incorporates nuanced arguments about travel time, wind currents and so on, and so can be used to explore actual travel time. The difference here is that we are simulating the mental model of the Roman world represented by the itineraries, and how long it might take is not the same thing as what it feels like to contemplate a journey. It might only take me six hours to get from Ottawa to Toronto, but for my friends in Toronto, the journey from Toronto to Ottawa just *feels* too far altogether.

Agent-Based Modelling and Simulation: Dynamic Space

In the rather simple simulation presented here, what is being tested is the effect of different patterns of connectivity on the diffusion of information. In the simulation, each individual agent is distinguishable by its starting place on the network. It is not very smart; it either has heard a 'message', or it has not. That is all it knows about its world. Does it matter what the 'message' is? Not really, since the purpose of this simulation is to explore the flow of information.

We could imagine that the message is a new religious practice, or a new style in pottery making (cf. Lawall and Graham 2018); whatever it is, it is secondary to the journey and is not the reason for the journey itself. This agent then travels through a region, following the pathways laid down in the itineraries. Other agents are travelling as well. Because each agent does not necessarily know the 'best' local route to get from one town to another along the itinerary, there is some randomness in the exact path each agent takes. In the two-dimensional simulation world, each route in an itinerary is modelled as a thick line against the map of the region, which makes it possible for two agents, travelling in opposite directions between pairs of towns, to pass each other without actually coming into contact (this allows the model to take into account the discrepancy between global and local forms of geographic knowledge; Graham 2006c).

When an agent who has not 'heard' the idea does come into contact with the 'carrier' (they collide), the idea is passed along and we now have two carriers spreading the idea. These are the only rules in this model: move along the path of the itinerary; pass the message to agents who have not heard it. Are these realistic rules? For the purposes of this model, it is not necessary for us to know how actual Romans transmitted knowledge one to another, or whether this knowledge was contested or transformed in the transmission; it is enough to know that it happened. We should not add any more complexity to the model than is necessary. 'Necessary' is the key word and is, of course, debateable.

I ran the simulation a number of times, at a wide variety of settings, to produce a 'landscape' of possible results for each region under study. Calling it a 'landscape' does not really do justice to what is happening here: if the model rules capture anything of the real experience of the perception of the connectivity of space in the Roman world, then the possible outcomes are histories that could have happened, with greater or lesser probabilities.

I compared each region against the other, based on the relative speed of transmission. Time in the model is defined in cycles. Each cycle is completed when every agent has run through its entire set of instructions. It would be possible to calibrate these cycles roughly against known travel times in antiquity based on the network structure of the itineraries and the various notices in the ancient literature on the speed of communications. For instance, in the consideration by Duncan-Jones (1990: 22–23) of the speed of communication for double-dated edicts from the Theodosian Code, he notes five instances of communications between Gaul and Italy where the average number of days was 39. This is twenty more days than the shortest average path between any two settlements in the empire-wide network discussed above, and so gives a rough indication that one link in network terms equals two days' travel (see Duncan-Jones 1990: 7–29 on the caveats involved, principally the effects of seasonality. ORBIS did not exist when I first created this model; it would be an interesting experiment for someone to run this model again against that representation of the Roman world).

Because no other variables are modelled in the simulation except the number of travellers, and the chance of an encounter provoking a transmission is guaranteed, the speed of transmission is therefore dependent on the structure of the itineraries themselves. Every region followed a broad pattern: it takes a bit of time for the first 10 per cent of actors to encounter the 'idea'. Thereafter, diffusion speeds up markedly compared to that original 10 per cent, until roughly half of all agents have encountered the idea. Finally, the diffusion rate slows down, as the last few who have not encountered the idea collide into those who have (some of whom will have heard it several times, a reinforcing process that could be explored in a more sophisticated model).

I want to highlight just two of the implications of this model:

1. Britain and Gaul are more 'fragile' and less cohesive than Iberia and Italy in terms of network fragmentation. This might indicate distinct northern (ignoring for the moment that Gaul has a Mediterranean coastline) and Mediterranean patterns of connectivity, with the provinces of the northern grouping less well known to the compiler or, alternatively, simply with fewer known routes to get from A to B. One consequence might be that it would be more difficult to overcome the perception of disruption and to find alternative routes. The perception of disruption could carry economic or political costs.

2. Iberia has the fastest internal diffusion rate, followed by Gaul. Britain and Italy are more internally consistent in their diffusion rates. This suggests that the adoption of innovation in Iberia and Gaul would take place faster than their geographical size might imply, and the adoption would not necessarily be as complete: the ability to reach all individuals rapidly along the network structures of the itineraries suggests that there were concentrations in particular areas. In Britain and Italy, on the other hand, the adoption would be slower than their size might suggest, but the adoption would be more thorough (the structure of the itineraries reflects a more even distribution of population).

These are two of the conclusions that I drew from the model that I thought might reasonably be tested or explored by someone else. I believed that these observations would perhaps help explain patterns in other categories of materials. With any model, there are at least two ways we could play the results. We could take the emergent results of the simulation as proof that the model's underlying assumptions are correct, and then use these results as new data points. As data points in their own right, they could then become the foundation for some other argument. Or we could take the emergent results as lenses through which we might examine other kinds of archaeological material, which is generally a far safer approach. In the original publication, I gestured towards some patterns in the epigraphic habits of these various regions that might be seen in a new light via my little model. There are patterns in the archaeology of inscriptions, in terms of their density and distribution, that are highly reminiscent of those in the model, which suggests that the cognitive arrangement of space evidenced in the itineraries does have a role to play in any explanation of the taking up of Roman culture.

But before such a model can be used as a data point, or evidence in its own right, the model ought to be taken to pieces by somebody else, run on a different kind of network generated from a different body of material. In fact, before the model can be used as a lens to deform our perspective on Roman history, before it can be used to gain a different viewpoint, it should go through that same process of being pulled apart! To that end, I made the model available and settled down to see what would happen next. That is the final step in any kind of work that relies on models: the source code has to be made available.

This model was my first attempt at building and publishing historical simulation work. The disenchantment I felt about archaeology, the estrangement, began to fade away. The virtual life I was able to breathe into these fossilized traces of the past – me! the brick stamp boy! – was empowering. This is critical: if we are going to speak for the past, tell the stories that structure and make meaning from the bits of the present that signify the past (the archaeological materials), we need to not be trying to do it from a position of ennui or disdain. We cannot hate the materials or the methods we use, because to do that is to do violence in the present.

Learning to write code, learning to explain what was happening within that code, learning to ask for help in public fora, learning to offer help: these were the things that began to re-enchant archaeology for me. The wonder and delight I found in building this model, which offered me new insights into the past that no one had encountered before, helped to move me towards that ethic of generosity that enchantment promotes.

It made me a better archaeologist.

Notes

1. Portions of this section are a reworking of Shawn Graham, 'Behaviour Space: Simulating Roman Social Life and Civil Violence', *Digital Studies/le Champ Numérique* 1, no. 2 (2009), DOI: http://doi.org/10.16995/dscn.109, CC BY 4.0.
2. Originally published as Shawn Graham, 'Networks, Agent-Based Modeling, and the Antonine Itineraries', *Journal of Mediterranean Archaeology* 19, no. 1 (2006): 45–64. Reproduced with kind permission of Equinox Publishing Ltd. Here I have edited somewhat to bring out some of the larger issues important for this volume.

CHAPTER 3

Add Agents and Stir

A network perspective is a powerful framework for understanding something of what was going on in the past. It is a skeleton, an articulation of relationships. As we have seen, when we reanimate some of the processes that might have taken place along those articulations, we can isolate the would've-could've-should'ves to a more limited set. This limited set acts like a lens through which we can view the material remains from the past in the present, deforming our own ideas and holding them up for systematic investigation.

We have moved from the network-as-a-metaphor to exploring the pattern of flow on actual networks, which could shed new light on the patterns we're seeing in the archaeology. But . . . we're still lacking actual people. The dumb golems from the previous model do not even begin to approach the complexity of human social structures.

When I was writing my PhD dissertation, I had those tonnes of bricks in that back shed. I had their fabric; I knew their geochemistry; I knew what was written on the stamps. But it was all dead to me. It was just so much . . . so much . . . stamp collecting. All PhD students will recognize that feeling when they're so deep into it they feel they can't quit, but whatever spark there was has been extinguished: it's just the grind, the determination to finish, that keeps them going. That's where I was when, in the third year of my work, I came across agent-based modelling for the first time through a chance conversation on a tour bus with a geographer. I had already started to have a dim perception that my sketches of which *dominus* was connected to what *figlina* and the movements of *officinatores* between them were, yes, networks. Recognizing them as networks gave me statistics! I could compare, say, the shape of the network under the Flavian dynasty with the shape under Hadrian. But these pictures were dead, lifeless, insects-pinned-to-a-corkboard. If I reanimated the patterns of connection implied by the stamped bricks, then the nodes would represent actual historic individuals. With agent-based modelling, maybe I could make them live again. A practical necromancy, if you will? That was the project I actually pitched for my postdoctoral work. With the simple model of information transmission under my belt, I returned to the bricks. I wondered, how did the networks that I found in the bricks change from one shape to another? What perturbed them? How robust were they?

Networks in Social Space[1]

'[Septimius Severus] . . . turned his full anger on Albinus' friends in Rome . . . each one was indicted for a crime; all who were prominent at that time in the Senate, or who were richer and more noble in the provinces were destroyed ruthlessly' (Herodian, III.8). Such passages are common in the annals of Roman history. Each one describes the extermination of various members of the city's elite, as one or more of Rome's factions vied for power. Under what circumstances did Roman patronage networks survive? Collapse? Transform? Let us raise the dead to explore how and why such episodes emerged in Roman society. This practical necromancy provides us a means to explore the consequences of social conditions actually and potentially extant at the time.

Roman historians have often drawn attention to the important role that friendship and patronage networks played in sustaining Rome's economy. Koenraad Verboven (2002), for example, characterized the Roman economy as the economy of friends. These networks, it has been argued, complemented and extended the market economy of Rome, fulfilling the role that banking and the transfer of financial capital played in modern economies. The pivotal figure in all of this was the patron, the man whose contacts, *fides* and personal power allowed him to protect and promote the financial and social welfare of his clients. Patronage is an asymmetrical friendship between individuals who have differing levels of social power. The practice bound different levels of Roman society together by creating networks of financial and political support and by imposing social obligations and debts that its members were required to pay. Each network revolved around the linchpin of its patron (Verboven 2002; cf. Wallace-Hadrill 1989; Saller 1989). Patronage and its resulting networks was the animating force of Roman society from its earliest days. The study of patronage practices and their consequent impact on Rome's social networks offers one way to explore the underlying DNA of Roman society.

This issue is important because Roman history is replete with instances in which the city's elite engaged in a process of self-extermination, a practice that seemed to present no fundamental consequences for Roman society at large. What was it about the structure of Roman society that allowed it to endure the loss of major figures in social and economic life? In a culture where the economy was embedded in social and political networks, the development and changing pattern of those networks has important ramifications for understanding historical change.

In this model, I take the archaeological evidence from one particular set of patronage relationships – the ties between landowners and brickmakers in the Tiber Valley, north of Rome (relationships that were recorded by stamps on bricks) – and uses these as the framework for 'reanimating' one sector of the Roman economy. I use the same number of agents in the model as can be attested archaeologically in the brick stamps. In order to explore this 'economy of friends', I have built a model of Roman social life whose fundamental 'procedure' is the morning ritual of the *salutatio*, the morning greeting clients gave their patrons. This ritual cemented the patronage networks underlying Rome's economic life, and it was one of the city's most ancient social rituals. Here I explore what such an economy might have looked like. I describe how spontaneous purges and proscriptions can be modelled and the circumstances under which they are generated. The initial results from this model point to gift exchange as a key factor in the emergence of civil violence in ancient Rome (and I consider the competitive building projects of the Late Republic, which were enormous gifts to the people of Rome, in this same light).

Salutatio

The morning *salutatio* was one of the most ancient traditions in Rome. The word 'salutation' is derived from the tradition, and it refers to the custom whereby the clients of a patron would formally greet the patron at the start of each day. The order in which a client was received stemmed from the status and esteem wherein he was held by his patron. An essential feature of this tradition was that outsiders saw it and, more specifically, saw the numbers of clients paying their morning respects to their patron (cf. Wallace-Hadrill 1989: 83). After the *salutatio*, the patron and his attending clients then proceeded to the Forum to conduct the day's business. The procession and activity at the Forum provided another opportunity for outsiders to assess the patron's prestige and status, through observation of the number and quality of his clients. (An excellent depiction of this daily show is in the Harris novel, *Imperium*, concerning Cicero and his clients.) The patron relied on his clients for political support. The client relied on the patron for financial, legal or other kinds of support.

It is important to note that the template of personal relationships described here was the template that Rome applied to govern its relationships with its conquered cities and peoples, a template embedded in the language of patronage. Indeed, it could be argued that this practice was a formative cause of the Late Republican civil wars. When new peoples were incorporated into the Roman system, they were described as clients of individual Roman statesmen, not of the Roman state. It was a practice that upset the balance of power among Rome's elite: more clients equalled more power. A model of the *salutatio*, therefore, is not just a model of individual activities; it also represents in a larger sense a model of how Rome managed its Mediterranean empire. It is impossible to understand Roman antiquity without viewing it through the lens of patronage.

Patronage, at its most fundamental level, can be understood as an asymmetric relationship between two people of unequal social status where there is a reciprocal, or two-way, exchange of goods and services. The relationship is not transient, as it would be in a modern commercial transaction, but instead is maintained by both parties for an extended duration of time and is distinguished by its personal quality (Saller 1989: 49). Patronage is a relationship that may be entered into voluntarily; a client may withdraw his allegiance and may have more than one patron (Garnsey and Woolf 1989: 154; Drummond 1989: 101). The central purpose of patronage, as Wallace-Hadrill (1989: 72–3) shows, is to control access to resources. Power is derived from knowing the right people, from giving and receiving favours. Archaeologically, we find evidence of this practice in the construction of the Forum Baths at Ostia by Gavius Maximus, Praetorian Prefect of Antoninus Pius. Over 90 per cent of the stamped bricks in this complex were supplied as a result of the contacts Gavius maintained with the Imperial family and with Asinia Quadratilla and Flavius Aper (DeLaine 2002). In the ancient Roman economy, the products of one's land were not things that one simply sold. Rather, they were 'bargaining chips' in a great game. Rome's economy was not a market economy; it was an economy of friends, a network of patronage relationships maintained through interlocking rings of well-connected people.

Salutatio is the crucial behaviour that is modelled in this simulation. I have imagined at least two ways that the historic impact of this practice can be explored. The first is to incorporate the practice into a randomly generated social network and then see how the simulated network evolves over time. The second method is to model the behaviour on top of the archaeologically known network of 234 individuals associated with a patronage network responsible for providing building materials to the City of Rome in the second century CE. In archaeology, it is rare to have the names of so many individuals and to be able to draw out the web of connections between them. However, what is extremely important about these individuals was not so much their number, but their social station. They were major landowners situated around Rome and hence the people closest socially and politically to the seat of power. Importantly, individuals from every stratum of Roman society were also participants in this network, from the emperor and his household on down. This network therefore – derived from brick stamps – provides a clear glimpse of Rome's social structure.

Network Theory and Patronage

The number of actors in a network is not the only important variable. The nature of their relationships was also a crucial concern. The dictates of patronage suggests that the relationships between individuals were unequal: Fortunatus's relationship with Quadratilla was not the same as Quadratilla's relationship with Fortunatus. Due to its unequal nature, their relationship, in a network model, would be expressed as two links. For the two hundred thirty-four individuals represented in our model, however, it was not always possible to determine the exact nature of the relationship between two given individuals. In such circumstances, one had to be content with the knowledge that a relationship had existed. Analysis of the network's changing shape and constitution, however, required some expression of the relationship, and in such circumstances relationships for the entire network were therefore expressed as single linkages. Various metrics can be computed and the nature of power explored, given the changing patterns over time. In terms of why a network might enjoy a particular shape, the driver of network formation most apposite here is 'preferential attachment'. It posits that an agent's chance of joining an actor heading a network is a function of the number of connections which that actor already has. In this conception, the rich get richer. Those individuals who are well connected find it easy to generate still more connections (Barabási 2002: 90–91). Here we can read 'patronage' for 'preferential attachment': there was no point for most Romans in becoming the client of a man who had few connections himself.

Behaviour into Code

Prestige and status were pervasive features of social life and the ancient Roman economy. Everything was filtered through the lens of prestige and status. Transactions were not framed in terms of pure economic exchange. Therefore, in our model, I encoded the following behaviours into our agents:

1. Agents were required to examine their own status level, which initially was a function of how many people they knew, and then pay respects to individuals whom they knew who had a higher status than themselves.
2. Agents knew that it was in their interest to receive high-status clients and accordingly were programmed to receive them when the potential client's status was relatively high to its peers.
3. Agents were programmed to seek an audience with a high-status patron, since they knew such visits would enhance their status.

These three rules constituted the fundamental procedures for agent conduct in the model. Together, they recreated the ritual of *salutatio*, the ritual of paying respects to one's social superiors. Two other rules were also incorporated into the model.

4. Agents were required to exchange gifts when paying respects. In the ritual of *salutatio*, gift exchanges served to cement the relationship between patron and client. They also facilitated the redistribution of wealth.
5. Agents were programmed to trade with counterparts at similar status levels, though trade was not contingent on each party belonging to the exact same rank.

After paying their respects, agents in the model manoeuvre through their world and seek to trade – to play the game – with others of similar status. I have opted to model the basic mechanism of trade in my model as a type of game where the agent's chances of gaining a favourable outcome depend on its social status. The mechanism is not a zero-sum game, wherein if one agent wins, the other must lose; rather, success depends on the agent's status level and the probability of a successful outcome imposed by a particular economic 'climate', which is set by the model's user. Both agents could win; only one could win; or both could lose. The 'climate' represents a host of individual, historic and economic contingencies. When two agents meet to trade, the climate indicates whether the agents have good market information, whether they are good dealers, whether one is having an off day, or any one of a potential number of competing factors that can influence whether an agent gets the best of any particular deal.

In the simulation, no specific good or service is 'traded' per se. Instead, I model the outcomes of economic exchanges based on the assumption that the more prestigious an agent is, the more likely he is to receive the best result from any particular encounter. If an agent wins, his money is increased by the 'risk factor', a variable that determines how much an agent stands to win or lose from a given transaction. Similarly, if the agent loses, his money is decreased by the same risk factor. Profit from a transaction can increase the agent's status in the simulation, but not necessarily. A great deal depends on the agent's status in the first place. Consider, for example, the fate of the wealthy freedman Trimalchio, a literary creation of Petronius. Despite his enormous acquisition of wealth, he gained very little status. Giving gifts can also enhance an agent's prestige in the simulation. While the act initially decreases the patron's wealth, it increases his chances of achieving greater economic success in the long run.

This simple model of Roman social organization displays interesting behaviours that may cast new light onto Roman history. When the model runs with only rules one through three, enormous disparities in status level emerge. When rules four and five are applied, the trading mechanism allows agents to make new acquaintances and learn of the existence of higher-status agents previously unknown to them. Through trade, agents gain opportunities to join new chains of patronage. The trading mechanism therefore opens up the possibility for social mobility. It is not success in trade that creates this possibility. Rather, it is the process of becoming known to new individuals. If the trade mechanism is turned off, the process of paying respects alone causes the overall social structure to ossify.

Generating Civil Violence

I began this section citing Septimius Severus's actions upon achieving the purple (that is, on becoming Emperor). Any mechanism I might generate to allow for the possibility of civil violence in this model is necessarily my argument-in-code, my procedural rhetoric, explicating my view on the sources of violence in antiquity. In early versions of the model, I had a 'smite' button. This button gave me the capacity to explore the effects of 'shocks' to the system through randomly killing high-status agents:

```
ask random n-of Romans with status = high
[die]
```

If the overall difference in social status between 'high' and 'low' agents in the artificial society was not great, social life continued – with agents at each rank ascending to the next level vacated by their dead predecessors. If the initial distinction in social status was great however, the artificial society quickly evolved into a despotic society, one headed by one high-status individual and populated by individuals of extremely low status. Agents ceased to pay respects to one another, and the society collapsed. In the emergent despotic society, random killings of agents seemed to have no effect, since all agents were equal in status – no one paid respects to counterparts or superiors; therefore, there was no possibility of changing status and ascending to a vacant social niche.

Obviously, the shock button was not a satisfactory long-term solution for the model. What are the sources of civil violence in the Roman world? The concern here is to identify a mechanism that could have generated civil violence from the normal operations – or failures of – the patronage system in Rome. The greatest expressions of civil violence – the Late Republican civil wars – can be viewed in this light as the competition between three or four 'great men': Caesar, Pompey, Antony and Octavian. Each man at different points in time attempted to expand their control beyond their own respective chains of patronage in order to incorporate all of Rome's patronage networks. The civil wars were a failure of patronage in that in the good of the state, the res publica became identified with the good of the individual general. Generals were permitted to oversee the pensioning and support of demobilized soldiers, and the allegiance of soldiers accordingly was transferred from the state to the person of the general. The arrangement permitted victorious generals to translate their military strength into political strength and subvert the normal workings of state machinery. Generals – as competing politicians – used the patronage system to stimulate urban riots, calling on their respective followers to contest legislation or elections through violence (Aldrete 2013).

Famines were another factor that precipitated civil violence in the Roman world. They also have been shown to be failures of the patronage system and political will, since these exacerbated crop failures and transformed them into the social disaster of a famine (Laurence 1998: 135). Ultimately, when Rome's political elite was confronted with environmental or political challenges, their response was consistently filtered through the lens of patronage. Technological change was rarely a disruptive factor in ancient Rome, largely due to the inherent conservatism of Roman patrons and their dependence on a slave economy.

At the individual level, Gregory Aldrete (2013) demonstrates that the mechanics underlying riots in Rome in the Late Republic and Early Imperial ages were generally not spontaneously generated; rather, they were often the product of professional agitators. The profession of agitator had its origin in the theatre. Individuals were hired to start the applause for a particular actor or performance. These 'claquers' – as they were also known – were subsequently appropriated by Rome's elite for political purposes, namely to provide 'spontaneous' support at orations and other political events. They were also hired to start demonstrations – demonstrations that potentially could tip into riots. When initiating a mass event, it was crucially important for the agitator to make the demonstration or riot appear as if it emerged spontaneously. The act of agitation required the presence of individuals who could be induced to riot if someone else appeared ready to do so, to initiate a band-wagon effect.

Work by Joshua Epstein (2002) on modelling political violence suggested a mechanism for allowing purges to emerge spontaneously from the model itself that seems analogous to the professional claquers in Rome. In Epstein's model, agents rebel if government legitimacy is perceived to drop below an agent's tolerance for bad government. They only spring into action, however, when other, similarly rebellious agents are situated nearby. Action in Epstein's model depends not only on an agent's internal state, but also on its social context. The social context for rebellion can be dampened by having 'police' agents who wander the world. In such a scenario, agents who fear arrest are less likely to rebel.

Epstein's mechanism depends on agents' responding to their internal states and to environment cues. While the modern context of Epstein's work does not map 1:1 to Rome, there are parallels, and the idea of an agent exploring its internal state against its environment is something with which we can work. I translated this mechanism into this simulation first by giving each agent a capacity to hold a grudge. Remember that a patron's status was enhanced by the social standing of those who visited him. It was therefore in the interest of patrons to ensure that their clients were suitably notable themselves before allowing them to participate in the *salutatio*. In the model, a patron's decision to deny agents the opportunity to pay respects due to their low social standing, thereby limiting their access to patronage networks, creates a state of 'grievance' in the affected agents and eventually lays the basis for political violence. Agents remember who has denied them the opportunity to participate in the *salutatio*. Each individual agent has its own randomly set tolerance for rejection, its own specific 'grievance' level. Its action on that grievance, however, depends on whether its neighbouring agents are also prepared to act. When does the simulation tip into violence? It does so when the global measure of patrons' legitimacy, their capacity to 'oppress' the clients over which they have charge, is exceeded by the number of agents ready to become violent. For each individual agent in the model, the measure of legitimacy is called *auctoritas*, or authority. *Auctoritas* is the measurement of an agent's wealth and prestige.

When agents become violent, death ensues. Agents in the simulation do not kill randomly. Instead, they target other agents against whom they have a grievance. Such targeted killings, however, can set off cascades of killing, since the removal of individuals alters the social environment for the *salutatio* by changing the levels of social prestige for the survivors, thereby changing the chains of connected individuals and altering the overall level of *auctoritas* governing the simulation.

Running the Model

As the model runs, 'reporters' record the number of patrons and clients, the amount of money in circulation and the division of the population into three classes based on status level. The reporters also show the emergent alliances between agents. These alliances are referred to as 'houses'. Initially, at the start of each run, each agent is assigned a unique colour. Once the agent joins a particular network, his colour changes to that of his patron. 'Mobsize' and 'oppression' (the collective *auctoritas* of the patrons) are variables that are also plotted over time. They enable the modeller to determine when the population has tipped into violent behaviour. 'Roman 23 is about to kill Roman 57. Roman 124 is about to kill Roman 98. Roman 200 is about to kill Roman 87 . . .' – the terrible litany prints out in the console window, as each Roman (agent) updates its status and its intended target. Various graphs and tickers start plummeting. Colours flash as alliances realign. Stability emerges for a while . . . and then the killings start over again.

It's a terrible enchantment, a terrible but compelling simulation to watch. If I run it using archaeological or historical data – an ancient social network – as a starting point, under which circumstances will violence emerge? Will the entire thing collapse? Or are there cycles? A complex system like this one can veer in different directions depending on the initial conditions, including the gifts that patrons give to their clients. Patrons in the model could keep a lid on the violence, even in the bad times and even when they took big risks with their money, so long as they redistributed their wealth in the form of significant gifts. In this model, bread and circuses really worked. However, this is only really true when the social network starts from a random position. If it starts from a historically known position, there are curious peaks of killing in the world where the overall economic system is generous, and a trough of peace in the world where the overall economic system is extremely harsh. The network effects at play – the channelling of resources into the hands of well-connected individuals and the inability of 'oppression' to be equally distributed – seems to lead to these outcomes.

Rome was not a static society. New peoples were added to the state constantly over time, and each new group or individual ideally was integrated into the existing networks of patronage, such as when Caracalla extended citizenship. When we add the possibility of new people joining the artificial society in our model, the situation changes dramatically. Newcomers try to join the game – find a patron, be received and enjoy the associated prestige and status – but opportunities are limited since, as new subjects of the empire, they carry little inherent prestige of their own. No patron wants the new clients. Consequently, grievances grow faster than the abilities of patrons to contain or mitigate them, and this leads to violence. However, the violence and killings open up new niches in the existing networks, thereby permitting the former newcomers to find roles. The problem is contained until the next generation of newcomers arrives. Starting with a network based on the pattern of friendship described in the writings of Cicero, and allowing for new individuals to join that society, the simulation eventually balances out with only marginally fewer people than when it started. The simulation produces a society that is top-heavy. By analogy, it looks rather similar to the state of Roman society at the end of the Republic and the beginning of the Early Empire. In history and in our simulation, Rome was the centre of a cycle where patronage networks were exposed to waves of killings and followed by the incorporation of new people who filled the network's empty niches; this surge of new people in turn set off another round of killing until a new society emerged.

Complexity theory suggests that the density and topology of connections can prove to be an Achilles' heel for networks. For some networks (as, for instance, with small worlds), the patterns of local and long-distance connections are such that the network generally proves robust in the face of random attack. When a network is subjected to external stress, the connections responsible for maintaining long-distance contacts within a network and between networks are generally not severed since there are relatively few of them. However, if an attack does succeed in severing one of these key agents, then the network may fragment. Agents who possess dense, long-distance connections with counterparts in a given network are able to support the establishment of multiple pathways for contact within a given network. If these are removed, however, new pathways for contact have to be established, which forces the network to attempt to sustain its operations using a reduced number of links. If a key agent is removed, then its removal may initiate a cascading failure within the network. Some surviving constituents will fail due to the reduced number of connections within the network, a failure that will initiate a second cascade. The extent of the cascading failure is determined by the importance of the first key agent to fail (Barabási 2002: 119–20).

Translating these insights into human terms, it suggests the central importance of the patrons in maintaining their social network. The obligations of patronage did not disappear when a head of household died, was exiled or was murdered. Instead, his functions simply devolved to the new head of household. If the new head proved unable to meet his obligations by creating new links with clients and finding powerful patrons for himself, then we might speculate that that failure could initiate a cascading process that would destroy his network in the end. The waves of killings generated in the agent-based model described here were also cascading failures, a function of the density or topology of the networks that were modelled.

Social change as social failure – the only thing lacking is actual humans. What if we could enter this simulation for ourselves?

Until the advent of agent-based modelling, counterfactuals were nothing more than thought experiments. The arrival of this methodology, however, enables us to raise counterfactual analyses to a whole new level by articulating our model with the rigor demanded by a computer. The models, and the process of building the models, are important in themselves for what they can show us about how our ideas interact. They are arguments constructed in code, a procedural rhetoric. For this reason alone, historians should be interested in building agent-based models, for if a model clearly reflects one's understanding of historical process X, then one can see the natural consequences of that understanding. Agent-based simulations force assumptions to be made explicit. Such models can be made to reflect not only our assumptions about the past, but also information derived from historical data. In the latter case, providing our assumptions are valid, there are grounds to suggest that the emergent results of such models must necessarily have some historical truth to them.

The agent models presented in this book, along with the more metaphorical use of 'network' as a tool to think with about provisioning the city of Rome, are not without their issues. They can – and should – be critiqued in terms of their handling of the data, the implementation of their rule-sets and the validity of the results. Then, as models, they provide a lens for (re)examining the archaeological data we find.

But despite decades of use in archaeology, agent-based modelling remains a niche pursuit. No one seriously engages with someone else's code, someone else's model at the level of the computation. While I find it magical to see the patterns emerge on my screen, perhaps it is not enough. What I find enchanting about it all – the emergence of larger-scale phenomena that I can use as a lens for looking at archaeology – is perhaps not enchanting enough for broader consumption. But maybe we can fix that: perhaps I'm just not making it clear why this confrontation with delight and disturbance enchants me.

When I first began to study Rome, I thought I understood its topography, its landscape. I understood the city as a backdrop to its history, a lovely painted scena. When I first arrived in Rome, with all of its cacophony, energy and compactness, I realized that I was so very, very wrong. Rome is no backdrop. It is an emergent player itself in the drama and culture and society that lives in and through it.

To study the past without taking into account how much human lives are entangled with the vitality of the world around them is to be impoverished. My agent models have so far been mere backdrop, and perhaps that's what's wrong with agent-based modelling more generally. Like Rome, I need to visit the models myself. I need to enter the simulation and interrogate my agents of enchantment directly.

Agents of Enchantment

'The contemplation of a Roman brick seems to leave me cold – quite cold. So I would dearly like to know why it is that you find yourself so enthusiastic.' This is the quotation (of Chief Inspector Morse in *The Jewel That Was Ours* [Dexter 1991]) I used as the epigraph to my

PhD dissertation. I put it there as a quiet rejoinder to conversations I had during my time in Rome, my passive-aggressive middle finger in the air. The contemplation of a Roman brick becomes the passport to deep time, for it is a nexus in a complex assemblage (of the kind described by Deleuze and Guattari 1980) in time and space. Its fabric pulls together the control of land two thousand years ago, the coppicing of wood for fuel, the climate and the power of the earth to nurture, to grow, the transport to the kiln site of raw clay (excavated by slaves in the fields), the smell of smoke wafting over the fields, the backbreaking labour to pound the clay into shape, the stacking and piling of bricks into carts and into boats, the long journey down the river, the disbursement of the kiln load to multiple building sites in Rome, in Ostia, in North Africa, the work of construction, the layering of mortar and plaster, the life of the building, its decay and destruction, periodic wars above balanced against the quiet of the soil below, the disturbance of the plough, of field-walking archaeologists. It is a nexus in the mining of rare earths in the Congo, the (sometimes compelled) labour of the rural emigrant poor in the factories of China and Taiwan and the American Midwest, the development of digital computing technologies against the backdrop of war and ballistics calculations and nuclear weapons' yields, the Home Brew Computing club and the escape of the game *Adventure* across the early ARPANET, the pedagogies of Piaget and Papert and the Logo programming language, the local elementary school and the purchase of some Commodore 64 computers, the evolution of Lisp and Logo and complexity theory into NetLogo. It is a nexus tying together a bus trip with a stranger, a workshop in Colorado, a postdoc on the Canadian Prairies.

When I run my simulations, it is almost impossible to speak of what is going on in the model without thinking of these things as creatures with their own agendas, broadly knowable but specifically, at any given point in time and space, unknowable to me. Bennett (2010: 99) argues for 'a touch of anthropomorphism' when we talk about these vibrant things because they 'can catalyze a sensibility that finds a world filled not with ontologically distinct categories of beings (subjects and objects) but with variously composed materialities that form confederations'.

The point of describing agents in an agent-based model this way is to free them from the confines of the computer. Their confederations of being (hence Bennett's [2010] term 'vibrant matter') extend well beyond the computer and enfold not just the materiality and history of computing but also my own history and my own being-in-the-world, and the being-in-the-world of named and nameless Romans so long ago, the landscapes and taskscapes and meshworks of lives lived and the world enfolding. The enchantment I feel when I encounter these confederations, that 'strange combination of delight and disturbance' (Bennett 2010: xi), is a kind of wonder at the emergent properties, of seeing fossilized patterns of social interaction spring back into a kind of life. Enchantment opens us up to recognizing that part of our way of knowing the past is in assemblage with the machines – that we are vibrant matter, too. Indeed, Bennett (2010: 11, 13) points out that if we look at humans not from the perspective of human lifespans, but from deep evolutionary time, we would see that the mineralization of soft bodies opened up new forms of being: humans are a by-product of mineralizations, a 'particularly rich and complex collection of materials. . . . If matter itself is lively, then not only is the difference between subjects and objects minimized, but the status of the shared materiality of all things is elevated.' What Bennett is arguing for is for us to see in these confederations of things a kind of distributive, emergent agency. She writes, 'No one really knows what human agency is, or what humans are doing when they are said to perform as agents. In the face of every analysis, human agency remains something of a mystery. If we do not know just how it is that human agency operates, how can we be so sure that the processes through which nonhumans make their mark are qualitatively different?' (Bennett 2010: 34).

This is what I find so enchanting about digital archaeological work. Chris Godsen (2005) once asked, 'What do objects want?' Following Bennett, perhaps the real question is 'What is the vibrant materiality at play as we consider things?' There are no objects, no things out there distinct from us. We are in productive assemblage with things, with distributed unequal agency across networks. Digital archaeology, more than perhaps other kinds of archaeology, shares authority in the co-creation of archaeological knowledge with quasi-independent algorithms. Archaeologists must consciously sink into the assemblages of vibrant matter that produce knowledge so that others can join them, so that the journey, the vista, is reproducible and replicable. There may be few other disciplines so situated to enable this to happen.

The Digital Assemblage

'To build is to hack, to hack is to break, to break is to build', says Roopika Risam (2019: 57) in *New Digital Worlds*. Risam (2019: 54) is writing in the context of discussing what a postcolonial digital humanities may look like, reminding us that knowledge making in digital humanities' approaches is as much about what emerges in the breakages and ruptures of tacit work with databases or code or creation of digital archives. She ties this to Samuels and McGann's (1999) ideas of 'deformance'. That is to say, in the performance of knowledge-making (because code has to be run in order for it to be meaningful, so that we only know its full potential in its consequences and affects), we also have to deform the things we study (Risam 2019: 57). Allison Parrish (2016) has discussed a similar idea when she says that 'programming is forgetting': in order for something to be encoded, we necessarily have to pare away at the core ideas. Ted Underwood's (2018) tongue-in-cheek assessment is that this is a triumph for the humanities, in that the machine-learning enthusiasts have finally had to realize that their models are so opaque they don't know what they're doing, and that human complexity has something to recommend it after all. We can also tie this into Croxall and Warnick's (2015) typology of the kinds of fails that one might encounter in a digital pedagogy. A postcolonial digital humanities, then, encourages us to dive deeply into the code, to expose its 'fictive neutrality' and explore the ways power dynamics of the Global North are embedded in the code, for the tools of the digital humanities 'are encumbered by the material conditions of their production: who designed a tool or project, what is its subject, who is the intended user, who built it, and how was the labour compensated?' (Risam 2019: 40).

Archaeological uses of agent-based modelling tend to not ask these questions, but rather take as self-evident that here is a tool that can answer questions about the past. While there is a recognition of the iterative nature of model-building (e.g. Romanowska 2014 provides guidance), the potential risk that our tools are blinding us to the ways these tools might be enacting colonial violence is unrealized, ignored or diminished. 'What forms of the "human" are sanctioned when artificial intelligence can reproduce human processes?' asks Risam (2019: 127). The entire apparatus of the Western world rests on a foundation of colonialism and exploitation; our digital apparatus continues to rest on a foundation of colonialism and exploitation. 'Asserting the ability of a text, algorithm, piece of software, or computer to "pass" as human presumes a universal definition of "human" and reduces the totality of humanity to the ability of a computer to perform a task in a particular way defined by a set of limits that reproduces dominant cultural norms' (Risam 2019: 136).

When I speak of agent-based models as being comprised of digital zombies I am making clear that I am not representing actual humans in the past, but rather entities who are performing certain things I think to be true about the past; however, I am also conflating the labour of these digital entities with the compelled labour-after-death of Haitian slaves. The 'zombie' in Western culture has long forgotten its roots in the slave plantations of Haiti. In popular culture, zombies are the perfect 'other' (Anderson 2019), humans without humanity. Thus I am wrong to conceive of the agents in my models as zombies. To think of them as zombies erases the material conditions of computing in the West, which depends on the forced labour in rare-earth mines in the Congo, the labour in bleak factories in China (see e.g. Merchant 2017), the underpaid labour of the Amazon warehouse worker in the American South (see e.g. Jamieson 2015). Instead, we have to highlight the artificialness, the created-beingness, of our representations in order to make clear just how much (or how little) we are amplifying 'normative forms of human subjectivity' when we use these digital tools (Risam 2019: 125).

But is it necessary to use some kind of metaphor to explain the actions of agents within a model? 'Agent' is itself a metaphor of a sort, but to leave it at that, I think, hides the fact that ultimately we are programming a set of rules to encode some kind of human. What form of human? We will see later that this question gains a greater urgency when we translate from an agent-based model to an 'archaeogame', but for the time being, one of the strengths of an agent model is that it forces us to recognize that we are not representing a human. At best, it is a bundle of appetites that respond to its position in an environment (an environment which can respond in turn to the actions of this bundle of appetites) and to its position vis-à-vis other bundles. It is a golem, a creature of clay that is activated by the words placed in its head and must obey those words. Thinking of these agents as kinds of golems forces us to not conflate the outcomes of our models with actual humans: it reminds us that we are dealing with fictive entities whose aggregate actions are lenses to help us study our world.

But Risam's (2019: 35) larger points remain: 'as models of the physical world, virtual worlds can provide iterative ways of accessing and understanding the world around us as they co-construct and co-constitute it. But will these worlds be ones that reaffirm dominant cultural values and knowledge hierarchies? Or will they be ones that imagine new forms of resistance through digital knowledge production?' All of that is to say, if we consider the results of these agent-based models as enchanting, we have to go deeper and ask 'Enchanting for whom?' Archaeologists have to interrogate not just the code they write for its fidelity to the archaeological phenomena they want to study, but also for how it might be playing into larger discourses of how we create and construct the world. Archaeology has a dark history of building virtual (nondigital) worlds of the past that serve to validate contemporary narratives. Enchantment can have its dark side.

Thus, part of what we have to do is examine our code and each other's code. Trevor Owens and Rebecca Mir (2013) performed just such a deep dive on the video game *Sid Meier's Colonization* and demonstrated how the agents representing various First Nations in the game were literally encoded as having lesser abilities, as being lesser beings. Various gamers left a series of comments on the original 2012 post by Owens and Mir on *Play the Past* (playthepast.org), accusing them of reading far too much into the code. One poster, Mrunimport, attempted to lampoon the argument by reframing it as being about the Goombas in Mario Brothers, substituting 'Goomba' for 'Indigenous' (the full exchange is at http://www.playthepast.org/?p=2509#comment-116540).

Mir's response patiently points out that the Goombas are clearly marked by the game developers as being of lesser interest – that the players are supposed to make common cause with the Mario Brothers and cheer them on. Anything goes with regard in how one treats the Goombas. The player's 'gotcha' argument actually goes to show why *Colonization* is controversial in a way that *Mario Bros.* cannot be, since Goombas are neither human nor marginalized.

Owens and Mir highlighted a structural element of the codebase that represented real humans as lesser creatures, and members of the gaming community took that to mean that they were accusing the individual developers of being racist. This disconnect – that our structures can be colonialist, can be racist, despite one's individual intentions – seems to be one of the hardest ideas to grapple with. What aspects of my agent-based simulations merely replicate the (unexamined) structural meshworks, the distributed agencies in my local confederation of things? This is why Bennett's (2010: viii) 'vibrant materialism' is necessarily political. 'What difference would it make to the course of energy policy were electricity to be figured not simply as a resource, commodity, or instrumentality but also are more radically as an "actant"?' (Bennett 2010: viii).

What difference would it make to archaeology if we took seriously that we co-create our understandings of the past through a vibrant materiality, a complex assemblage with digital things which stretches over time and space?

This is where agent-based modelling becomes archaeogaming, because archaeogaming more neatly enfolds, more tightly binds, the archaeologist with the distributed agency of the assemblages we study and are part of. Let us build some archaeogames from these agent-based models. Archaeogaming, as Reinhard (2018) has conceived it, requires us to look at these games with archaeological eyes, to consider not just representation in the games but also the performance of archaeology within it – not just playing as an archaeologist, but considering the games as archaeology, both from within and from without. Considering games and their agency and how they affect us and effect change means thinking of them as vibrant matter in the sense that Bennett has proposed. It means considering them in a more expensive definition of 'assemblage' than is normally meant in archaeology, but a fully multimodal networked intertwining of entities. And not just human entities, either. Archaeogaming is an invitation to consciously sink into the assemblages that produce knowledge and effect change in the world. The syllogism might be that assemblages are a function of vibrant matter; vibrant matter leads to enchantment; enchantment leads to awe; awe leads to creativity as a way of knowing.

Note

1. Originally published as Shawn Graham, 'Behaviour Space: Simulating Roman Social Life and Civil Violence', *Digital Studies/le Champ Numérique* 1, no. 2 (2009), DOI: http://doi.org/10.16995/dscn.109, CC BY 4.0., but here edited to highlight another way of raising the dead . . . and then setting them loose to die. This paper was originally written in 2007 and published in 2009.

CHAPTER 4

Archaeogaming

To recap where we've been: I've been outlining one perspective on digital archaeology that begins by drawing out the networks visible in the archaeological materials and then reanimates those networks as the substratum on which we model higher-level social processes as a way of both enchanting the archaeological record and of asking impossible questions of the archaeology. Those first two sections of this book brought together several strands of my research as an archaeologist and as a digital humanist, and are more or less unremarkable approaches to studying archaeology digitally (even if both network analysis and agent-based modelling remain niche pursuits within archaeology).

In this chapter and the next, I want to illuminate where I think these perspectives could go, and so I enter a more speculative mode. I will take you through how I imagine we can make the shift from agent-based models to archaeogaming, and then give an example of one possible way to fold such a manoeuvre into your teaching, even if you are not a 'digital person'. I will then wrap up in the final chapter by exploring some other technologies we may wish to fold into our archaeogaming to heighten the possibilities for enchantment.

This might not work. But it's worth a try. Let's play.

On Play and Failing

In 2010, I was one of the first contributors to a new group-authored blog, *Play the Past*, devoted to exploring the intersection of play and cultural heritage. One of my first pieces explored the colossal failure of my first foray into integrating a video game into my teaching. I had built a scenario for the game *Civilization IV* that simulated the civil violence surrounding the Year of the Four Emperors, when Galba, Vitellius, Otho and Vespasian all vied for the throne. I wanted students to play the scenario and log the events that happened in the game to contrast them with what they knew from their textbooks. I wanted them to see the gaps between the simulated experience and the 'actual' history, and to understand that what happened in the past was not foreordained. Things did not go well:

> Play a game, or write an essay? I figured it would be a no-brainer. . . . The response was . . . well, you know that odd uncle you have, who turns up at family gatherings, and everyone tries to humour him without causing too much disruption? It was something like that. 'I enjoyed it Sir, it really made me think differently about what was going on in AD69 . . . but if it's alright with you, I'd rather write an essay' was a typical response. (Graham 2010).

Failure, whether it is in our teaching or in our research, is never a welcome experience. The value, however, in a perspective that embraces archaeogaming is that failure is a baked-in feature: there is no avoiding it. It forces an experimental mindset that draws from the experience what worked and what didn't and why, and uses this to try again. Good games balance that cycle so that the failures incite the player to play again; bad games cause the player to throw the controller down and turn the machine off.

Representing the full complexity of human history in a game is not possible. Instead, we are distracted by things like visual fidelity to an imagined 'authenticity'. For archaeogaming, and for learning, graphics get in the way. Even simple text-based games (nowadays called 'interactive fiction') can be far more powerful learning experiences and simulations about the past (McCall 2018; Moll 2018) because they require the imaginative leaps to occur within the player's head. Infocom, the early giant of the video games industry, had it right when in an advertisement they showed a human brain with the tag line 'We unleash the world's most powerful graphics technology'.

However, the focus on ever more powerful graphics, ever more realistic depictions of explosions and splatters, spurred a technological revolution and the invention of the graphics processing unit. The powerful chip architectures necessary for producing beautiful, photorealistic graphics also turn out to be extremely good at other kinds of simulation, including neural networks. Neural networks are a simulation of an idea of how the brain processes information. They have spurred a torrent of innovation in the areas of machine learning and artificial intelligence. Curiously enough, this puts us in a situation where the best representations of the world are not those that add more detail, but those that forget. Ted Underwood (2018) writes,

> To learn a language, toddlers have to generalize from specific examples (a familiar tabby cat) to a looser category (cat or animal). This requires a subtraction of detail, since animals aren't always tabby-colored, don't always purr, and so on. We may not be conscious that learning requires subtraction, since forgetting details comes naturally to human beings. But computers find it easy to remember details, so if we want them to grasp general patterns, we have to explicitly tell them to condense a long list of emails (or animals) into a usefully fuzzy model. The success of machine learning depends both on gathering data and on condensing it, but the second, subtractive step is the part statisticians call 'learning'.

In the humanities, we are not good at consciously thinking through the process of 'subtraction' and its ramifications. We are not good at making it clear why we choose to forget the various details or aspects of what we are studying in order to create our models. That is why we need to build pedagogies of failure into our work. If we have license to break things – to fail – then we better understand why a particular representation of the past is appropriate, what its limitations are, and how the code and hardware we have used focus attention on some aspects but not others. But we need to be cautious. Risam (2019: 17) points out that it is precisely the act of forgetting, of encoding some understandings but not others, that makes it possible for the entire digital project to become a colonialist undertaking. Who gets forgotten, and why? Erasure is political. It is not just that what gets digitized or encoded is a function of what's out there: it is also how it is out there. Archaeological knowledge that is the result of looting materials from African countries for display in European museums is becoming transformed into 3d photogrammetric models, available for consumption or sale on various digital platforms: this digitization can 'rehearse colonialist knowledge production' (Risam 2019: 17). In Risam's formulation of postcolonial digital humanities, the task is to push back by asking how the projects are designed, how the materials are framed and managed, and what forms of labour have created them. Risam (2019: 33) goes on to remind us that the humanities has long been about worldmaking: 'Colonialism itself is a world-making project, reflected in and constructed through a variety of methods, including the maps that outline the shape of the world; the link between textuality and the production of colonial discourse; and the legal, juridical, and political apparatuses that produce ideological conditions for a colonial world.'

Our agent-based models, our virtual worlds, our archaeogames, are part of this tradition. We're literally making virtual worlds. Our pedagogy of failure then needs to consider digital work as inherently colonialist, and one way it can do that is to *not* hide the labour and decisions and breakages, but instead present the virtual worlds we make as wonderfully fractured potentials.

Pedagogy of Failure

To have that license to break things, it is helpful to have a taxonomy of the different kinds of 'fails' that one might encounter. Knowing the kind of fail means that we also have a sense of how to extract the useful lesson from the fail, making it productive. Croxall and Warnick (2015) provide just such a framework. I have often referenced this framework in my writing and teaching precisely because, in the academy, we have socialized our students to hide their failures, to recoil from discussing what doesn't work, as if we each of us didn't have things go wrong every day. So let us learn how to fail properly. Following Croxall and Warnick (2015), there are four kinds of failure. Two of them are as one might expect: first, the technical failure of the software or computing platform, its glitches; and second, a lack of framework to contextualize the results (when the software or hardware works) – that is, the 'so what?' question cannot be answered.

Where the pedagogy of failure comes into play is in shifting failure from something that happens to us to something we seek out. Their 'third tier' of failure asks students to consider where the breakages or failures are in others' tools or projects and treats the failure as an artefact to be studied within its larger social or technological assemblage, while the fourth tier involves actively breaking the software or technology, pushing it far beyond its intended uses or using it against the grain or in vastly different contexts. I've often thought of this last level of 'fail' as being the starting point for experimental archaeology and for that reason see archaeology as having a natural affinity for much of the digital humanities.

A pedagogy of failure then tries to move students from the first two tiers of failure into the more metacognitive tiers of thinking of the digital as artefactual, or as an epistemology. When we encounter agent-based models, it is easy to get hung up on the first two tiers of failure. We fight and labour to get the software to work properly. We validate the models; we test them to make sure they're doing what we think we've designed them to do. We struggle to publish our models – to answer Reviewer Two's pointed 'so what?' question – and we have of necessity had to develop a literature to point to as the scaffolding, the framework. While we are wandering between these two tiers, it can be hard to discuss what hasn't worked, what has failed, or to invite someone else to reimplement our code or engage with its arguments at the level of code. The article is published; it duly appears in others' literature reviews (whether or not its conclusions actually support the use to which the citation has been deployed).

To move to thinking of failure as an artefact to study or an epistemology to be deployed, we need permission to *play*. To break things. To push the technology and our engagement with it out beyond the end of the pier. This has been part of the agenda of this book: you can blame me. You have my permission – my blessing! In the next section, I will reframe a model we encountered earlier as a game, and we will look at what that might tell us. I conclude the chapter by showing this pedagogy in action. Then, I will suggest you stop reading the main text to explore Appendix A, where I walk you through one of the simple agent-based models that come bundled with NetLogo as we consider it as an artefact. In that appendix we will try to mash different pieces of code together to make/build/break a new model, concluding with a reimplementation of the Itineraries model discussed earlier (the complete code for which is in Appendix B).

Games That Play Themselves[1]

Archaeologists have been simulating past societies via computation for decades (for recent overviews, see Wurzer et al. 2015; Costopoulos and Lake 2010). It is nothing new for us to perform a kind of practical necromancy to raise the dead to see what they can tell us. Archaeogaming introduces a new actor into these artificial societies: living humans. There are dangers to guard against and opportunities to seize when we co-write the past with our digital homunculi. In this chapter, I draw on some of my own experiences to suggest a path forward on this quest.

Heads Will Roll

Consider life in a small society run along patriarchal lines. Some families dominate; the head of household's word is law in these families, even over the people in a chain of lesser families connected by kith and kin. All depends on your relationship with Him. Now consider a situation where He is suddenly removed – perhaps a sudden death. Your world wobbles a little bit, but succession rules quickly allow us to figure out who is now in charge. It is a rigid structure, yet it works. Most of the time.

For now.

But what would happen if many heads rolled, all at once? If the heads died in infamy and shame? How much damage can such a social world sustain before it collapses, recovers or transforms? I am thinking now of the social world of the Romans in the Late Republic or the early days of Empire, a world self-consciously rigid in the way I described, yet one that manages to carry on regardless. Let us, then, kill some Romans. It is perhaps one of the best ways to understand the ways in which Roman society was resilient to the frequent pogroms and proscriptions of the Late Republic and other eras because we can see what happens next.

Romans must die for me to explore the ways Rome's social network reacted under stress. This does, of course, present some obvious practical issues, but through simulation, ones that are tractable. The kind of simulation I used was an 'agent-based simulation' (ABM). Think of an ABM as a kind of giant self-running, self-organizing petri dish. Each 'agent' is its own program, coded to react to its environment and/or the presence of other 'agents' (Lake 2015). Agent-based modelling allows me to raise Romans from the dead over and over, and give them patterns of interaction known from the archaeology (for instance, the stamps on Roman bricks in and around Rome fossilize nodes of social interaction, as it happens). I raise these digital Romans up; I give them artificial life; and then I kill them. Since the agents are programmed to interact based on social networks known to have existed in the past, aspects of their emergent behaviour are necessarily tied to that past (cf. Epstein 2006: 31–33). Thus, since I wish to know under what circumstances this society might collapse, I have them interact in an economic and social world as known from the scholarly literature. My agents harbour grudges; they nurse wounds and social slights. Their primary motivation is to find chains of patrons and clients to whom they can attach in order to obtain resources; that is, a classic rich-get-richer effect is in play. Those who have not, get shut out. They take their revenge. And then I start to put this world under stress to see what happens next.

There is something mesmerizing as I watch this artificial life creep and fight its way across the screen. As described, it is a giant petri dish, where my intervention is limited to setting up the pieces, writing the rules and flipping the 'on' switch. But . . . wouldn't you want to play this game? *Climb the social ladder in Rome! Help your clients and find yourself better patrons – but make sure you don't make too many enemies along the way or you, too, will lose . . . the Game of Togas.* It doesn't take much to flip an agent-based model into a video game; it is simply a matter of whether or not the player/researcher has any active agency in what happens on the screen. In this regard then, archaeologists are already gamers. They use ABMs to explore the past, but remove themselves from the action: thus an ABM is just a species of video game that plays itself. In which case, there is little reason why games-qua-games shouldn't be another kind of experimental petri dish to help archaeologists to write the past.

The Seductive Lure of the Digital Landscape

As I watch the screen and tell the story of what my digital Romans are up to as they live and die, it becomes easier and easier to believe that I'm actually watching something true about the past. In *Foucault's Pendulum*, Umberto Eco tells a story where the protagonists feed a computer with vast amounts of information to devise a conspiracy theory, for their own entertainment, to determine a 'truer' story of European history. Things take a turn for the worse when the men begin to believe that the simulation is mapping out an actual 'real' truth – and, even more dangerously, others come to believe in it too.

   This, it strikes me, is a problem common both to gaming and to simulation. It is all too easy to succumb to the beauty of the digital landscape, a world that turns around *me* the player, *me* the creator. In both video games and agent-based simulations, we have a kind of control, an agency, that we do not have in other aspects of our lives. This seductive power blinds us. When we are very good at a game, when we can anticipate what happens next and hit that state where the game is just challenging enough to keep us pushing forward, we have internalized the rules that govern the game and its story. To be 'good' at a game is to perform (uncritically) the vision of the world that its creators have encoded in the rules, in the mechanics. When we are very good at simulation, we similarly have internalized the ways in which code can be used to tell stories of the world. In which case, if we are interested in *archaeogaming*, it might be worth thinking about the methods that have evolved to guard against this tendency in modellers. If we are interested in mere simulation, it might be worth thinking about the methods used to understand games in order to guard against this tendency in gamers.

It is useful to expand, therefore, on some of the ways agent-based modelling and video gaming might intersect, particularly in terms of how we evaluate the success or failure of both to 'do good history', as a contribution towards the methods of archaeogaming. After all, archaeology has always been concerned with understanding virtual worlds, whether those worlds are built from stone, wood or concrete; it's just that now we must understand the worlds built from sand and electricity as well.

Perspectives on Space and Time

The difference between games and agent-based simulations is not so vast. An agent-based model, in fact, is a special class of video game where the player does not actually play. She sets it all up, and she watches to see how that world reacts. She's interested in the whole-world interrelationships; the player of games, on the other hand, is necessarily interested in the reactions to his own actions. In some respects, one could make the analogy to social network analysis: simulation is to whole-network analysis as a video game is to ego-analysis (cf. Weingart 2011 on network analysis). That is to say, the difference is one of perspective.

If archaeogaming is going to be a serious pursuit, then the first lesson we can take from agent modelling concerns *time* and *space*. The way that time is treated in agent-based models is critical; time is malleable so that there is time *for* something to take place. It makes a difference to your model whether or not your agents update themselves one at a time, each one running its procedures sequentially, versus in parallel. Emergent effects that can seem profound or meaningful might only be an artefact of how 'time' is imagined. Then there is the time *within which* something might take place. Terry Pratchett's (2001) *Thief of Time* calls this the 'universal tick', or the time it takes for *now* to become *then*. Agent-based models tick in time with the computer's clock: does processor clock time have any meaningful analogy to 'historical time'? Similarly, agent models happen in a kind of space. This space can be a flat, two-dimensional world subject to edge effects that can muddy the waters; in some models, the left-hand side of the world connects to the right-hand side, and the top connects to the bottom, which gives us a torus. In others, the space is the gaps between social actors – that is, a network. How does space work in the games we are analysing from an archaeogamer perspective?

Aarseth et al. (2003) years ago devised a typology for video games that depended upon considering several axes of analysis – space, time, player-structure, control and rules. As we begin to devise the methods for archaeogaming, I want to suggest that we pay attention to space and time in their formulation: space contains 'perspective, topography, and environment'; Time contains 'pace, representation, [and] teleology'. Whether the virtual world we are analysing is in 'meatspace' or cyberspace, these categories usefully force us to concentrate on what space and time are doing in the game/simulation in meaningful ways. Consider my simulation of Roman social life where the Romans must die. In terms of 'space', the simulation has an omnipresent perspective: I see all; I can peer into each agent's life at will. The environment is geometric; the world in which these Romans move is static, and the conditions do not change during the run. In terms of 'time', the pace is turn-based (each Roman updates in turn), time is mimetic (it takes time for the Roman to achieve something), and time is teleological in that the Romans have clear goals and ambitions in mind. As table 4.1 shows, my simulation occupies an interesting space between *Caesar IV* and *Civilization IV*, two well-known games that also contain useful simulations of Roman society.

Table 4.1. Comparing time and space in games and an agent-based model. An expansion of Kee and Graham (2014), table 13.2.

Space/Time	*Caesar IV*	*Civilization IV*	*Game of Togas*
Perspective	omnipresent	vagrant	omnipresent
Topography	topological	geometrical	geometrical
Environment	dynamic	dynamic	static
Pace	real-time	turn-based	turn-based
Representation	arbitrary	mimetic	mimetic
Teleology	finite	finite	finite

Let's put the shoe on the other foot. How do *Caesar IV* and *Civilization IV* hold up against the standards used to understand agent-based models? Let us use Iza Romanowska's (2014) framework for evaluating agent models (see also her longer discussion 2015). For Romanowska, the key elements to usefully evaluating the success of an agent-based model are

1. scope
2. appropriateness
3. resolution

4. how complicated is it?
5. parsimonious parameters
6. utility

Scope and appropriateness deal with research questions. Scope: Are we building a model to explore a hypothetical or to understand patterns in the data? *Caesar IV* clearly has a research question at its heart: how does experience in the provinces make a man fit to govern in Rome? When I reframed 'Romans must die' as a game in my opening – help your clients succeed; find a patron to help *you* succeed – I was framing a question about the role of patronage in generating social structure in Rome. Appropriateness: is a resource management simulation an appropriate tool for answering the question about governance? Resolution: *Caesar IV* shows me individual Romans, with whom I have to interact. That may be too low a level given the scope and appropriateness. Parsimonious parameters: how many knobs and dials can I twiddle? What and where are the feedback loops? Complexity theory here teaches that simpler is better (Romanowska 2015). Utility: not 'is this a fun game', but rather 'what have we learned?' 'How are we changed?'

Archaeogaming and Simulation as a Kind of Digital Public Archaeology

Finally, I put it to you that one of the most powerful ways that archaeogaming could intersect with a digital public archaeology becomes evident if we consider the original purpose of the NetLogo agent-based modelling environment (currently, the most widely used ABM tool in archaeology). NetLogo was originally designed to teach students about complex phenomena by getting them to observe the ways small parameter changes could affect the global behaviour of the complex system (Wilensky 1999). The *Evolving Planet* archaeogame (Rubio et al. 2017) takes this approach. But we could go further. What if we put the players into our agent-based models? Not just tweaking the global, but engaging the first-person? Holistic and egocentric at the same time? NetLogo comes with an extension called 'HubNet' that allows individuals to take on the role of a single agent within an otherwise fully digital simulation. The NetLogo developers call this 'participatory' simulation'. Is there room in archaeogaming to merge humans and machine-made societies? That tools change us and change what it means to be human is a truism of archaeology: archaeogaming perhaps is a way to understand what this digital moment is doing to our humanity.

Archaeologists are naturally gamers already. We have been building virtual worlds long before video games emerged. We have already developed methods and techniques for understanding the virtual worlds of the past; the things we see as archaeologists in the virtual worlds of the present accordingly can be grounded in the methods and techniques of archaeology. This section has suggested a framework based on typologies of time and space coupled with perspectives on agent-based modelling validation techniques to help guard against the seductive lure of the digital, so that when Romans must die, they die usefully.

Making as Empathy[2]

Sometimes, the point of games might not be in the playing, but in the making, and in the failing to make. Tara Copplestone, one of the leading figures in archaeogaming, has for many years advocated for archaeologists and game designers to collaborate to write archaeology, to write history, via games. In her ethnographic work alongside game designers, she points to a number of ways that academics interested in games miss the point of the problems and approaches that game designers face (Copplestone 2016). In short, it is not easy to make a game. It is not easy to make an agent-based model, and it is even harder to take that model and turn it into an experience that a person may explore first-hand. This is the kind of 'hard empathy' that Perry (2019: 13) calls for, 'deployed . . . such that [the archaeological record] reaps an ethic of generosity and considerate action in/on the world'. Let us consider then one way of approaching the problem of fostering the kind of enchantment, the kind of empathy, that Perry calls for. Over the last several years, I have tried to design my teaching around this exact problem. I am not talking about writing essays. I am talking about making video games – or more accurately, about learning to write history through algorithms. In my classes, I ask students to explicitly think about how one could set up the rules, the recipes that engage with the historical or archaeological materials, to allow for a kind of emergent storytelling. Think about a small child who is playing with a Lego playset, and the stories the child tells as she plays: that's emergent storytelling (see MacDougall 2010).

This kind of writing is alien to how we normally teach our students to write, for it explicitly demands that the 'writer' think about how the 'reader' will make the story in the process of 'reading'. William Urrichio (2005) pointed out the ways that video games represented history. He was not overly concerned with the graphical representation of the past (period-correct clothing and architecture), but rather with the ways that the rule-sets of the games allowed for different understandings of history itself to be represented. He suggested that historians should engage with video games, and the point of intersection was historiography. The rule-sets of games directly correspond with the historiographic traditions – the rule-sets of historical practice – within which historians write.

Ian Bogost (2007) coined the phrase, 'procedural rhetoric' to express much the same thought. The idea that the processes of computation embody a kind of rhetoric and representation of how the world works is also a kind of cosmology. One can learn a lot about how game designers view the world by closely reading their code (Sample 2011). I set out to explore these ideas with a seminar called Video Games and Simulations for Historians.

Let us agree that the rules of games represent something of how the game-makers/players view the world's workings. I put it to the students that what we were engaged in, in learning to write history-through-algorithms, was akin to a kind of oracle or riddle building, a way of describing the world that the player – the reader – needs to explore. In this way, the reader may construct or build their own understandings not by reading and intellectually understanding arguments, but through experience (Kee et al. 2009). Because we are engaged with the human past, it is also a kind of necromancy in that we might summon the spirits of the past forward, recreated and resubstantiated in digital form. These spirits of the past represent our own best ideas about the past, not the past directly, which of course we can never know. We project onto historical actors our best understandings. So, too, with these digitally substantiated simulacra: the meanings of the past emerge from our playing with these digital spectres. We are more familiar with these when we encounter them pinned to the pages of a book or essay; but in silicon they write themselves through interaction with each other and with the player.

There was a bit of attrition during these first few weeks of the class. There are a couple of reasons for this. Angela Cox (2014) identifies one of these when she writes about her own experiences treating games as texts to be analysed in a composition class. On Cox's reading of her experience, one point of resistance is our colonization of what students perceive as a nonacademic space: academics don't play games. It may be a surprise that this first issue should emerge in a classroom where 'video games' was in the title, but, according to Cox (2014),

Postcolonialism may in fact provide the best explanation for some of the most frustrating student behavior I have witnessed in these classes, because if we see students as the marginalized group and the established academics as the center then student resistance to classroom activity and homework becomes a colonial struggle at the margins. . . . Videogames are outside the center's power and must be defended from further colonization. That is, [students] are resisting cultural appropriation.

Bill Caraher (2014) has reflected on similar themes of student resistance to what and how we teach. He situates one location of resistance in student perceptions of the 'trivial' – that the learning is not 'serious' enough. This accords well with my own experience in another class (where we wrote for Wikipedia; Graham 2013b), where resistance emerged amongst my most historically minded students: what we were doing neither looked nor felt like what history was supposed to be about. Kapell and Elliot (2013) identify a similar theme in the academic study (by historians) of video games and other simulations of the past, within intersections of historiography with ludology and narratology. If the process of history is composed of both selection (of facts) and assembly (of a convincing and sound narrative), then the kind of assembly that a video game allows is both good history and good pedagogy because the player actively constructs (reads) 'history as a process' rather than as a grand narrative. The objection then, such as it is, is that video games allow the 'non-professional to do her or his own "assembly" of the past' (Kapell and Elliot 2013: 14). Historians and students object, and resist, alike.

The Assignment

The students had one major project to complete over the duration of this course: to design what the ideal game would look/feel/behave like (the parameters of this project were inspired by the work of Mark Sample's Videogames in Critical Contexts course, HNRS 353-002, Spring 2012, at George Mason University, http://samplereality.com/gmu/hnrs353/). My assignment prompt was this:

In small groups (assigned by the instructor), you will produce a 40 to 50-page game design document for an ideal history game (or meta game; a game about games) that distils what you have learned about telling history through interactive media. This document will also demonstrate in passing what you have learned as a result of this course. You will need to reference the appropriate games, history learning, games and history, design, psychology, cognitive science or other literatures to explain and show how your game/simulation would achieve its desired ends. For the purposes of this course you do not need to produce the actual game, although you may wish to create a playable mock-up or 'beta' of what the game might look like. It should demonstrate key concepts or gameplay mechanics, and be about 10 minutes worth of play. If you create a mock-up along those lines, your written document can be correspondingly shorter.

Such a big project holds much potential for running off the rails. Numerous checkpoints were established throughout the term to keep the project on track (our term ran for twelve weeks). The idea was that the students could then reuse these checkpoint materials in their final project-design document. The first checkpoint was 'the pitch', where they would be constrained to a single short paragraph to describe the game and their intended historical outcome. The next checkpoint asked them, in a single page, to identify the 'problem space' (McCall 2012) and the principle game mechanic for addressing this space. The problem spaces of a game are the challenges that the player must overcome; hence, to think of 'history' as replete with problem spaces forces the student to think of how actors in the past were 'confined by resources and rules of interactions with others' (McCall 2012: 12). This is a crucial benefit of writing history with video games: it forces understanding that the past was contingent and not preordained. Moreover, video games foreground the act of (re-)creation of the past in the present, focusing on the contingent rather than the grand master narrative (Kapell and Elliott 2013: 14).

These two checkpoints were due during the third and fifth weeks of the term. It was not until the seventh week (over halfway) that students produced a document that finally addressed the game structures and the relationship to the 'skin' of the game (that is, the difference between what the game is ostensibly *about* and what it actually *does*). The final checkpoint (week nine) described in detail the player's experience at each stage of the game: what they experience, feel, learn and do. Two weeks later, each group had to present their work in progress in lightening timed presentations; each group had ten minutes and thirty slides (set to auto-timer) to cut to the heart of their process. Writing algorithmically is about writing spare, keeping it lean and using the most effective amount of code to get the job done. While these students did not write code per se, they wrote academic code in a way that mimicked computer code, in contrast to that normal tendency to fluff, to expand, to meet page requirements.

Again, in keeping with the desire to promote lean and effective coding, the students also had to blog weekly, reacting not only to the readings and the class discussion, but also to what was happening in their groups. 'Accuracy' is a recurring theme. In the earliest posts, 'accuracy' is conceived in terms of visual fidelity to the props of history, such as proper uniforms, correctly rendered architecture, period-appropriate speech (that is, with the 'skin' of the game rather than its underlying rhetorics). Roughly halfway through the course there is a pivot. I had the students play *Depression Quest*, an interactive fiction (text adventure) by Zoe Quinn (2013).

Depression Quest is an interactive fiction game where you play as someone living with depression. You are given a series of everyday life events and have to attempt to manage your illness, relationships, job and possible treatment. This game aims to show other sufferers of depression that they are not alone in their feelings, and to illustrate to people who may not understand the illness the depths of what it can do to people.

Working through how interactive fiction can produce emotional impact wrought a change in the idea of 'accuracy' held by the class. By removing the graphics, by confronting them with a story generated by their own choices that focused on the experience of an illness, the earlier lessons of the course began to click with the students. Subsequent discussions in class were richer and nuanced (and the video game fandom element receded somewhat). As one student put it during a class discussion, the ability to make meaningful choices in the narrative fostered historical empathy and care; the characters ceased to be puppets and became actual people again.

Outcomes

At the end of the course, there were six group projects submitted. Did the students see how algorithmic writing could produce knowledge, understanding and empathy for actors in the past? Did they make the connection between what they were doing and the way information on the web is presented to them? For the most part, yes. One project ultimately missed the point entirely, but another project, The Medic's War, exceeded all my expectations. Using a digital bricolage approach, these students used an interactive fiction platform to handle character interactions, triggered by code phrases discovered while exploring a top-down isometric pixel-style depiction of a battlefield and a camp. The sound of battle was ever present. Its creators wrote in their final submission that they consciously chose to highlight the tragedy of war, rather than glorifying it, by putting the player in the role of the field medic who must recover the wounded. No matter the side, the field medic has to deal with the carnage, the futility of it all. It was a profoundly moving game to play. There were no winning conditions.

I had worried about these particular students. In one regard, they had bought in to what we were doing in this course too much. Every checkpoint document was vast and complicated. In their zeal to create the perfect game they had adopted a kind of kitchen-sink approach. The moment with *Depression Quest* was powerful for this particular group because it was also alienating. Angela Cox (2014), in her class teaching games as texts, notes (when introducing older games and their conventions), 'The notion that they had to type commands into the older games was utterly foreign to them; they struggled with it in much the same way that students struggle to read Middle English when we assign them Chaucer'. The zenith of interactive fiction occurred before these students were born; interacting with *Depression Quest* confronted the students with something that bewildered in its restraint. To drive home the idea of restraint, I had this particular group resubmit each of their checkpoint documents in the style of a tweet (140 characters only, in those days). In their resubmissions, they recognized that engaging with algorithmically generated (and read) texts could be used to create in the player the sense of confusion and despair that they identified in the diaries and letters of First World War soldiers and civilians. Thus, by writing not at the level of narrative but in the construction of possible outcomes, these students designed an emergent narrative to evoke the pity of war.

Our last few sessions included a discussion about how the lessons that this course taught translated into other digital media, including Google Scholar, Wikipedia and even the robots who can write the sporting news (see Levy 2012). Another student, who was a self-described nongamer, wrote about how her ideas about 'accuracy' in digital media had changed over the duration of our course: it wasn't about ever greater visual fidelity or obsessive attention to details. Rather, it was about experience. She had come to see that the 'immersion' part of immersive media was the extension of her mind into these digital places. She reflected on how learning the rules of these spaces by *being* in these spaces meant that she had to *become* the kind of ideal person for whom the space is constructed.

This is the value of encouraging students to use technology to learn how knowledge is produced, how history is constructed and how values are passed on. In this digital era, we enchant our students best by teaching them to pull back the curtain and look at what happens behind it.

At this point, feel free to interrupt your reading by trying your hand at building an agent-based model by following along the code walk-through in Appendix A.

Notes

1. Originally published as 'On Games That Play Themselves: Agent-Based Models, Archaeogaming, and the Useful Deaths of Digital Romans', in *The Interactive Past: Archaeology, Heritage, and Video Games*, ed. Angus A.A. Mol, Csilla E. Ariese-Vandemeulebroucke, Krijn H.J. Boom and Aris Politopoulos (Sidestone Press, 2017), 123–31. In this section, I reframe the model discussed in chapter 3, Networks in Social Space, as a kind of game. The difference between agent-based models and archaeogames is – or could be – a very narrow gap.
2. Originally published as 'Pulling Back the Curtain: Writing History through Video Games', in *Web Writing: Why and How for Liberal Arts Teaching and Learning*, ed. Jack Dougherty and Tennyson O'Donnell (University of Michigan Press, 2014), 149–60. There have been some gentle edits.

CHAPTER 5

The Fun Is in the Building

Building an Archaeogame from an Agent Model

In our ideal game powered by an underlying archaeological agent-based model, every decision that the player makes is meaningful in that the other agents in the game take actions or make decisions as a result of that choice. Contrast that with what happens in many big-budget games that manage player interactions with non-player characters (NPCs). The only meaningful choices are the ones that push the player further along the scripted path, giving the illusion of agency. These kinds of interactions are playfully skewed in the 2017 film *Jumanji: Welcome to the Jungle*, where the heroes, transported into the video game representation of the evil board game, encounter an NPC:

> NIGEL. Welcome to Jumanji! Nigel Billingsly at your service. I've been so anxious for your arrival.
> BETHANY. What's with this guy?
> SPENCER. I think he's an NPC.
> BETHANY. A what? English, please.
> SPENCER. A non-player character. He's part of the game. So anything we ask him, he only has his programmed series of responses.
> FRIDGE. Got it. It's all clear now.
> NIGEL. Franklin 'Mouse' Finbar! Welcome to Jumanji!

The entire film is a clever send-up of the many tropes of big-budget video games. The heroes could seemingly do anything in the world, but find that they are constrained by the game's overwhelming need to push them along a particular script. Solve puzzles, avoid dying, and perhaps they'll escape the game. When they are killed inside *Jumanji*, they regenerate by dropping from the sky, a traumatizing version of 'respawning'. Big budget games often use cutscenes to move the story along, little mini movies that the player has to watch. In *Jumanji*, the heroes are forced to follow along with the narrator (often Nigel) as he relives the cutscenes.

On a personal level, I find that kind of gameplay extremely boring. As *Jumanji* so deftly shows, to actually live in such a space would be terrifying. I can describe, as I did earlier, what my ideal video game might look like – one that takes the agency and emergent consequences of agent-based modelling as its core engine – but would such a game actually be entertaining? Or a better question: would such a game be meaningful? Would it make for a digitally enchanted engagement with deep time?

Andreas Angourakis is an archaeologist who builds agent-based models. Together, we tried to turn an agent-based model into a playable experience. We began by considering one of the most well-known archaeological models, Artificial Anasazi (Dean et al., 2000). This model also comes bundled with NetLogo in its models library. This exploration of the Ancestral Pueblo peoples tries to simulate their response to a changing climate, some fifteen hundred years ago in the American Southwest. The model contains within it data concerning the physical geography of the Long House Valley, its hydrological and agricultural potentials. The model simulates individual households and their decisions on where to live within the valley and how much land to cultivate. As the simulation progresses, the changing environment (as known through palaeoclimate data) has an impact on the households' decision-making. Households migrate to other parts of the valley, and, inevitably, these simulated households die off or survive given their decisions in the face of a changing climate. Thus the simulation makes an argument that a changing palaeoclimate alone as the major driver for settlement change and collapse in the Long House Valley is not sufficient.

What better way to explore the effects of climate change for people today than to embed them within an archaeological simulation? Murphy's Toast Games, a collective of archaeologists and game designers, asked a similar question but in terms of human evolution. In their game *Evolving Planet*, the player guides, from a command post on a spaceship in orbit, a group of beings as they begin to colonize a planet. The point of the game is to teach evolutionary principles to the player by having the player try to place the beings (quasi-self-aware robots that are not aware of the player) in environments on the planet that will force certain kinds of evolutionary strategies. The robots that survive become progressively better adapted to their planet, eventually gaining full sentience and culture.

The initial choice before us was how to integrate the player into the simulation. We could devise a conceit where the player is somehow outside the simulation but affecting it. Or we could imagine what the simulation might look like from the inside and try to give that experience to the player. One of the issues that we have experienced with publishing agent-based models in traditional journal formats is that people simply do not play or engage with the model itself. The journal article reports the aggregate behaviour of the model. The code, as an artefact of research, is little examined (and, of course, not always published or made available itself, but see Janssen 2009). The French archaeologist Jean-Claude Gardin (who according to Dallas 2016 should be seen as one of the earliest figures in digital archaeology) argued for 'performative, interactive mechanisms . . . allowing active access to descriptions and interpretations of the archaeological record, conceived as a schematised sequence of inferences between propositions organically connected with supporting archaeological data' (Dallas 2016, on the work of Gardin).

Gardin developed schema and methods allowing for this kind of work; we might argue that archaeogames of the kind we are building here should be included in this kind of framework. By translating an archaeological model into a game, we enable the player of that archaeogame to perform our understandings or their own, if the game rules/mechanics allow for it (game mechanics as distinct from archaeological mechanics represented in the game; cf. Bogost 2007; Urrichio 2005). Turning to the Artificial Anasazi model in NetLogo, we can ask how closely the model adheres to Gardin's idea of 'allowing active access'. On the surface, the player/user can only fiddle with broad demographic parameters, setting fertility rates and 'death-age', proportions of the harvest held back each year, and the relative 'harvest variance'. In Janssen's (2009: 5.1-5.5) reimplementation of the model, he found that the single biggest factor in the model that enabled it to reproduce the known climate and archaeological data was tweaking the carrying capacity variables. This tweaking does not match the kind of 'active access' that I think Gardin had in mind. Janssen (2009: 5.3-5.4) notes,

> There are many more additions to the model possible such as social interactions between households (reciprocal exchange of food, kinship relations). It is also likely that households do not make decisions to leave the valley completely independent of other households if they are part of a social fabric.
>
> . . . The fact that the Long House Valley abandonment cannot be explained by environmental factors is demonstrated by the original

Artificial Anasazi, but it could also be explained by calculating the carrying capacity of the valley. A more comprehensive question like whether exchange networks increase the resilience of settlements in the US south west may need to be addressed by a series of models, including stylized models that simulate various possible landscapes. Such a model would be based on assumptions that rely less on quantitative measurements like the Artificial Anasazi, but more on ethnographic interpretations of possible social mechanisms.

Andreas and I studied the NetLogo code for Artificial Anasazi and began to imagine what active access to this simulation might look like, especially in the light of Janssen's comments on 'social fabric'. We began to ask 'why' questions. When we ran the simulation, we saw households moving to new locations over time. Why did they move? What prompted that decision? Did that disrupt the family, and, if so, how? Did they know people in the new location? Did kin matter in the decision? The model, of course, represents this as a mathematical function; it cannot answer these questions in a way that makes human sense. But perhaps a game could do it. We wanted to create an enchanting, uncanny and ultimately moving engagement with this deep past. We wanted players to *care* about these households. And so we undertook to translate the model into a first-person perspective (what gamers call a 'first-person shooter', but minus the shooting) to envelope and immerse the player in the world of the Long House Valley, to allow the player to speak with these households, to find out more about them, to worry and care for their wellbeing. In this we were influenced by the Emotive: Storytelling for Cultural Heritage project (https://emotiveproject.eu/):

> In heritage locations, narrative tends to be used narrowly, as a method to communicate the findings and research conducted by the domain experts of a cultural site or collection. It's typically a single-user experience and can often lack emotional resonance or impact.
>
> . . . Emotive works from the premise that cultural sites are, in fact, highly emotional places. That regardless of age, location or state of preservation, they are seedbeds not just of knowledge, but of emotional resonance and human connection. ('Background' 2016)

Game Design Is Hard

In studying the ancestral Puebloans via simulation, we would run the model over and over again, sweeping the parameter space (e.g.

if a model has two parameters that each run from 1 to 10, then there are [10 x 10 =] 100 different setting combinations to explore) to understand how the model works, and then mapping those outcomes against what we know of the archaeology to better understand the past. Andreas then translated the core model from its NetLogo representation into the language of video games, C#, using the Unity3D game engine. This act of translation is rather like all acts of translation in the tension between a literal word-for-word representation of the code from one language into another versus a more interpretative approach that captures the general thrust. Some things are lost in the process, but some things are gained. One of these is in the performative aspect of getting to know the simulation. In playing the game, instead of exploring the parameter space by looking at the results of the simulation runs as individual data points in a spreadsheet, you have to explore the behaviour space through immersive exploration, discovery and meaningful dialogue with the non-player characters. 'Meaningful dialogue' is perhaps where enchantment comes into play in that the player is going to read into the dialogue their own understandings of the past, or perhaps have these confronted and challenged (on emergent dialogue in procedural storytelling, see Ryan 2019).

However . . . game design is hard. We knew we wanted to bring the player into the Long House Valley. We knew we wanted the player to speak with the people in the households – but that created a problem right there, as there are no people, no individuals, in the underlying simulation! We knew we wanted the player to be able to affect the state of the simulation, but it had to be by persuasion rather than fiat. That is, the player could not affect the global state of the world, only the local situation in which the player happened to be. We needed, in fact, a story to tell that would make it sensible for all of those things to *be*.

Thank goodness for the time travel trope and a childhood of watching science-fiction TV!

How do we explain that the player has somehow materialized in the past? All time-travel games have this problem. *Evolving Planet*, which is really about human evolution on earth, reframes the problem as one of being on another planet that we are colonizing with humanoid self-aware robots. In our game, there is an accident in the archaeochronophysics lab that disassociates the player-character's consciousness from her body, but somehow makes her corporeal enough to interact with the people of the Long House Valley. Play is through a chain of incarnations, a conceit influenced by the old TV show starring Scott Bakula, *Quantum Leap*. In that show, Bakula's character, Dr

Samuel Beckett, would 'incarnate' into the body of a historical figure and be trapped in a particular situation until he 'solved' whatever the issue was. In our version, players incarnate at various points in the on-going simulation, and can query and interact with households, trying to understand why they are doing what they are doing, and trying to influence and change their decisions. The player might interact with the descendants of characters they interacted with in the previous incarnation. The player knows the 'true' history of the Long House Valley, and the goal is to try to avoid environmental collapse. We are trying to account for, or at least give a space for, all those other potential social mechanisms gestured at by Janssen (2009).

NetLogo has blocky graphics that don't have to be particularly good because they are merely ciphers for representing the simulation's dynamics. Translating the simulation into a photorealistic first-person environment, on the other hand, carries the expectation of extremely high-resolution graphics. We are not graphic designers or artists. Instead, we found digital elevation models from the US geological survey and imported that into the space. We learned how to generate procedural ground cover, vegetation, trees and rock falls so that the landscape looked realistic (e.g. if the slope was sufficiently steep, the game would generate a scree of rubble at the base of it).

The problem of how to represent the player within that world is a bit more complex. We never see the player character; their embodiment is not quite completely physical. How do we make the player interact with a household? In the original simulation, households regenerate like a single-celled organism, with five 'individuals' winking out of existence, and another five individuals winking into existence at the end of the household's lifespan, with certain variables and values transferring to the new household. Since our player incarnates in the game at different years, the way that households replicate can make for jarring discontinuities. We added a 'character' variable to a household so that the player encounters a manifestation of the 'character' variable rather than the agent (the household) proper. This permits the illusion of continuity; the character can pass down knowledge of past interactions and can be made to speak for the household as a whole.

When speaking, the 'character' for the household selects appropriate text and responses using a procedural text (a replacement grammar of the kind developed by game designer Kate Compton; see tracery. io) partly determined by the household's variables and decision making. A 'replacement grammar' functions rather like those fill-in-the-blanks worksheets that children sometimes play with – select a noun, a verb, another noun and so on, then place them into the text in the appointed spot (although what can be achieved with a replacement grammar can be far more complex). The player speaks with the households and tries to influence the probabilities that a household makes a decision one way or the other. The dialogue builds a unique engagement each time, fostering empathy and attachment. The replacement grammar is sufficiently large and complex to generate many snippets of broader stories, which the player completes in her own mind by filling in the gaps. In this way, the player herself completes the illusion of intrusion into a complex society and its history (but we will return to the possibilities of non-player characters in chapter 6).

Once the player 'releases' the scene by choosing to disincarnate (the player may feel that she has exhausted the opportunities for conversation, or decide to stop trying to influence the households because she feels the probabilities are now right in order for x, y or z to happen), the game play pauses, and the simulation is allowed to continue with these new changes. In these interstitial scenes (analogous to a cutscene in a 'normal' game, though conceptually very different) the player can see the effects of their intervention against the baseline version of the simulation. The task for the player at this point is to choose when to stop the simulation from progressing and where to intervene again, incarnating back into the Long House Valley.

So, is it . . . fun?

Maybe. It certainly is a different way of writing the history of the Long House Valley. The simulation contains within itself the archaeological and palaeoclimatic evidence and other kinds of ecofacts and artefacts that we, standing in the twenty-first century, know. Putting a person into that space highlights so much of what we don't know, what we can't know, and so it should be an arresting and discomfiting experience. It should make clear some of the limits of what archaeology can know, and remind the player about what we want to know – the lives of these people who made decisions about where to live and how to live that made sense to them. It humanizes the simulation and, perhaps, humanizes the past.

If this section leaves you cold, it might be because neither Andreas nor I are game developers. We just don't know how to do it properly. Should we not just call in the experts? After all, if we are seeking to enchant people's engagement with the past through digital means, isn't this really the point where we're better off leaving things to the developers? Tara Copplestone (2017) has examined this question in some detail, conducting interviews with archaeologists, game developers and archaeologists who develop games. The way that the developers tell it, they design systems and experiences allowing for *a* past to be told, while archaeologists tell *the* past. In their view, developers set up the how, while leaving the player to develop the *why* (Copplestone 2017: 86). This would seem to be broadly congruent with what Andreas and I were trying to achieve with our quantum leap–style game. Copplestone (2017: 88) reflects on her own archaeological practice and how she will use these tools and approaches of the developers and yet still build something that feels very different from what 'official' game developers build:

> I was initially trained to do archaeology through pen and paper context sheets, illustrations, 2D maps, and monograph reports. The internal affordances of these media forms involved in my practice have had a significant impact on how I think archaeological data and narratives *should* look or feel. As such, the way which I think, and the outputs that I create, will tend to fall in line with this worldview – regardless of the scope of affordances of the media I am using or the thing which I am studying.

This sets up the tension we as archaeologists feel when we expand into nonlinear or playful modes of representing – remediating – the past; that tension is present as an undercurrent in the question 'But is it fun?' What we really mean is 'But is this actually expressing good archaeology given the affordances of this medium?'

A mouthful, I know. Copplestone (2017: 90) goes on to argue that the media forms we are accustomed to using to express the complex theoretical ideas we value (e.g. multivocality, ideas on reflexivity, agency and so on) are undermined by the use of media forms (paper journals, linear writing perhaps) that simply don't match. She writes, 'Different programming languages, engines, styles, genres, and narrative structures produced distinctly different possibility spaces to those which we traditionally engage with. . . . Thus, creating a game through a particular language requires thinking through how that coding language operates. . . . [The] tools themselves impact what *can* be made and *why*' (Copplestone 2017: 91-92).

Copplestone and her collaborator Luke Botham demonstrate these points via their 'ergodic' literature game *Buried* ('ergodic' from the Greek *ergon*, work, and *hodon*, path; a text or game requiring effort to read and make sense of; Aarseth 1997). *Buried* was built using Twine, a platform/engine for creating choice-based narratives. In the game, a meditation on being an early-career and/or precariously employed person in archaeology, there are seventeen potential endpoints, generating between 1,000 and 10,000 words of text from a corpus of

150,000 words of narrative. The game's very choice-based structure highlights what can and cannot be done – the agency or lack thereof experienced by newcomers to the field – making a powerful comment on the power structures we work within.

Perhaps our playable Artificial Anasazi can never work because it is simply nontranslatable into the ways a first-person shooter constructs knowledge. Perhaps our game should have been framed more like a management simulation of households, rather than from a first-person shooter perspective. The correct genre to reframe Dean et al.'s Artificial Anasazi might be *SimCity* rather than *FarCry*. Yet the management simulation genre is not without problems for our goal of an enchanted digital archaeology. Thinking about management simulations, and *SimCity* in particular, brings us back to that original vision of the City of Rome as a process, an entangled network stretching over time and space.

SimCity, Roman City

If there is a game designer who might understand what enchantment via the digital means, it's Will Wright. In an interview in 2005, Wright discussed how he came to design *SimCity* and some of its various spinoffs (Phipps 2005). He mentions how he was inspired by how kids are entranced by ants and the kind of spontaneous self-organization that ant colonies exhibit, calling it 'almost magical': 'I began wondering, could we build a more robust simulation of human behavior if we adopted this ant model, where we distribute the intelligence not through the agents, but through the environment?' (in Phipps 2005). This idea led him towards a model where the player creates the environment, experimenting with different configurations, and the agents respond accordingly. The blanks-in-the-story that this creates naturally are filled by the player's imagination, making the player and the computer co-creators, each playing to their own cognitive strengths.

Something almost magical. Something fascinating when we experiment. Distributed intelligence. Spaces that react to the assemblages put within them. Coproducing meaning by letting the computer *and* the person tell the story through the gaps. All of this tells us that *SimCity* is a vector for a digital enchantment that can change the way we see the world.

SimCity has had an extraordinary amount of influence in the game design space, arguably creating the entire management-sim genre. Rollinger (2015: 4-5) calls the kind of history encountered in a game space a kind of 'affective history' and thus a source of a potentially different kind of historical knowledge, and considers what kind of affective history the playing of the *Caesar* franchise of games permit. In all of the *Caesar* games, the core mechanic is the same: it is a city-builder set in a vaguely 'Roman' time and place. You as the governor have to lay down where every workshop, insula, bathhouse, shop and so on will be. In this way, you attract colonists, who go about their lives. It is explicitly colonial: previous inhabitants of the area turn up from time to time as barbarians at the gates. The inhabitants of your city pay taxes; you use the taxes to build more of the city. Every building requires different 'classes' of people to perform different roles; you must balance their needs and desires to keep them happy citizens who do not quit your city in disgust (or die, as sometimes happens). Rollinger considers carefully where this representation of 'the Roman city' falls on the spectrum of plausibility. Some mistakes can be forgiven for the purposes of playability; but a deeper issue that Rollinger identifies is that the kind of city that is depicted here is *not* an ancient one, but a city of the late twentieth century United States. As a clone of *SimCity*, how could it be otherwise?

Will Wright famously invented *SimCity* as a result of finding the terrain editor tool he was working with to build a shooter game, *Raid on Bungling Bay*, more compelling than the game itself. To make that terrain editor into a game, Wright drew on a lot of mid-twentieth-century planning theory in a bid to make the cities he laid out *play themselves*. In particular, he was inspired by the 1969 book by Jay Forrester, *Urban Dynamics*. Forrester had decided that (American) cities were broken. Forrester's book made the argument that cities could be 'fixed' not by government but by incentives for business. Prior to his foray into planning, Forrester had designed computers and management systems to solve problems of modelling production and distribution in industrial firms. In 1968, he encountered John F. Collins (the former mayor of Boston). As a result of their conversations, he began trying to use the same methods he had developed for industry to create a system dynamics model of the city of Boston. The result was called DYNAMO. DYNAMO imagined that there were three classes of people who mattered in a city – managers, workers and the underemployed. Forrester's assumptions about what the underemployed were like conditioned how the underemployed were represented in the model. He did not think much of them: they were modelled as a drag on health and other resources, offering little to the city in return. Thus if low-income housing was introduced in DYNAMO, the simulation duly found that it was a bad idea: 'According to the model, these programs increased the local tax burden, attracted underemployed people into the city, and occupied land which might otherwise have been put to more economically healthy uses' (Baker 2018). In which case, if one wanted to help the underemployed, the model would naturally suggest counterintuitive solutions, solutions which naturally accorded with small-government assumptions about the world. The authority and supposed objectivity of a computer model also permitted a certain amount of handwashing – 'it's not us, it's the computer!' – which helped guarantee its popularity in certain corners of the Nixon White House. It helped give cover to the idea that counterintuitive notions would give the best results. 'Forrester's arguments enabled the Nixon Administration to claim that its plans to *slash* programs created to help the urban poor and people of color would actually, counterintuitively, *help* these people' (Baker 2018).

The popularity of *SimCity* and its undeniable influence in fostering and promoting particular visions about land use (indeed, *colonialist* visions of how cities should work) that continue to the present day (*SimCity* appears in many planning curricula as a laboratory for students to develop their own theories of urbanism; see for instance Wilson 2014) demonstrate the power of digital enchantment to impact far beyond the confines of a game.

Roman City-Builder Games

I wonder, too, how much influence *SimCity* has had on the study of the Roman economy? It would be a subtle influence, an influence of the kinds of possibility spaces we might envision for studying Rome. I am certain that my hours playing the game trying to solve the problem of getting *my* cities to work 'properly' led directly to my master's studies in the City of Rome programme at the University of Reading with Janet DeLaine and Ray Laurence (scholars whose work is synonymous with understanding ancient Roman cities). My master's thesis was an exploration of the problem space of building an aqueduct to Rome – of organizing the labour and materials, of sequencing those materials on site so that this monstrous machine (an aqueduct) for moving water could be built in a timely way. That influence remains in my work. The description of Rome as a kind of rolling process, a weight on the world (see chapter 1, 'The City as Network'), can be seen to be influenced not only by the hoary chestnuts of Roman economics, the primitivist versus modernist debate, but also by some of the embedded assumptions of *SimCity* – that it is possible to have a global overview of what's going on in the city at any one time, and that the planner can intervene at will at any time. Moreover, we are always dealing with *terra nullis*; the environment does not matter; and it is only the tastes of the wealthiest citizens that matter (Schooler 2010). The impact of *SimCity* on planners deciding to become planners is well attested (e.g. Roy 2019), and its impact on the wider video game industry is indisputable. Where it concerns us right now is in its impact in terms of archaeogaming. There are many clones of *SimCity* dressed up with ancient clothing; let us return to explore one iteration, the *Caesar* series.

In *Caesar*, the effect of its parentage in *SimCity* is present in the ideas of 'zoning'. While in *SimCity* zones are explicit and their effects can be known fairly quickly, it's only through play that their analogues can be deduced in *Caesar* because the zoning is hidden behind the graphics. Industries must be put on the edges of the city, and the city must have a glorious monumental core. Students of the Roman economy have asked for years whether Roman cities are producer cities or consumer cities. The only kind of city that ever works in *Caesar* is one that it is a 'practical' city, a machine optimized for commerce. Such a city is the only city that ever really wins the game (Rollinger 2015: 27-28). 'The consequences of this for the mediation of supposedly antique aspects are obvious: the playful efficiency is deeply ahistorical' (Rollinger 2015: 29).

Another major ahistorical element is the treatment of slavery in the game. That is to say, slavery is entirely missing in the game. A historical simulation of a Roman city would have to have slavery, but no modern game could represent slavery as a playful mechanic. Games always reflect the current social and political mood. Rollinger points out that *Grand Ages: Rome* (published by Kalypso Media in 2009) has slave market, but its influence is not depicted visibly in the game (rather, the game provides buildings within a certain radius with slaves), nor can the player interfere with how they are distributed. Slavery is tidied away, just another economic calculation (Rollinger 2015: 30).

If I were to design a Roman city-builder game, for I, too, am enchanted by the same idea that Wright had, that a city plan is a kind of skeleton of the city waiting to be reanimated, I would try to achieve certain things. In my view, an ideal Roman city game *should* represent the core truth of studies of the ancient Roman city: the idea that we don't actually know, at a macroscopic level, how the ancient city actually worked. It should have microlevel events that we *do* know from archaeology (evidence of buying, selling, producing, consuming; of colonialist impacts; of indigenous resistance and accommodation) but let the player combine these within competing frameworks for explaining the macroeconomy – consumer city, producer city, Roman bazaar and so on. The interactions of the different parts would be operationalized depending on what kind of macro framework that the player has selected.

Why It Matters

Remember why Wright was ensnared by Forrester in the first place. Forrester's work gave Wright a way of making the static things he was creating in the terrain editor for *Raid on Bungling Bay* dynamic, to turn them into something that could grow and change, to match Wright's imagination. Foster's work operationalized Wright's enchantment. Foster's theories were constrained by his own background solving production and distribution problems, and, as long as one could frame the problem in those terms, his simulations were a useful answer. But as we have seen, they carried within them – as a result of the various vital materialities of the computer punch card, the military industrial complex, the rising tide of feminism and the expulsion of women from computing roles (see Hicks 2017 on 'programmed inequality') – a procedural rhetoric that was seductive at a political level. The result of that seduction was the implementation of this algorithmic knowing into the real world.

Forrester's ideas about society and the proper way to model it had consequences in the real world in terms of public policy. But it also influenced Will Wright, who used it to translate his awe, his sense of enchantment, into a more portable simulation so that others could feel the same awe. Copycats and clones changed the skin of the game, but not the underlying mechanics. The popularity of these games normalizes and hides what otherwise might be subject for huge debate. Humans enter into assemblages with these games, and the vast networks and ties transform the world not only to make it possible to play these, but also to enable some visions of what could be possible, and to forestall others.

The powerful lesson here is that in his search for enchantment, in his search to communicate his awe, Wright settled onto a useful computational tool that was freighted with serious baggage. This is why enchantment when it is concerned with digital things has to also provide the tools for disassembling those things, to break them, to reconfigure them in new ways. Part of why *SimCity* continues to enchant is that its original source code was released on the internet as part of the

One Laptop Per Child initiative (which, given the political impacts that *SimCity* has had, might not necessarily have been a good impact to spread in the world any further; fortunately, the initiative largely flopped). By releasing the source code, tinkerers and game makers can study its code and try to make something new.

A seed for a NetLogo model that might start you building your own city simulation/game is my little Golems in the City model, the code for which is in appendix D. Golems in the City could be a model for building a self-organizing ancient city management sim. It loads up a city's footprint, then turns the golems loose within that armature of streets. It only has one mechanic in it right now that is moderately playful – the golems like to gossip. One could measure the time it takes the message to percolate using various kinds of cities – perfectly orthogonal, like a Greek or Roman colony; more organic, like pre-Roman Pompeii; towns that grow along a line, like a Phoenician city; or what have you. A market mechanic could be developed in it. A daily rhythm could be added, sending the golems to different parts of the city to satisfy various social or economic needs (as decided by the individual golem). In this way, designing and playing with the model allows you to enter into a coproduction relationship with the computer, to enjoy coauthorship status with your machine in the way that Wright imagined when he said, 'We're actually levering the player's imagination as a co-processor to fill in the blanks where the computer is weak' (in Phipps 2005).

Where the computer is weak here is what makes this archaeogaming. The player would bring their archaeological experience, their knowledge of ancient history, to fill in the gaps. It is a kind of emergent storytelling that enables a productive digital enchantment. Enchantment in this sense opens us up to recognizing that part of our way of knowing the past is in assemblage with the machines, that we are 'vibrant matter' too (Bennett 2010: xi). The assemblage that produces *SimCity* and, by extension, many of the commercial city-builder games on the market today is one that extends across women coders working on the mainframes of the 1960s, the industrial military complex of the immediate postwar period, the patterns of middle-class education and professional advancement at the expense of women in computing in the 1960s and 1970s, nostalgia in the 1980s for the Last Good War or fear maybe of the Soviet Other (Wright's coding of *Raid on Bungling Bay* in the broader context of 1980s war films looking backwards at Vietnam or forward to a Soviet invasion), the developing networks of digital components designed in California but manufactured elsewhere from elements mined in Africa – the list could go on.

All of these coalesced in the figure of Will Wright and his level editor. Pushing outward in time from that point, we have an entire new genre of game, and we find progressively more complicated (but not complex) simulations and representations of city life. I remember visiting my brother at college in the early 1990s. He had his own computer(!) and, on it, two games: *Civilization* and *SimCity*. We came from a small village on the edge of the cultivated land in the Ottawa Valley; we already had this sense of being on land that could potentially develop into anything, if it just had a chance. Playing the game together gave us that chance. We built Shawnopolis. Gordtown. We turned our village into a metropolis. We debated how the game was responding to our choices, and why. Playing the game tied what my brother was studying (Canadian history) to ourselves and to our county, and gave us a sense of power and possibility. Every town we built was an opportunity to try out what we believed about how things *should be* and what we believed things to be *in the past*.

Agent Model to Board Game

Making the shift from an agent-based model to a polished video game is very difficult. I can imagine using a variation of the tactic my students used in their game, 'The Medic's War' where they used different kinds of platforms in combination to get the effect they did not have the skills to program but wanted for their experience. This kind of bricolage, of putting together different pieces of other bits of software, points to another element of digital work that is somewhat counter-intuitive: that digital habits of thought do not have to be expressed in digital media. The agent-based models that one can build using the materials in the appendices in this book could be used, for example, as the generators of a kind of procedural history that one could build a card game or board game around. Events in the simulation would trigger events on the game board. Or alternatively, you could use the discipline and framework of simulation-building to generate a complete board game, which is how FORVM: Trade Empires of Rome (Brughmans, Romanowska and Graham 2018; http://forvm.ca) was designed. I'll say it again: one doesn't have to code or write or build a digital experience from scratch to employ usefully computational habits of thought.

Pandemic (Z-Man Games 2007) is a board game where the players are playing against a kind of networked cellular automaton. The players are trying to coordinate to stop epidemics spreading across the map of the world, where travel and connections are represented as a network graph of nodes and edges pinned to the map. In each turn, there is a stage where the diseases spread from one node to another in a kind of cascade (this is the 'cellular automaton' part of the game: each node's – each location's – state is updated depending on the state of the nodes to which it is connected). The players try to inoculate, quarantine or otherwise disrupt the diseases' progression. It's rather like the Virus-on-a-Network simulation bundled with NetLogo, with added player agency. It is a brilliant cooperative strategy game.

When Tom Brughmans, Iza Romanowska and I set out to create a board game simulating the Roman economy as a networked expression of power and control, we had played a few rounds of Pandemic in the past and had seen the connections with agent simulation immediately. We knew we wanted to create a game that expressed our ideas about the Roman economy, but we hadn't yet settled on how we would do that. Inspired by the connections we saw in Pandemic with networks and agent models, we began by writing pseudo NetLogo code on a giant piece of paper. By 'pseudo code' I mean code that expressed what we wanted to happen, that more or less followed the conventions of actual NetLogo simulations. Expressing our intentions as code-like steps meant that we could always see how the procedures interconnected, and we could role-play the interactions we wanted to see happen to make sure that the possible outcomes were constrained by our knowledge of Roman society and economy. We were building a digital experience, but dispensing with digital tools to express that experience.

We knew that we wanted players to be constrained by the actual ways cities and towns in the Roman world were connected. We obtained the network representation of the Stanford ORBIS model (Meeks and Scheidel 2012) and simplified it a bit, plotting it out on an A3 sheet of paper. Then we started playing out the rules of our simulation by taking those instructions we would normally have forced our digital golems to follow, and by trying to follow them ourselves. Our rules:

1. Move agents around the empire, one town at a time
2. Commit social intrigue (marry off children for better alliances, for example)
3. Collect the windfalls of local trade
4. Build improvements to make trade more profitable
5. Deal with the daily life
6. Convert your wealth into prestige

7. See if you've won the game

8. Deal with fate, omens and the gods

We included in the rulebook for FORVM an 'intellectual agenda' for the game that centred on the idea of making and changing the rules as an act of scholarship (Brughmans, Romanowska and Graham 2018). A video game has an impartial referee interpreting the rules for the player; this interpretation is so invisible, so seamless, we sometimes can't tell what the rules are except through conscious acts of trying to break the game, find the glitches, expose the flaws in the machine's logic. Board games, on the other hand, are entirely transparent. The rules are written on the page, and their interpretation is subject to discussion and negotiation by the players. A board game is an analogue simulation that has fuzzy edges. This also makes it an extremely valuable pedagogical tool, because its interpretation and abstraction of some kind of historical phenomenon into playable rules is totally open: one doesn't have to play by the rules if the rules are somehow wrong or if all the players decide on a change: 'Hey, this game could be even better if we did *x*!' A digital simulation is concerned with making historical phenomena operational, while an analogue simulation is concerned with making those phenomena playable and balanced. In our board game, we designed rules that we felt achieved a balance between something that was playable and something that was faithful to the underlying idea about Roman economics that we were trying to model. In our rules for FORVM we encouraged players to question those decisions and to dispute them. We encouraged players to publish their enhanced rules or even to modify the game wholesale – to use its board and representation of Roman economic space towards entirely different ends.

Agent-based modelling can *start* in a computer, but can become a framework for your own playful explorations of the past with pen, paper and some wooden tokens. That is how we move from agent-based modelling to archaeogaming. In the final chapter of this book, I turn to digital making more generally, especially procedural generation where what we make are things that make things themselves. We set our digital golems free to have a bit of agency on their own, and then ask them to tell us about the past.

CHAPTER 6

Artificial Intelligence

I had been scraping Instagram for several days, collecting tens of thousands of images that had been tagged with a variety of labels connected with the trade in human remains. People buy and sell human remains on Instagram, and they have to find each other somehow. I had seen how many of these posts were quite circumspect about what was going on or why the picture was being posted, but often it was quite apparent to my eye that some pictures were posted for their curiosity value, while others were meant as explicit enticements to purchase. With my colleague Damien Huffer, we wanted to see if there was a way to understand at scale (i.e. not having to look at every single picture ourselves) the visual rhetorics used by this community interested in the dead. This led me to exploring computer vision and the use of neural networks to identify and caption images. The community of research around computer vision is huge, and interest has been running high for a number of years now, and so the literature (and code!) is now vast. I eventually learned how to get the machine to make pictures for me of *what it thought it was seeing*. The first time I got that code to run, it seemed to take forever. I watched as the ticker counted upwards through each iteration . . . run 1 of 25 of epoch 10; run 2 of 25 of epoch 10; . . . for 500 epochs. It took a while.

And then . . . the computer started generating image files and opening them one by one, tiling across my screen. Every single one of them a detail from a Hieronymus Bosch-esque world, one gleaming skull on a pedestal after another, this one in three-quarters view, that one without part of the occipital bone, that one just a cap, every single one of them with a jagged colour profile making it look like an oil painting not quite done.

It was extraordinarily creepy.

But is it digital archaeology? Is this digital enchantment? How did the machine *do this*? Is this a digital artefact in the way that Reinhard (2018) argues? And if so, what does it mean? Or rather, what are its meanings?

'Digital' is just too big a word. A 'digital' archaeology – like 'archaeogaming' itself – runs the gamut from an archaeology of how digital technologies come to be and are used, to explorations of material culture effected through digital technologies, to archaeologies conducted inside and of virtual worlds created by procedural algorithms, to reflections on what the affordances of digital media are and how they come to craft what it is we can know about the past.

Again, 'digital' is too big a word. In this final chapter, I want to focus on the ways *new* affordances of digital technologies – their ability to learn about the world, untrained and unsupervised – open up new venues for archaeological creativity and playful engagements. The way they learn about the world again is founded on a networked representation of knowledge. I want to sketch out some of the ways I think this might intersect with enchantment. The point of enchantment, of being open to enchantment and the connections that span across these vibrant materialities, is to move us away from the crisis mode of archaeology (Perry 2019). Archaeological creativity is, as I see it, a counterpoint to the ways the results of archaeological knowledge-making – let us call it archaeological data – are used to support, for instance, settler-colonial narratives about land use. Archaeological creativity turns our normal archaeological rhetorics upside down and perhaps injects some whimsy and humility.

Archaeological creativity can *use* or *emerge* from digital work, but it is entirely possible to have archaeological creativity that isn't 'digital', as we saw with the Forvm board game. Consider Alyssa Loyless's 2019 work, 'Visualizing the York Minster as Papercraft'. In this piece, she describes how and why she developed a paper (cardstock) model of the York Minster as a visualization aid, as a piece of public outreach and as a study of the history of the minster. It is clear that digital technologies made it possible for her to design and print the complex pieces that make her three-dimensional paper model. But is it a digital archaeology? Ian Dawson and Paul Reilly (2019) reflect on the life and afterlives of a 3D (digital) model of the Winchester Old Minister as a nexus of physical and digital interpenetrations. Here, the ontological shifts that different remediations of the model into and out of various physical and digital media permit, and the ways these shifts force Dawson and Reilly to think differently about the minster (and our own actions as archaeologists, creating and destroying all at once), clearly situate *their* creative work as digital archaeology.

It might be that the key element that makes something 'digital' is that the intersection of different networks of power, materiality, mediation and knowledge are keys to the work. If this is so, we are firmly entangled in Bennett's vibrant materialities, assemblages, that open us up to enchantment. The importance of networks as an armature for all of the work discussed in this volume can't be overstated. And networks, it turns out, are also fundamentally important because controlling the flow of information, transforming it, and changing in reaction to the differing weights of connection in reaction to stimulus are together the same thing as computation. Once things that can compute/react/process information are linked together and can pass information back and forth, we enter a new realm of complexity. The future of digital archaeology is one where the humans are only one part of the assemblage, and perhaps not even the most in-control part.

Giving the Golem a Voice to Speak and Eyes to See

One of the more fascinating aspects of computational creativity in recent years is the emergence of neural networks. A neural network approach to machine learning (sometimes also called artificial intelligence, although the uncritical use of 'AI' as a label has a pernicious rhetorical effect of distancing responsibility from humans to machines) creates 'layers' of computational neurons that fire together in particular patterns when exposed to stimuli. The analogy with biology is explicit, even if we don't always understand how neurons and memory and learning works in the biological world. In a convolutional neural network used for image recognition, the neurons are mathematical functions that take particular inputs from the previous layer of neurons in particular weights or strengths. If we exposed the neural network to an image, one layer of neurons might fire in response to areas of high contrast, and pass what they are seeing up to the next level. Another might respond to the presence of an edge of colour; a third, to a curve. Later levels respond to combinations of the inputs from the lower levels. The particular architecture of a neural network can be quite complex, with some layers feeding backwards, others forward. A neural network can be 'trained' on text or images or sound or any other kind of data. The 'learning' happens at the end of the chain of layers of neurones. If the neural network is exposed to a picture of a dog, that pattern of weightings and connections that lights up can be associated with the label 'dog' – and thus the neural network can be used to sort through millions of pictures to assign labels.

Archaeological applications include the work of Iris Kramer and colleagues (2017) from Southampton University, who are using neural networks to identify archaeological features in Britain's New Forest. Caspari and Crespo (2019) apply a similar methodology to the Eurasian steppe looking for Saka culture tombs. Historians Melvin Wevers and Thomas Smits (2018, 2019) have been using neural networks to understand the patterns in the evolution of newspaper advertisements in Holland over the twentieth century. This alone is quite an accomplished use of computation, but Wevers and Smits has taken it one step further, asking the machine, What is it that you, the computer, are actually *seeing*? To achieve this, they use what are called 'generative adversarial networks'. They want the machine to generate its *own* advertisement.

In a generative adversarial network, there are *two* neural networks at play. The first one identifies images. But the second one sets out to *fool* the first. The first is a detective; the second is a forger. The forger sets out to generate an image, putting random colour information into an image file. The detective rejects the forger's work as unrecognizable, and it gives a measure of just how unrecognizable it is. With this information, the forger is able to try again, tweaking its composition. Over time, the forger generates a piece of work that the detective allows through. In Wevers and Smits's work, their forger is able to make things that *look* similar to the source images (cars, for instance), and is able to arrange the things in ways that vary similarly to the source advertisements. The machine has learned something of the visual rhetoric of advertising!

Neural networks can also be trained on text. In this approach, the patterns that light up are not about image data (that is to say, a fixed input), but on the probabilities that a given sequence of letters follow other sequences of letters. When we train the neural network on a body of text, it is learning a distribution of probabilities for how the different letters are likely to be combined over the corpus that we feed it. We can then 'sample' from the model to get it to *generate* new text.

I fed an early draft of the entire text of this book to a neural network. It worked away, learning the likelihood that the letter 'a' would be followed by a 'g', then an 'e', an 'n', then a 't' *when I'm already talking about agents*. If I'm talking about something else, well, that's an entirely new set of probabilities. Which one it will draw from when it generates new text depends on the seed text I give it, the germ from which to grow. We can even tell it how creative to be by tuning the 'temperature' – if we tune it way down, it will only ever select the next letter with the highest probability. That is to say, it becomes very conservative in its guesses. Turn the temperature way up, and it tends to go for the more unlikely combinations.

```
> Temperature at 1:
> the model is not the model of the city of the past , the
agents are only a client.
Temperature at 1.5:
> i am a particular event , it is a network
```

The neural network *knows* me.

It can be very amusing to feed the neural network various texts and to see what emerges. But we can also use these as a kind of lens to deform our texts to see something else – a kind of process that Mark Sample (2015) has termed 'weird digital humanities'. Say we trained the neural network on *The Decline and Fall of the Roman Empire*, by Edward Gibbons. With the temperature turned way down, we end up with a kind of base signal, the urtext if you will, for Gibbons's work:

```
> The senate was the senate and the senate and the senate
and the constitution . . . . The provinces of the Romans
were supported by the soldiers who had been subsisted by
the emperor the senate, and the provinces of the emperor
was confined to the provinces of the senate, and the
constitution of the emperor was supported by the soldiers
of the Roman empire
```

If we dial the temperature (the creativity) up:

```
> The provincials indeed maintained a soldier, the fleet of
the Christian sufficient exploits to the approaching honours
of the nation. The military wars were subject to the field
of public manner, and rather than the soldiers in the most
support of the disorders, and not alarmed by the man. The
great river, the provinces were the most particularly under
the slaves of the most liberal presence.
```

The magic of neural networks is this ability to learn style and voice. For instance, I fed it the text of the plays of Sophocles; it produced the following (the bolding and odd formatting is something the machine has also learned[!] from the conventions of my source texts downloaded from The Gutenberg Project website):

```
> O more of the breath of the shore,
And here and rended the stranger gods,
When the speed and the fight to the child,
Threatened disclear and to me
II 2
The clamour and the sea--come, when the sacred father
haste,
When he will be endowed in the way,
When of his father taught his father's wards
And who shall your seas a prade
The eagle as terror of the face,
And we must still me not as the steed of the storm,
But of the bride and the earth, who revealed
And where it from the daughter of the doom,
And Zeus is a distracles here,
Suffer out and here with shame.
And then the terror of the shores and the son!
```

The shock of this work – *the enchantment* – is when it generates text that makes sense and causes us to pause and reflect on the original sources (Zeus Distracles!). Janelle Shane is a scientist who in her spare time explores neural networks as part of her practice. One of the things she delights in reporting back on her blog 'AI Weirdness' (http://aiweirdness.com/) are her investigations into how neural networks know things, and what *precisely* they see/know. One of her favourite tools to interrogate is VisualChatbot. VisualChatbot (Das et al. 2017) takes a neural network trained on 120 thousand captioned images from the Common Objects in Context dataset (Lin et al. 2014) and pairs this text with a chatbot trained to answer questions about the image. You can upload an image to the VisualChatbot and then ask the bot about the image. If you give it a picture of kittens, you can ask it how many kittens it sees, and it will tell you.

Shane has found instances when the bot will bluff when it is confronted with an image that is not like the images in its training set. She has found that if you ask it about the colour of something in the image and it does not know the answer, it will simply lie and report 'it's a black and white photo so I can't tell'. If you ask it how many giraffes are in a picture *that contains no giraffes*, it will always give you a number because in its training, humans never asked questions about giraffes when there were no giraffes present. Hence, to ask about giraffes *must* mean, to the bot, that there's a giraffe in the picture some-where, and thus it will bluff.

Think about that. The machine has learned how to see, how to talk about what it sees, and how to lie about what it isn't seeing. (Incidentally, this puts paid to the idea that algorithms are unbiased: all algorithms reflect the inherent biases in their training data or in how they are designed to learn. Work like Shane's, while humorous, gives us a strategy for countering narratives of algorithmic omnipotence.) The machine does exactly what it has been optimized to do, and in this case, the shortcut it has found is *to lie*.

If you are designing a neural network to identify pottery, or using a neural network to identify human remains (Huffer and Graham 2017) in social media posts, or otherwise trying to employ these technolo-gies in your archaeological practice, can you trust your digital collabo-rator? The problem here is that we want to use these neural networks for justification (i.e. to give us answers) when what they are suited for is deformance. The VisualChatbot points the way to a solution. When we chat with the bot, we are not presented with 'The Result' with a probability or with the semblance of scientific authority. Rather, we encounter a being with a personality, with flaws and strengths, and we respond to it like a human. In this enchanting encounter, we know not to take everything at face value. We have a kind of empathy with it, and part of being empathic is giving the benefit of the doubt. In the same way, as with agent-based models, the results of neural net-work–powered investigations are not about finding 'The Answer', but a landscape of answers.

When I was a kid, we had a Commodore 64 computer. We swapped cassettes and later floppy discs with other kids at school, and some-how we ended up with a copy of ELIZA.

```
> Load "ELIZA",8,1
> Run
> Hello, I am Eliza
> * Hi Eliza, I'm Shawn
> Do you believe it is normal to be Shawn?
>* Yes
> Are you sure?
```

Eliza is regarded as one of the first chatbots (Tzouganatou 2018). She was designed by Joseph Weinzenbaum in the 1960s to mimic the questioning of a psychoanalyst. It was – and remains – a magical piece of software, not least because it works by triggering stock phrases given the user's input. In the interaction above, it recognized 'I'm' as part of its 'knowledge' of feelings and emotions – but not entities with names. And yet, despite its stupidity, there's something charming about the encounter. Ten-year-old me spent hours playing with Eliza, telling it stories, trying to get it to repeat forbidden words, wondering how I could make something like this myself. Fast-forward several decades, and our world is replete with chatbots. Conceptually, most of them are not much more complicated than Eliza. If you've had the misfortune to try to 'chat' with tech support on a website, you've likely interacted with a bot populated with stock phrases and trigger words. The VisualChatbot described above is similar, even if it is more sophisticated in how it recognizes how to react to the user's questions, giving more of an illusion of sentience. Many museums and heritage sites are now using chatbots to handle basic information retrieval requests. These bots are plumbed into the Facebook Messenger system and can be configured to ask questions that resemble the conversation trees we see in video games. They do not go off-piste, as it were.

The same structure can be used to create bots that function more like an interactive fiction text adventure. Provenancebot was a bot I programmed to live in Facebook. It used a series of choices to set off branching narratives. Crucially, many of these branches left lots of the story unsaid, which forced the human to fill in the gaps with their own understanding, their own reading of the silences. James Ryan, in his 2019 Ph.D. thesis on procedural generation and narrative, calls this 'curationist emergent narrative' (his thesis asks if it is possible for the game world to do the curating *itself*). In successful experiences, humans are willing to take this task on (that is, it is this willingness that makes the experience, not the experience that fosters the will).

This would make for a different experience for each person. In a similar vein, archaeologist Sierra McKinney programmed a chatbot aimed at schoolchildren that functioned more as a facilitator than a storyteller, an archaeological Eliza to promote discussion among the humans (McKinney 2018). More complicated chatbots can be created by teaching the machine the likely probabilities of characters going together by training it first on a corpus of materials using neural network approaches (see for instance the work and teaching of Allison Parish, whose semantic similarity chatbot code has been linked to the Open Digital Archaeology Textbook Environment GitHub repository, https://o-date.github.io/). Imagine feeding the machine all of the written work of Mortimer Wheeler, as well as transcripts of all of his appearances on *Animal, Vegetable, Mineral?* Train the machine also on the *responses* to things he said or wrote. Then, wrap that knowledge in a chatbot interface. The resulting creature is a pseudo-Wheeler and will respond not according to a decision tree or set of canned responses, but through an assessment of the likely probabilities of character/word responses given the particular input.

The pseudo-Wheeler chatbot understands what you say and responds appropriately *in the voice of Wheeler*, if not his exact words. It is a *would-have-said*. In many respects, this is how Alexa, Siri and their ilk already behave, having the entire power of Google or Apple or Amazon behind them. In the hands of the major info-barons, this is troubling and frightening; but in our hands, we have another avenue for enchanting encounters with the past. Feed the entire corpus of Cicero – his speeches, his letters. Feed the entire corpus of his contemporaries. Feed the graffito, the slurs, the poems, the vernacular, and you will have a first-century Roman you can chat with. (But keep in mind the work of Risam, Owens and Mir, and Bennett: where could this possibly go wrong?)

From here, it is but a short computational step to enable that chatbot to carry out actions that could affect a game world or an agent-based simulation. Indeed, our ancient chatbot could be one of the agents in the simulation. Perhaps there are *many* such chatbots within the simulation. The technology now exists for our simulations of the ancient world, set in procedurally generated landscapes and architecture, to respond in nonlinear ways to our embedded presence within them and for the likely voices of these agents to be richly endowed with knowledge about their world.

But there are troubling ethical problems with this, which we will turn to in a moment.

The Digital Resurrection of Flinders Petrie

Between when I wrote those words above and when I received this manuscript back from the peer review, the field of natural language processing and generation had made enormous leaps in modelling how language works. Let's circle back for a moment to the idea of simulating the 'voice' of the dead.

The code that I used to generate pseudo Gibbons and pseudo Sophocles modelled the probabilities of different letters following one another. While sophisticated at the time, that approach is now little more than a toy. With the increase in computational power and complexity, these newer models open up tricky ethical issues for us, and in particular if we use them to try to give our digital creations their own voice to speak. Let me sketch out how these new models work, resurrect Flinders Petrie, and then we'll examine the aftermath.

More complex models of language now try to work out the 'rules' of language by 'masking' whole words and working out the probabilities to deduce the hidden word from the words that sit to either side. Others try to represent a word as an 'embedding' in multidimensional space (using a model built by Google). But the most complicated model, and the most successful, as of this writing, is probably the GPT-2 model, developed by the OpenAI foundation. It was trained on webpages found from outward links on Reddit that Reddit users scored as highly useful, some eight million websites. The sheer *size* of this data let OpenAI develop a model that contains 1.5 billion parameters. Because of the potential malicious uses of the model, OpenAI did not release this model, but instead made available a series of smaller models – a 'small' model with 117 million parameters, and a 'medium' model with 355 million (there is a 'large' model available, but it is too large to run on a typical laptop).

Jesse Vig (2019) from the *Towards Data Science* group blog has a post exploring how this model generates text. He begins by experimenting, trying to break the model (an 'alchemical' approach, as Rahimi 2017 laments), feeding it two distinct sentence prompts:

'The dog on the ship ran'
'The motor on the ship ran'

The model completes the first sentence with 'The dog on the ship ran **off, and the dog was found by the crew**'. It completes the second sentence with 'The motor on the ship ran **at a speed of about 100 miles per hour**'. The model understands the difference between dogs and motors, and the likely probabilities of different words completing the sentence. The model has what its creators call an *attention* mechanism, which focuses on the linguistic idea of the 'head' of the noun phrase. There are other linguistic patterns captured by the model, arranged twelve to a layer across twelve layers. It is this attention mechanism and the learning of linguistic patterns that accounts for this model's success.

I fed the opening chapter of this book to talktotransformer.com, an interactive front end for the model. The first paragraph is what I wrote; the second paragraph is the machine's:

This is a book about enchantment and digital archaeology. It is a book about trying to pull together the connective threads on nearly twenty years of work in simulation, agent modelling, video games, and Roman economic history. These are not, on the face of it, 'enchanting' topics. But hear me out. It's about trying to remember what it was that was magical about archaeology when I first began, and why I find digital approaches to archaeology to still be magical.

> In this book, I'd like to trace out some of the elements
that underpin magical engagement with archaeology. I would
like to show you some of the tools digital archaeology
(D-arch), and computer archaeology have developed in
order to be able to address specific aspects of magical
engagement. But it isn't hard to imagine that if you
were an archaeologist working in the digital frontier
of archaeology a lot of these new tools might not have
occurred to you. To me, it's about being able to be
enchanted by the methods that a new medium has provided to
the archaeological enterprise.

I don't know whether to be pleased or worried by this result. It could almost be the blurb on the back of this book's cover. It gets a lot of things *right*.

Salesforce, a marketing company, has built their own model, called CTRL, on top of GPT-2 and released it on GitHub (Keshar et al. 2019; https://github.com/salesforce/ctrl). This model has 1.6 billion parameters 'trained to condition on control codes that specify domain, subdomain, entities, relationships between entities, dates, and task-specific behavior. Control codes were derived from structure that naturally co-occurs with raw text, preserving the advantages of unsupervised learning while providing more explicit control over text generation' (Salesforce 2019). Presumably, Salesforce is not as concerned about malicious weaponization of their model as OpenAI is.

This elaboration of the GPT-2 model can be prompted with, for instance, a URL (real *or* fake) and, told that the prompt text is a 'link', it will generate text informed by the metadata contained in the link (Woolf 2019). For instance, using Woolf's code for interacting with CTRL, I fed it the fake URL https://www.cnn.com/world/09/19/2019/ evidence-for-atlantis-found-in-suburban-ottawa-backyard. This URL does not point to anything at CNN, but it does mimic the structure of a real CNN story. But the words in the page title are understood by CTRL as controls in that 1.6 billion dimensional space on the *kind* of language that would be appropriate, collapsing the probabilities to 'news story' dimensions. The result:

> Evidence of Atlantis found in suburban Ottawa
MUST WATCH

```
Story highlights
The discovery was made by a man who lives on the
property.
It is believed to be one of only two known locations where
ancient artefacts have been discovered.
(CNN) A Canadian couple has uncovered evidence that
could help solve an age-old mystery — and possibly prove
Atlantis' existence.
In what they say is the first time such a find has ever
happened in Canada, a husband and wife from Ottawa,
Ontario, stumbled upon a cairn . . .
```

I fed the same model fake URLs patterned after my university department's faculty biography pages. I created two names, 'Sarah O'Connor' and 'Stuart O'Connor'. Sarah's biography was utterly glowing, but listed the many service organizations that Sarah belonged to, while Stuart's biography put its energy into listing all of his books. The model understands the gendered and hidden labour of the academy it seems – should you play with talktotransformer.com and experiment with sexualized or racialized language, do not be surprised when it generates toxic or not-safe-for-work text, reflecting our current world view back at us (at least, current as represented by the internet in 2019).

The text that models like GPT-2 and CTRL can generate demonstrate an incredibly sophisticated understanding of how the English language works and the interrelationships of different concepts (seemingly without limit!) that might be the *subject* of conversation. GPT-2 and CTRL are not just *language* models, but *knowledge* models.

And somewhere in there is archaeology.

The experiment with using CTRL demonstrates that my thought experiment from earlier in this chapter, building a digital pseudo-Wheeler whom I might want to interrogate about his worldview, is feasible *now*. What's more, the CTRL codes show that it is possible to collapse the multiverse of possible generations to a local universe conditioned on a particular worldview. In neural network work on images, you might be familiar with the idea of photos that get 'painted' in the style of Monet or Picasso via 'style-transfer'. This is the same idea, but with text.

It is worth pausing for a moment and noting that the antecedents for this kind of work stretch back at least as far as late antiquity and the book of Jewish mysticism, the *Sefer Yetzirah*, or, *Book of Creation* (Zweig 1997). This text shows how the letters of the Hebrew alphabet could be combined, via what we would now recognize as a graph or network, to make immediate God's creative generation of the world. The original

Golems of European Jewish folklore were given life through this combinatorial magic. The thirteenth-century Christian mystic Ramon Llull was aware of and influenced by these Jewish traditions of combinatorial generation and devised the *Ars Combinatoria*, a system for understanding the relationships between theological and ethical concepts in a way that would guide reflection and insight. Llull's *Are Combinatoria* eventually provided some of the insight and inspiration for Leibniz's calculus, and so on, into the era of digital computation. Nowviskie (2014) draws direct parallels between Llull's system and the ways that digital humanists use algorithmic agency to deform and otherwise interpret the texts that they study. The application of a neural network artificial intelligence to generate a kind of 'life' that we as archaeologists may then interrogate and play with (the 'ludic algorithms' that Nowviskie mentions) has a deep foundation. 'Emergence, rather than derivation, is in fact the hallmark of Llullian method' (Nowviskie 2014: 166).

> Llull invented a device for putting new ideas into the world out of the fragments of old ideas and constraining rule sets, but left the (inherently subjective) evaluation and explication of these emergent concepts up to a human user – a person explicitly figured in his writing as an artista. Llull's machine generates 'truthful' formulations equally with falsehood, and makes no claim about or evaluation of its own output. (Nowviskie 2014: 143)

Let us make a new device using the GPT-2 model of the world. I used Max Woolf's code for retraining the GPT-2 'medium' model (with 355 million parameters, 1.5 GB in size) on Flinders Petrie's (1892) *Ten Years' Digging in Egypt 1881–1891*, creating a model of Petrie's language and – potentially – worldview (I would have used Wheeler, but Petrie's writings are already available in the Gutenberg Project website, readily digitized, whereas Wheeler's are not.) Then, I ask this simPetrie some questions about archaeology. The dialogue below represents our 'conversation'; each question by me was a prompt to the model to generate text. *None of simPetrie's responses have been edited.* As you read simPetrie's responses, reflect on what they (may) reveal about the doing of archaeology in the late nineteenth century. Given that Flinders Petrie is celebrated in archaeology for the development of both field and analytical methods, let's ask his digital doppelgänger for its thoughts on the matter:

SG> Professor Petrie, What is the key finding of your researches?
SimPetrie> The only way to find out what is the key to every mystery is to know everything about it, and then to try to

discover the mystery as far as possible by deductions from
what is known. When we come to the real problem, how do we
find the real in the unreal?

SG> Professor Petrie, could you describe your methods for
us?

SimPetrie> I have always tried to be fair to the student,
and to give as much information as possible. I have tried
to give as many facts as I can remember; and then try to
match them with each other in the various accounts, so
as to arrive at some general idea. People often ask me
where the evidence for a fact comes from; and that is no
easy matter, when the evidence is so scanty. I have often
thought of writing a work on probability, in which every
fact might be found, and the numbers by which they must be
numbered, by heart, according to their weight in evidence.
I believe I have found the right ratio; and the more I
think of it, the more I see that it will not only be right,
but will be of great service to our subject.

   This method of ascertaining the amount of evidence is
the only one that seems to me entirely consistent with
scientific accuracy. It is easy enough to find the average
of thousands of facts; but it is much harder to find the
average of the facts themselves.

SG> Could you describe for us the role of local labour in
your excavations and surveys?

SimPetrie> The local labourers, who live and work under
me, are the most intelligent and hardy people I have met.
They live by digging, and having to earn their living by
selling the finished product to other local people who use
it to make shoes, &c. Though they are often exploited
in this business, they never trouble about it too much,
and are content with what they can get for a good wage.
Their only ambition is to live as cheaply as possible. The
knowledge which I have gained from their labours has been
of great service to me in my excavations, and I have always
been glad when one of them has told me how he has improved
his skill, or found a new construction, by improving the
methods of his fellows. I should be sorry to see such
methods go to waste for want of improvement and improvement
of the methods of my neighbours, for the end in view is the
same.

SG> Professor Petrie, what are the sorrows of archaeology?

SimPetrie> The sorrows of a dead man. I have seen the dead.
All that is preserved is what is in their power to leave
behind them.

> The remains of the temples, though they may be exposed,
> are of no use. They are only patches of stone, in a country
> where there are many other buildings. If the dead man had
> been a sculptor, he would have had no need of the temples;
> nor is it likely that any one could have made any use of
> them except by accident. The temples, then, were but a sad
> sacrifice to an unmeaning king.

SimPetrie is startlingly coherent. The original Petrie's concern for rigor and consistency in his archaeological recording and systemization of materials appears in the digital Petrie. The use/abuse of local labour is hinted at, with a touch of the colonial condescension we might expect from a nineteenth-century Englishman. The overly – to our ears – florid language of the period comes through.

When we ask simPetrie about 'his' world, the neural network takes our question as a signal of how to collapse the possibilities for the generation of its response. Careful questioning and attempts at breaking could reveal the limits of that simulated worldview. How does that worldview map back to the original Petrie's? How far can it be pushed before it breaks? Much like an agent-based model has to be run through all of its possible combinations of parameters to understand the simulated worldview, the simulated history's 'behaviour-space', we have to figure out a method for doing the same for this neural-networked model. One way perhaps of doing this might be to deploy data mining and text analysis. I could imagine asking simPetrie the same question a thousand times at each 'temperature' or creativity setting between 0 and 1. Then I would topic model (look for statistical patterns of co-occurrence of words in a response) these responses and map how the discourses found therein persist or evolve over the creative landscape of simPetrie's responses. That might begin to give us a map of the territory that we have stumbled upon. It will require much work and indeed play, experimentation and the wilful breaking of the models to expose the sharp edges.

However, some of the things we wish to play with, like the GPT-2 and CTRL models with their billions of parameters, are perhaps *too big* for enchantment. Is this where we spill from enchantment to terror? These models, after all, now that they've been generated (and consider the energy and environmental costs of training such models is estimated to be five times worse than that emitted by a car over its entire lifespan, or approximately 626 thousand pounds of carbon dioxide equivalent [Strubell et al. 2019; Hao 2019]) can now be deployed so easily that a single scholar on a commercial laptop can use them. The technology behind these models is not that far removed from the technologies that can simulate and generate perfect audio and perfect video of *things that never happened or were never said*, so-called 'deepfakes' (these too depend on neural network architectures). We will need to develop methods to deal with and identify when these models are deployed, and quickly. By the time this book is in your hands, there will be new models, larger models, of text generation, of language, and they will be deployed across a range of tasks. It will be exceedingly hard to spot the work written by the machine versus that written by a human. Our golems are getting out of control. But there are other ethical issues, too.

The Ethics of Giving the Golems a Voice

'When we teach computers to write, the computers don't replace us any more than pianos replace pianists', writes Ross Goodwin (2016); 'in a certain way, they become our pens, and we become more than writers. We become writers of writers.' SimPetrie asks, 'How do we find the real in the unreal?'

In *Feet of Clay*, Sam Vimes orders Igneous the Troll to rebuild the shattered golem Dorfl and this time to give it/him a tongue to speak with; shocked, Igneous responds that everyone knows it is 'blasphemy' if golems speak. In a world where our digital golems can be creative on their own, 'authorship' is not about putting the words down on the page, and 'scholarship' is not necessarily about marshalling facts about the world in a logical order to make an argument. Instead, they become an act of creative composition and recomposition, or the re-mixing and selecting of texts for training and of hyper parameters to be tuned. In fact, the same skills and techniques and scholarly work informs the creation of agent-based models. This kind of generative, computational, creative writing is not really about making a machine pass for a human, but, much like the agent-based models discussed earlier in this volume, it is about discovering and mapping the full landscape of possibilities, the space within which Petrie *could* have written. These *particular* questions prompted the machine to collapse the possibility space around how archaeology was conducted and around whose voice mattered in that work; thus the results perhaps give us access to things that were so obvious they were never written down. What is the evidentiary status of a mapping of the behaviour space of the model? There could be a fascinating Ph.D. thesis in that question. It reminds me of Terry Pratchett's idea of 'L-Space', outlined in his novel *The Last Continent:* the idea that 'the content of any book ever written *or yet to be written* may, in the right circumstances, be deduced from a sufficiently close study of books already in existence. Future books exist *in potentia*, as it were'. But this dialogue with sim-Petrie also raises, for me, some interesting *ethical* issues that so far in digital archaeology – in the work of people like Meghan Dennis (2016) or Lorna Richardson (2018) or Colleen Morgan (2009, 2019) – we are only beginning to dimly understand.

Tiffany Chan, for her M.A. thesis in English at the University of Victoria, used a recurrent neural network to map out the space of one particular author. She writes,

> What could we learn about our object of inquiry (in this case, literature) if we broke down, remade, and compared or interpreted it either alongside or as if it were the original? Articulated in Victorian terms, this project is like conducting a séance with a computer instead of a Ouija board. The computer mediates between human and machine, between the dead and the living. If, as Stephen Greenblatt suggests, literary study begins with 'the desire to speak with the dead' (1988: 1), then [this project] begins by impelling the dead to speak. (Chan 2017).

Colleen Morgan (2009) wrote, a decade ago, in the context of video games that use historical persons as non-player characters (NPCs) to decorate the games, that

> NPCs are nonhuman manifestations of a network of agents (polygons, 'modern' humans, fiber-optics, and the dead person herself) and the relationships between these agents and as a result should be studied as such. But does this understanding of an NPC as a network make it ethical to take such liberties with the visages of the dead? What does it mean when Joey Ramone comes back from the dead to sell Doc Martins?

In these two passages, we find many of the threads of this book. We see 'networks' as both a literal series of connective technologies that thread the digital and analogue worlds together. We see an impulse to raise the dead and ask them questions, and we see something of the ethical issues in making the dead speak. For instance, Petrie plainly did not say any of the things the simPetrie did in our dialogue. What if simPetrie had said something odious? It's entirely possible that the model could extrapolate from hateful speech collected in its training corpus, triggered by passages in the small body of text of Petrie with which I perturbed the original.

What if that text gets taken out of context (perhaps for an academic book or journal article) and is treated as if Petrie actually *did* say these things? In a conversation on Twitter about simPetrie, the computer scientist and sometimes archaeogamer John Aycock raised the issue with me of desecration: similar to the way human remains can be desecrated and ill-used in the real world, could this use of computation be a kind of desecration of a person's *intellectual* remains? Lorna Richardson (2018) points out that the creation of any kind of visualization of archaeological materials or narrative 'is a conscious choice, and as well as political act'. If these models are the instrument through which I 'play' the past, as Goodwin (2016) suggests, then I am responsible for what collapses out of that possibility space. The ethical task would be to work out the ways that collapsing possibility space can do harm, and to whom.

The advertising and entertainment industries have the most experience so far with raising simulacra of dead celebrities to sell us things and to entertain us. Tupac Shakur raps on stage with Snoop Dog years after his death. Michael Jackson performs from beyond the grave at the Billboard Awards. Nat King Cole sings a duet with his daughter. Steve McQueen races a 2005 Ford Mustang. These uses of the dead, and their resurrection, are more troubling than portrayals of historical figures in films or video games because of the aura of authenticity that they generate. Alexandra Sherlock (2013: 168) argues that

> the digital individual continues, irrelevant of the death of its author and prototype, and since the relationship that viewers have with this social entity was always conducted through representations and images anyway, nothing about this relationship actually changes . . . in popular culture the media persona becomes divorced from the actual embodied celebrity and their representations become a separate embodiment of their own – an embodiment with which people are able to identify and bond with in an authentic and real way.

These representations of dead celebrities worked because they depended upon, and continued to promote, parasocial one-sided relationships; the public was so used to the feeling of being connected with the *idea* of these individuals that their digital resurrection proved no obstacle, no barrier to enjoying the performance. Sherlock (2013: 170) discusses an episode where the digital resurrection of a celebrity *did* go wrong – the resurrection of Orville Redenbacher, of popcorn fame: 'Rather than promoting the enchanting notion of immortality, Redenbacher's advertising agency had accidentally and rather embarrassingly reminded viewers of the mortality of Redenbacher, and themselves by extension.' The advertisement fell into the uncanny valley, the term from robotics that describes when a robot is so human-like that the few errors in the depiction (lifeless eyes, for instance) generate a feeling of creepiness. Sherlock (2013) calls this entire process of using the images of entertainers, whether as holograms or on film, 'digital necromancy' and attributes some of the success (or failures) to the idea that, in addition to profiting from a parasocial relationship, the revenants fill a need for answers, a need for reassurance in the face of death, given that Western culture largely avoids talking about death:

> A form of necromancy does exist today, precisely in response to the marginalization of death. One might perhaps consider the technicians who created the Bob Monkhouse advertisement [where the comedian tells the audience about his own death from cancer] as modern necromancers – reanimating the digital remains of the deceased Monkhouse to impart his knowledge concerning his own death. It is as though the ancient art of necromancy has resurfaced in the practice of digital resurrection. (Sherlock 2013: 171)

All of which is to say that simPetrie could become 'real' in the same way the personas of entertainers and celebrities become 'real', and the views and opinions expressed by the digital doppelgänger could be given far more weight than is warranted. 'Subconsciously, their appearances may appeal to embedded beliefs that the dead are wise and knowledgeable: if they speak or show themselves to us, we should pay attention. Somehow the dead seem more believable', writes Sherlock (2013: 172).

When 2K Games, the makers of the game *Civilization*, included in its sixth iteration the Cree Pîhtokahanapiwiyin (Poundmaker) as one of the playable leader characters, they put words in his mouth. Milton Tootoosis of the modern Poundmaker First Nation said, '[This representation] perpetuates this myth that First Nations had similar values that the colonial culture has, and that is one of conquering other peoples and accessing their land. . . . That is totally not in concert with our traditional ways and world view' (Chalk 2018). While the depiction and lack of consultation with the Poundmaker First Nation is troubling enough on its own, imagine if the game-character of Pîhtokahanapiwiyin was coded in the way simPetrie was, and imagine further that the developers did not consult with the Cree on which texts to use for training – or whether to do this at all. The danger of the neural-networked power representation is in its liveliness, the possibility of fostering the kind of parasocial bonds that make the examples drawn from the advertising and entertainment worlds work. A neural network–powered representation of a key figure in Cree history would run the risk of becoming the version of Pîhtokahanapiwiyin that sticks; thus, who builds and designs such a representation, and for what aim, matters. This neural network approach to giving voice to a video game's non-player characters, to an agent-based simulation's agents, is exceedingly powerful. If we are building simulations of the past, whether through archaeogaming or agent-based modelling, we either need to make our software agents mere ciphers for actual humans, or we need to think through the ethics of consultation, representation and permission in a much deeper way. The technology is racing ahead of our ability to think through its potential harms.

There is also the ethical issue in the creation of the training data for GTP-2 in the first place, the creation of the possibility space. The authors of those eight million webpages obviously never consented to being part of GTP-2; the material was simply taken (a kind of digital colonialism/terra nullius). The use of Reddit as a starting place, relying on Reddit users' selection of 'useful' sites (by the awarding of 'karma' points of three or more to a link), does not take into account the demographics of the Reddit user community/communities. The things that white men ages eighteen to thirty-five living in a technophilic West see as interesting or valuable may not be the kind of possibility-space that we really want to start baking into our artificial intelligences powering the world. Taking a page from information ethics, Sicart (2009) argues in the context of video games that permitting meaningful choices within a game situation is the correct ethical stance; where are the meaningful choices for me who 'plays' the GPT-2 model, or for me whose website may be somewhere inside the model?

A framework for considering the myriad ethical issues that might percolate out of this way of raising the dead and giving them a voice again might be the 'informational ethics' of Floridi and Sanders (1999, 2004), as interpreted by Sicart (2009) from the perspective of video games. This perspective considers 'beings' in terms of their data properties. Data properties are the properties of relationships and the contingent situation of a thing. That is to say, what makes the rock on my desk a paperweight rather than merely debris is its relationship to me, our past history of a walk on the beach and the act of me picking the rock up, and the proper ways of using objects for holding down papers on desks (Sicart 2009: 246, citing Floridi 2003). Compare this with Ingold's (2007: 15) 'material against materiality', where he invites you to pick up a stone, wet it, and then come back to it a short while later:

The stone has changed as it has dried out. Stoniness, then, is not in the stone's 'nature', in its materiality. Nor is it merely in the mind of the observer or practitioner. Rather, it emerges through the stone's involvement in its total surroundings – including you, the observer – and from the manifold ways in which it is engaged in the currents of the lifeworld. The properties of materials, in short, are not attributes but histories.

The meaning of data entities lies within the web of relationships with other data entities, and all *things*, whether biological or digital, are data entities (Sicart 2009: 128–30; Morgan 2009). From this perspective, there is moral import because to reduce information complexity is to cause damage: 'Information ethics considers moral actions an information process' (Sicart 2009: 130). The information processes that give birth to simPetrie, that abstract information out of GPT-2, that collapse the parameter space to one local universe out of its multiverses, are all moral actions. For instance, these language models and these neural network technologies are predicated on an *English* model of the world, an English approach to language. Models like GPT-2 obtain part of their power through their inscrutability. Foucault (1999: 222) wondered what an 'author' might be and concluded it emerges in the condensation of physical and cultural influences, that 'the author function' disappears instead to be experienced: 'What are the modes of existence of this discourse? Where has it been used, how can it circulate, and who can appropriate it for himself? What are the places in it where there is room for possible subjects? . . . What difference does it make who is speaking?'

That is the ethical question posed by archaeogaming, because the 'who' isn't just humans anymore.

Augmented Reality

According to game expert Douglas Ruskhoff (2005: 415), 'The frightening news is that we are living in a story. The reassuring part is that it's a story we're writing ourselves. Alas, though, most of us don't even know it – or are afraid to accept it. Never before did we have so much access to the tools of storytelling – yet few of us are willing to participate in their creation.' Let's think about the implications.

Some time ago, inspired by the work of people like Helen Papagiannis (2012) and Stuart Eve (2011), I became interested in location-based augmented reality. My ability to build immersive experiences was limited however, and I lost many weeks of work trying to engage with 'magic eye'–type augmented reality, where the window of your smartphone would overlay digital data onto the picture. At the same time, I was also toying with interactive fiction authoring using Twine, a platform for text-based storytelling where the story unfolds by clicking on the choices presented. I realized that these two streams of experiment could be combined by giving the interactive fiction access to my handheld device's geolocation data. Passages in the story could be triggered by the location in space of the player. I called it 'low friction' augmented reality for two reasons. One, it reduced the chore of programming the interaction, for once I had worked out the bugs, the mechanic could be copied and pasted by other creators (it is now part of the Twine Cookbook at https://twinery.org/cookbook/). Two, it relied on sound files and text to create the heightened sense of the weird and enchanting, rather than graphics. Get rid of the graphics, and suddenly many more creative possibilities will emerge.

It was more of a proof of concept than anything else, but the demo story I created, 'The Ottawa Anomaly', tried to not so much *tell* a story, but provide echoes of events in key areas around Ottawa's downtown with incomplete bits of text and dialogue and clues of where to go next, such that each player's experience of the story would be different – the sequence of geotriggers encountered would colour each subsequent trigger's emotional content. If you heard the gunshot first and then the crying, that implied a different story than if you heard them the other way around. The opening tried to frame a storyworld where it makes sense to hear these echoes of the past in the present, so that the technological mediation of the smartphone fits the world. It also was trying to make the player stop and look at the world around them with new eyes.

I once set up a treasure hunt around campus for my first-year students, a playful way to make them familiar with the history of the place. One group, however, interpreted a clue as meaning a particular statue in downtown Ottawa; they returned to campus much later and told me a stunning tale of illuminati and the secret history of official Ottawa that they had crafted to make sense of the clues. Same clues plus different geographical setting (by mistake) equalled an oddly compelling story. What I'm getting at: my audio fragments could similarly evoke very different experiences not just in their order of encounter but also given the background of the person listening.

It is getting easier and easier to develop quite sophisticated augmented reality experiences that incorporate sound and visuals and geolocations. The thing about hand-held augmented reality that overlays digital graphics on the image is that you, the creator, have to craft a compelling account for *why*. Why this device? Why are you looking through it at a page, or a bill board, or a magazine, or what have you? It's not at all natural. Here's one attempt:

> Shawn dusted off the old diary. *Smells of mould,* he thought, as he flipped through the pages.
> *Hmmph. Somebody was pretty careless with their coffee.*
> *I think it's coffee.*
> *Hmm.*
> *Doesn't smell like coffee.*
> *What the hell? . . . damn, this isn't coffee.*
> Shawn cast about him, looking for the android digital spectralscope he kept handy for such occasions. Getting out his phone, he loaded the spectralscope up and, taking a safe position two or three feet away, gazed through it at the pages of the diary.
> *My god . . . it's full of . . .*

In the passage above, I'm trying to make that hand-held AR experience feel more obvious, part of a story. That is, *of course* you reach for the spectralscope – the diary is clearly eldritch, something's not right, and you need the device that helps you see beyond the confines of this world.

Without the story, it's just *gee-whiz, look at what I can do.* It's somehow not *authentic.* That's one of the reasons, I think, that various museum apps that employ AR tricks haven't really taken off (work, however, continues; the Emotive Project, emotiveproject.eu, frames their AR experiences with a Roman window frame, as known from excavation: a 3D-printed version of the Roman window smartphone-sized frame holds the device to make a literal window on the past). The 'breaks in presence', the things that jar us out of the experience, can be tolerated for only so long (Turner, 2007). Breaks in presence that you might have already encountered in the hand-held, image-led smartphone AR widely available might be the constant juddering of the 3D object as the app strains to find the ground plain, a lack of appropriate shadows, or blocky cartoony graphics. Good storytelling can account for *why* these aspects of the experience are happening (the old 'not-a-bug-but-a-feature!' strategy). Augmented reality can't be divorced from the tools and techniques of game-based storytelling. Augmented reality is as much about *affect* as it is *effect* (Graham et al. 2019). Indeed, there is good reason to believe that *aural* augmented reality, where physical space is overlaid with soundscapes and other forms of audio, can be a much more affective and arresting intervention precisely *because* its breaks in presence are much less abrupt or obvious, and clever design can play with the breaks in presence to *enhance* the desired effect. The Voices Recognition prototype, an app that gives voice to the dead in a cemetery in York in the UK, plays with loudness and cacophony juxtaposed against the 'busyness' of the monumental landscape. Mass graves have no markers and are areas of seemingly empty grass, but the cacophony of shouting voices forces us to stop and look at the area again with new eyes (Graham et al. 2019: 232–33).

With regard to the smartphone-based visual AR experience described earlier, the narrative about the spectralscope serves as an entry point to the experience, and any AR experience will need that framing. The mechanic of the game or the experience should be illustrative of the kind of historical truth we are trying to tell. William Urrichio (2005) pointed out that game mechanics map well onto various historiographies. What kind of truth then does an augmented reality application tell? A chatbot or any other digitally playful, creative experience has to be embedded and explored within the wider context from which it springs in order to achieve that shock of the unfamiliar that helps move us towards enchantment (Roussou et al. 2019; Tzouganatou 2018).

When Machines Create

This book starts off with its feet firmly on the ground, using a well-established methodology for thinking through the intersection of computation and archaeological ways of knowing, with agent-based models. Those chapters recount quite complex pieces of work, and those models make nuanced arguments about Roman history. How then can such work be 'practical'? All these computational ways of raising the dead, or of creating digital golems, require time, energy, exploration – and play. This playfulness is at its heart an enchanted mode of engaging with the past, and it delights in the surprises and chills that computation allows. It co-creates ways of knowing about the past that sit at the uncanny interface of human and machine.

The day that I trained a generative adversarial network on several thousand images of human remains being bought and sold on social media was a moment of chilling enchantment. As already explained, I was trying to see what I could learn about this trade by getting the machine to generate photos based on this corpus of materials. Letting the machine churn away for a day and a night heightened the anticipation; what will happen? In the morning, I opened the terminal and examined the result. The computer had painted a series of images of human skulls, each one looking like a memento mori of the kind present in renaissance oil paintings. Each one staring directly at the 'camera', at me. *Here we are*, they seemed to say, *the Ghosts in your Machine.*

If we let the machines show us how they see, tell us what they hear, describe what they've learned and explore for us the consequences of our just-so stories of the past, what kind of archaeology will we have created? It will be an archaeology unlike any we have encountered yet, an enchanted archaeology, a powerful archaeology for pushing our stories into the world.

Imagine. Imagine hearing the voice of the dead, whispering in your ear as you walk around the site. Imagine that voice reacting to where you move, how you move and what you do. You ask the voice questions, and she laughs softly and answers you with a question of her own. Can you trust her? Is she lying to you? She sees what you are seeing, sees how you've touched the historical site marker, and comments on it. Another voice pipes in – he flatly contradicts her, and the difference colours your experience of the site, and the site changes as you change. Other voices speak to you as you move around, remember what you've said, what you've done. As you approach the mass paupers' grave, the clamour grows, the shouting, the whispers merging into the roar of the dead (see also Eve et al. 2014).

What game are they playing? What are the rules? The only way to know is to enter the game. Will you play?

I'm describing an aural augmented reality where the NPCs and the site are activated as an agent-based model, but what they say and how they react to you is generated via a neural network trained on imagery and archival letters. The content is generated on the fly; each person's experience of the site is dynamic and emergent. It would be a very powerful enchantment – a practical necromancy indeed: agent-based models to archaeogaming, to artificial intelligence. The dead are reanimated, and, from the probability space they inhabit, there are things to learn in this one reality, this one collapsed set of things-that-actually-happened.

The experience I have described sits somewhere between storytelling and what has been called 'transhumanist' or 'posthumanist' archaeology. What is 'posthuman' here is the focus on allowing the machine its own creative agency. Thus posthumanism in archaeology can be seen as an approach that asks these questions:

How can we work with digital technology to transcend (disrupt) perceived boundaries and develop new understandings of the self and others, agency, life, or embodiment? Can we work *with* digital media and technology to develop new perspectives on more-than-human pasts? Can other-than-human agential entities be grasped and fostered via digital media and techniques to create multisensorial experiences? How is the digital shifting relationships between archaeologists, the archaeological record, and the public? (Díaz-Guardamino and Morgan 2019)

The inclusion of sensorial experiences within these questions reminds us that enchantment is both a mood and a sensation/emotion, and that storytelling is ultimately what we do to achieve it. Perhaps the greatest storyteller among practicing archaeologists right now is Ruth Tringham. Tringham's (2019) most recent experiments directly connect this kind of transmedia and computational explorations of knowledge-space with enchantment as a physiological response. Tringham has long written about the possibilities and problems of putting words in the mouths of the long-dead (see for instance Tringham 2015a, 2015b; Joyce and Tringham 2007), but has recently turned to thinking of the power of emotive storytelling through nonverbal interjections – the verbal hmms and ticks and shrieks and shouts that underline the emotional content of a message, some of which seems to be cross-cultural, drawing on the work of Sauter et al. (2010). In Tringham's (2019: 345) recent experiments, she does not try to put words in the mouths of the dead, but uses their nonverbal interjections to inject *feelings* into *us*: 'I was interested in exploring this possibility by putting aside background music and dramatized acting and, instead, exploring whether the image and sound from the archaeological and heritage data themselves could be used to create such emotional triggers.'

Tringham draws an intriguing connection with the phenomenon of Autonomous Sensory Meridian Response (ASMR). ASMR is described by those who encounter it as a feeling of warmth, a tingling on the surface of the skin, and it can be triggered by whispering or other certain repetitive sounds or visuals (which can either calm or excite the person experiencing ASMR responses, citing Poerio et al. 2018). Tringham's experiments remix the work of archaeological illustrator Alice Watterson (2015), which critically explores archaeological uncertainty and ambiguity in terms of visualization, with potential ASMR triggers to try to generate emotive engagement. She has also experimented with remixing her own earlier work in nonlinear storytelling. She concludes about her experiments that

focusing the story on the utterances makes us more aware of the powerful emotional evocation that is contributed by these 'marginal' aspects of speech. We cannot see or hear their details, but we can get very close to them in order to conjure up their emotions, without having to think in terms of clear textual content. The close proximity that is a characteristic of my quasi-ASMR videos creates a feeling of almost touching the past. (Tringham 2019: 350)

This is an exciting development, for it ties the physiological experience of enchantment directly to digital enchantment. I am clearly captivated by the power of the machine to create affecting and immersive worlds in the sense of how the neural network pulls together its understanding of archaeological knowledge (and the idea of training a machine additionally to understand and use ASMR triggers is exciting and frightening); but also, and just as clearly, there are other routes to digital enchantment. Tringham (2019: 350) goes on to say, 'There are still many ways in which the ambiguity of archaeological data could be celebrated and a dynamic human-scale past expressed that have yet to be explored creatively with digital formats.' Now that we have nearly reached the end of this volume, where will your enchantment of digital archaeology take you next?

Conclusion

Enchantment Is a Remembering

In the fields and bogs near my home, deep time ruptures the present. I live in a city now, and even here deep time pushes through in uncomfortable ways. The university sits on a wedge of land between a canal (a world heritage site, even) and a river. The campus slopes upwards to the point where the canal and river diverge. This land was 'waste' land, owned by a newspaper mogul, but inhabited by squatters pushed south from the developing city. He donated the land to the nascent university, and construction began. A wash connected the canal to the river, bisecting the planned campus. Early plans wanted to incorporate it – a lagoon, a pond, a parkette – but eventually it was merely built over. Tunnels connect the buildings of this campus from its highpoint to its low: to traverse the tunnels means walking on the original ground surface. Every time it rains, every year the snow melts, the tunnels get very wet indeed. The earlier landscape pushes through. On the other side of the river, there is now a park operated by the National Capital Commission. Along the river banks there is evidence of the deep time, for those who know how to look, of where the Anishinabe camped and groomed the forest. Indigent and Indigenous, side by side, poking through layers of institutional Ottawa.

'Enchantment', as an archaeological concept, is in some ways easy to grasp when we are physically confronted by deep time. But what about digital landscapes? Where are the deep time ruptures there? Some of them come from the realization that the languages we code with developed in and were developed by the Cold War and the dictates of nuclear simulation (see MacDougall 2014). Some of them come from the sexism and classism of twentieth century Britain and the death of the computing industry in the UK (Hicks 2017). For me, another source of enchantment in the digital is the realization that digital artefacts are still *human* artefacts, subject to entropy and decay. Old websites that still work, code that can be made to run in emulation via the Internet Archive, digital agents like 'Eliza' who have achieved a kind of immortality through always being ported forward to the next platform . . . these confront us with the weirdness of our digital past and hint that there are digital futures that do not have to be like our current toxic digital present.

This book has hinted at that aspect of decay, though I believe that topic requires another entire book. The agent models that I held up as examples of moving from networks as metaphor towards networks as computing things in their own right are already dead. To bring them back to life requires revivification of computing hardware and software from the early 2000s. I can still install the earlier NetLogo environments on which I wrote and developed those models, but the underlying hardware is different, and the way it might generate, for instance, the pseudo-random numbers that simulation depends on might be subtly different, affecting the results and the ways my code might be interpreted. Enchantment requires being alive to, and sinking into, the vibrant materialities and networks of assemblages that give life to digital work. Our digital artefacts decay, rot and, like all artefacts and features, need to be understood as contexts describing particular interventions/actions in particular times and places (see Mark Sample's [2019] recent postmortem on a number of his twitter bots and how they died).

Digital archaeology doesn't do this yet (notable exceptions are Perry and Morgan 2015; Moshenska 2014). We worry about preservation and create trusted repositories and publish data, but there are very few who are considering what the actual *decay* of digital debris (not just the hardware, not even the software, but the *things* themselves) says about our current moment. Historians and archivists are more active in this field (see, e.g., Milligan 2019; the Archives Unleashed project, archivesunleashed.org; and the Documenting the Now project, docnow.io). Milligan has written persuasively about the 'historical event horizon' and what counts as 'history', pointing out that the 1990s and the first great floruit of widespread engagement with digital technologies is now largely beyond the ability of historians to study, save for what was preserved of particular places and spaces like GeoCities.com (which incidentally was explicitly founded and operated on 'homesteader' and 'colonization' of terra nullius metaphors, which presages the current neodigital colonialism of data extraction that people like Risam [2019] are concerned with). While this enchantment of digital archaeology has largely been concerned with fostering a mood of engagement with what digital creativity can tell us about the past, there is space for an enchantment of digital archaeology that deals with the decay of our digital present. There are ruptures where the deep past intrudes for both.

Programming is forgetting; enchantment is a remembering.

Programming Is Forgetting

Allison Parrish (2016), poet and programmer, gave a talk called 'Programming is Forgetting: Towards a New Hacker Ethic', where she took an extended look at Levy's (1984) history and celebration of early computing culture, *Hackers*. The book documents a male-centric history of early computation and recounts an 'ethic' that very much guided the first few decades of personal computing and early internet culture. One aspect that she identifies of this early culture is its celebration of a 'hands-on' ethic. Parrish (2016) unpacks the troubling hubris of this ethic:

> One is that the world is a system and can be understood as being governed by rules or code.
>
> Two, anything can be fully described and understood by understanding its parts individually – divorced from their original context.
>
> Three, systems can be 'imperfect' – which implies that a system can also be made perfect.
>
> And four, therefore, given sufficient access (potentially obtained without permission) – and sufficient 'debugging' – it's possible to make a computer program that perfectly models the world.

Parrish goes on to draw out the implications of this worldview, a kind of logical positivism where if enough data, enough rules, are gathered together, a perfect model of the world will be arrived at. One might argue that the hands-on ethic celebrated in early hacker culture – unpacked for us by Parrish – is what continues to underpin a lot of what agent-based modelling and archaeogaming also celebrate – a doing, a coming to know in the process of doing things, that drives towards ever greater fidelity to the 'real' world. In doing so, we generate code that replicates a worldview at odds with our goal of understanding or explicating the past (see Risam 2019 on the kinds of humans envisioned in 'digital humanities'). The hands-on ethic is a lie because nothing can ever be fully described: the act of programming is itself an act of forgetting, Parrish tells us. What we 'forget', in order to make messy reality tractable for our model, is in accordance to our own blinkered worldviews. How easy it is to be seduced by data, in the way Gavin Smith (2018) warned us. But if 'programming is forgetting', then, according to Parrish, the world can't be debugged: the programs we make are *interpretations* of the world.

Bethany Nowviskie (2016), in 'Resistance in the Materials', reflects on the difference between building a tool oneself – knowing the ways it resists or moves with the grain of the materials one is working on – versus the resistance encountered when we work with tools that others have built for us. The forgetting that is done in order for the tool *to be* is apparent in the first case and invisible in the second. But for large-scale take-up of some kind of digital approach, what with all of the different demands on a person's time and energy and resources, only the second kind of resistance will be encountered by most of our students and peers.

So we are in a quandary. This book has been arguing for a deep engagement with a hands-on approach to playing, tinkering, exploring, crafting and storytelling; of making small toy models and delighting in the enchanting aspects of the work. One source of the enchantment lies in the building, in the joys and frustrations of the making, and the sharing. But such making is not equally available to all, and, at a certain scale, the things that are enchanting cease to be visible.

The solution, maybe, is to recognize that we are talking about different levels of complexity here. Not everything has to be built from scratch. We can find enchantment by *breaking* the tools we are given, by playing *against* the toys we are given. Janelle Shane's experiments with 'giraffing' a neural network show us ways that we can see the cleavages and ruptures and the forgotten in the programming we encounter ('to giraffe' in her formulation is to break a neural network, referring to asking a neural network if it sees a giraffe in a photo: it will always say 'yes', which points to the limitations in its training dataset). Playing a video game by trying to do things the game does not allow – exploring and finding these forbidden unimagined or forgotten activities that by rights should be present – is another way of testing and pushing. Glitching images, making memes, passing what data we have to websites like musicalgorithms.com to hear rather than to visualize: we can begin to find digital enchantment by *not* doing what we are supposed to do. We might begin by just cobbling together toys and digital tools analogously to the writing game 'exquisite corpse'. In this game, the first writer writes a sentence, then the next writer writes a sentence building on the first, and so on. Imagine building an agent-based model that way! Eventually we might find our way to more complex modes of generating, finding or identifying enchantment, but it may well be that the most practical of practical necromancies is a digital variant of the exquisite corpse.

This book is an experiment building towards a practical digital necromancy. It started with networks, as a kind of all-purpose metaphor for understanding what might emerge from a given pattern of relationships within a broadly construed assemblage of things, flows and entities. It walked you through how such series of relationships could be made operational in an agent-based model (and indeed in the appendices goes into great detail, so you can build your own agent-based models); these models, it is important to note, did not capture every element that could be captured. Instead, they were toys to think with, that sought to make the familiar weird again, and to limit what emerged to that which I might reasonably explain. In casting these things as toys, as simple models, I demonstrated some of the complex insights that they can foster. Agent-based models that are too complex go too far in pushing a Western rationalism, a hacker ethic as deconstructed by Parrish, into the past. By calling these things 'toys', I point to the simplification, the *programming-as-forgetting*, that makes strange, that remembers we are not simulating the past but our *stories* of the past. In crafting digital creatures to enact the patterns I found in the archaeology, I found enchantment in the emergent behaviours. This playfulness, I argue, should be channelled into games, archaeogames, where the player can sink into a context for those behaviours. The mood of playfulness and the fact that no one person can be expert in all the things encourages an openness, a willingness to fail in public and to be collaborative, which I argue here and elsewhere (Graham 2019) is another feature of what enchantment can offer for digital archaeology. I argue that with the neural network revolution in artificial intelligence approaches, we can push these toys further and find ways of making them see and speak, an artificial intelligence that could make for enchanting encounters with the deep past. Each step in this process requires an ethical sensibility that is alive to the potential for damage: who might this hurt? The artificial intelligences that we can even now create on our laptop computers are on the cusp of escaping our control, especially if we make them available on the internet. The work of the archaeologist, in raising the dead, has something political to say in this current moment where artificial intelligences are being touted as the solution for very nearly every question. Enchantment, if it is not tempered with ethics, can be dangerous. Seductive. Beware.

This book began with an odd question, on the face of it: in archaeology, what are computers *for*? I found inspiration in the work of Jane

Bennett (2001, 2010) and Sara Perry (2019), both of whom are arguing for an enchanted mode of engagement that, for me, finds the wonder of archaeology in computational representation. I had to tell you the stories of my disenchantment with archaeology, with how the ways I was being trained to be an archaeologist left me alone and alienated. By taking you on that journey from disenchantment to showing you some of the wonder that the digital work has for me, I have tried to show you the sources of enchantment.

Digital archaeology, more than perhaps other kinds of archaeology, shares authority in the co-creation of archaeological knowledge with quasi-independent algorithms and recipes set in perpetual motion. Stephen Ramsay (2010) once said, 'algorithms are thoughts; chainsaws are tools'. The tacit knowledge, the unspoken bits about working with these digital golems, these thoughts-encoded: that's the part of the craft that needs the most work right now. It's in this tension that I find enchantment in our digital work. There are other routes to enchantment in digital archaeology; to speak of enchantment is necessarily to foreground your own reflective, open, warts-and-all practice – the successes and the failures. My hope is that this book inspires you to find yours and to share it with the rest of us.

Digital archaeology, as I have conceived it here, is not about computation in the service of finding *the answer*. It is about deforming, and thinking through, the various networks and distributed agencies that tie us to the past and simultaneously make it strange, that enchant and confound us. There are any number of courses in the catalogues at universities around the world, any number of tutorials on any number of websites, that will walk you through how to do *x* using software package *y*, and, when you know exactly what it is you need to do, these can be enormously helpful.

The best strategy for *deformance*, however, is *to play*. Play around – you're allowed! Try things out. See what happens when you do *this*. But we – as the academy, as the guardians of systemized knowledge – have managed to beat playfulness and wonder out of our students. Our systems are built on disenchantment. What's more, when you're just starting out and you're not sure of the terminology, not sure of even what it is you're after or what question you're really asking, it is easy to succumb to information paralysis – too much information means you're not able to act at all. The strategy I take with my own students is to make it safe to fail, safe to play around, what Stephen Ramsay (2014) famously called 'the screwmeneutical imperative'; to do this, you need to have someone model productive failure, to have someone to point to who is trying things out and reporting back on what has worked and what has not. Beyond this, there is no magic recipe, no silver bullet.

'Should I learn python or R or javascript or . . . ?'

'No. You should identify the problem at hand and then use whatever it is that works for you' is the answer. The truth is, you exist at this point now with access to these particular resources and this particular digital environment. Be archaeological, generate meaning from context. You use what you have now to see more of the landscape of possibilities. Fold what you already know how to do into a cycle of experimentation. If you want to get started in digital archaeology, develop the habit of note-taking and reflective practice every time you sit down with the machine. *Do not* remove yourself from the reporting. As Mark Sample (2015) once wrote, citing the Oblique Strategies creativity-promoting card deck of musician Brian Eno, 'Your mistake was a vital connection'. You will find in your mistakes your own sources of enchantment, of vibrant materiality – indeed, your own practical necromancy.

Coda

It's a cold dark rainy Tuesday in October. There hasn't been much sun today, and the air is heavy with mist. I've opened the window, but everything is muffled, as if I'm hearing the world from the bottom of a deep hole. It's a day for introspection and falling leaves and spirits. I'm thinking of ghosts and monsters. I'm thinking of that vampire skeleton, that person from the fifteenth century I met in the late twentieth. How it must have been terrifying, to see one person after another succumb to . . . something . . . that was killing them. Mutilating the corpse of the first person to die, a magical action whose utility was that it relieved the emotional terror of being at the hands of . . . a monster. As I write this, I am working on another research project, a project which means that there are tens of thousands of pictures of skeletal remains lying inside this machine, one click away, many bearing evidence of wounds or deliberate post-death cutting, mounting, transformation from being a being to being a thing. Deep time, trauma and rupture erupt transubstantiated through wafers of silicon and electrical pulses. As I sit here at my keyboard, I type words that will be read by people I will never know. My mind reaches out to yours through the mechanical-electrical-digital assemblage of machines and power and chance, over space and time. But my mind is also in another space, somewhere between memory and memorialization;

there's a PDF in another window on the screen, a paper about avatars, monsters and machines. It describes what I am experiencing: 'While immersed in archaeological interpretation, you are not completely in the present, but also not wholly in the past, but inhabit an interstitial space' (Morgan 2019: 326). Living in this interstitial space is rather like those encounters with deep time with an Irish crannog that Fredengren (2016) wrote about as being a way into enchantment. This computer, this tool that I think through, is part of my thought, my extended cognition, similarly present but not here, a node in physical space and in cyberspace. You, me, the present, the internet, the vampire, my bricks, the nameless dead – we are all smeared together and through each other. Information entities. Morgan (2019: 326) calls this a 'cyborg archaeology', where 'the perceived boundaries between machines and humans, nature and culture, and the present and past are inevitably permeable'. Archaeological monsters, for Morgan (2019: 331), are human and inhuman aggregates.

In my re-enchantment of archaeology, I am become one of Morgan's archaeological monsters. 'Successful ventures into cyborg interpretation should not be a seamless, transhumance integration of machine and body to transmit ideas about the past', she writes, 'but should invoke a monstrous disruption, interfering with both our understanding of the past and current sense of self' (Morgan 2019: 329).

She goes on to say, 'Monsters, in their sensuous, ambivalent in-betweenness, can be an expression of creative impulse, subversion, or evidence of play within archaeology. . . . To creatively transgress within archaeology is delightful', and 'Play is an underrated but deeply important part of creative digital practice in archaeology' (Morgan 2019: 330). She contrasts this cyborg archaeology of avatars, monsters and machines with the cold emptiness of 'digital' archaeology, that mere use of computation in noncritical or reflective ways. Morgan's (2019: 234) work, as she says, aims 'to make trouble'. This, I think, is the final part of the story of my re-enchantment with archaeology. When I distanced myself from my materials, when I tried to hold myself apart because of my disdain, my scholarly immaturity, my faux objectivity, I could not feel enchantment, and I could not find the people whose lives were lived through these materials. A disenchanted archaeology, what I had been taught was archaeology, put me and the work apart from each other and from the communities I was working in but never with. The alienation had both professional and personal costs. Sinking into the assemblage, recognizing the multiple powers and perspectives of 'networks' in the materials (and the ways that networks can themselves compute) opened myself and my approaches to the value of productive failures, of creative explorations, of play, the craft of digital work and storytelling. Morgan (2019: 329) reminds us that 'archaeologists must consider the full implications of our resurrections. . . . What are our responsibilities to the people of the past?' This enchantment of digital archaeology, this progressive layering of networks with representational and computational power, this resurrection of the dead, makes our responsibilities to the dead even greater than we may have previously thought. We have the power to give the dead voices that speak out of the possibility-space of things-they-may-have-said, but I don't know that we're ready to fully grapple with this yet.

Here be monsters; welcome them in.

Afterword

Guidelines for Developing Your Own Digital Archaeology

Digital work is craft work, and, like all craft, requires learning some amount of tacit and embodied knowledge. How do you get started? These guidelines will help, but remember, there is no rule book for digital archaeology.

- First of all, recognize that digital work is *slow*. Computation itself might happen quickly, but getting to the point where you're doing what needs to be done in order to do x, y, or z is a slow process. Understanding what the results might mean is similarly slow. Opening black boxes of algorithms (recipes, step-by-step instructions) and understanding what someone else has coded is slow, painstaking work. To encode something necessarily means that something else has to be forgotten. Ask yourself: what has to be forgotten in order for this to work?
- Play. Modern computers and devices are by default largely locked down by Apple and Microsoft. You are not supposed to do anything outside of the ecosystem of apps and software that are provided to you. Push against this. Learn to open the hood. Find the terminal, find the command line. You will be pushing here against modern techno-capitalism (you anarchist!). This will be the hardest part.
- Keep track of *everything*. Write down what you did, why you did it and what aids, tutorials, blog posts and walkthroughs you were reading.
- Search the exact error messages you receive – copy the error message and search – with perhaps a bit of context. Chances are someone else has already had this error before and has posted the solution.

• Share this information, within the boundaries of what is safe for you to do given your particular situation. As a white, middle-aged, tenured man, I can be far more open about my failures online than other people because I am privileged, and so I keep an open research blog at electricarchaeology.ca (and if you are a white, middle-aged, tenured man, why aren't you making it safe for others to share what works and what hasn't?).

• The framework that Brian Croxall and Quinn Warnick (2015) developed for discussing 'failure' in the context of digital pedagogy can be usefully employed to provide structure to your notes and reflections. Understanding *why* and *how* something failed, the *type* of failure, is a necessary precursor to developing your digital craft.

• Carefully detail when things *do* work, in the context of what hasn't worked in the past. Not only will you have a handy reminder of what to do the next time this particular task presents itself, but you will also have a record of your own progression, your own development over time, which will help keep you motivated.

• Attend to enchantment. These moments when you are confronted by the uncanny and the delightful are signals of deeper assemblages of distributed agency in your materials. Where you find enchantment, there you will find that you are learning something deeper about the world. Digital archaeology is amazing. Why shouldn't you find enchantment, joy, in your work?

A vital resource for learning the tools of digital work for those of us in the humanities is *The Programming Historian* (programminghistorian.org), a set of peer-reviewed tutorials that continues to grow (and is also available in French and Spanish). Survey the lessons there to see various hands-on walkthroughs of tools or approaches that you might wish to use on your own materials. Begin with the lessons by Ted Dawson (for PCs) and Ian Milligan and James Baker (for Mac) on the command line and the terminal. Lemercier and Zalc's (2019) *Quantitative Methods in the Humanities* might also be a good spot to start, as well as the various agent-based modelling and network tutorials collected by Tom Brughmans on his blog, https://archaeologicalnetworks.wordpress.com/resources/. For agent-based modelling in particular, download NetLogo from the Center for Connected Learning at Northwestern University, https://ccl.northwestern.edu/netlogo/, and work through its tutorials (Wilensky 1999). The Open Digital Archaeology Textbook Environment covers many different computational tasks from an archaeological perspective and also comes with prebuilt computational environments that can be launched with a single click (hence taking care of the problems of installing software packages and allowing the reader to jump into learning rather than spending time toiling with configuring their own machine); it may be found at http://o-date.github.io.

Digital archaeology is a team sport: let people know what you're doing. Ask for help. Collaborate. Share what has worked and what hasn't. Fail productively!

Appendix A
Tasks for Golems – Building an ABM

In this appendix, I am going to walk with you as we build a simple archaeological agent-based model. My ambition here is that you will find the experience as similarly enchanting as my students, but without perhaps the angst of having a grade attached to the exercise. Then we're going to add some playful elements to the model, making it not quite a game but also not quite a simple simulation anymore. We will also build a *reimplementation* of the core model dynamics for the Itineraries model discussed in chapter 2, 'Reanimating Networks'. We are not writing code from scratch. Instead, we are going to use the code snippets that come bundled with the NetLogo modelling environment. It's a bit like using Lego blocks from different Lego sets to create that Star Wars / Harry Potter mash-up you've always wanted.

The point of doing this is that there is *enchantment* in the process of building. Moreover, when you build an agent-based model, you are giving your digital golems instructions that they will carry out (if they are well expressed – i.e., the instructions are syntactically correct), which may not necessarily mean they do what it is you wanted. Are they expressing some unanticipated outcome of the story you have told in code, some logical necessity that throws new light on the archaeological material, the archaeological story that you're seeking to resurrect? Or is it just another damned bug? It's at this point that you need a mode of wonder, of enchantment, to figure out what is a meaningful outcome of what you have encoded and what is an undesirable artefact of your thought. That is, what kind of 'fail' have you encountered?

You may skip ahead to the finished code if you want, but do try to work through the process below. We're going to start with a completed model that can be thought of in archaeological terms. Then we're going to back up and figure out how to load archaeological network data into this environment. Once we have an archaeological network, let us pretend that it is a network of sites connected to each other, over which we are interested in exploring the consequences of a simple trade in pots. We will then build into the simulation a pair of playful buttons: one to erase sites from the network and one to build more connections. We'll finish off by modifying this network to use the information on the 'strength' of the connections as a proxy for damage-in-shipment.

I rarely write a simulation from scratch. What we are doing here is the way I have learned to build simulations: from the bric-a-brac of others' work, using found code that might be retrieved from NetLogo's own library of models and code snippets or that might exist out there on the web (one spot to start looking is at OpenABM, hosted at https://www.comses.net/).

Golems with Colds

One of my favourite demo models in the NetLogo environment is 'virus on a network'. In this section, let's explore its code and see how we can put a player into the simulation. NetLogo is available at http://ccl.northwestern.edu/netlogo. (In what follows below, I am using NetLogo version 6.0.4). Download and install the environment for your computer. Open it up, then under 'files', select 'model library'. Under 'sample models', select 'networks' and then 'virus on a network'.

This model simulates some kind of connected system (cities? countries? ports? individuals?) into which a virus has been introduced. The nodes – individual agents – can be susceptible to the virus, infected by the virus, or resistant to the virus. Nodes do not know right away that they've become infected, and there's always a chance that they might become resistant. (If you click on the 'info' tab, you will find a description of what all the pieces of the model do, which incidentally makes this an example of 'literate' programming, where the analysis and paradata of the model can be included in the model file itself).

Run the model with its default settings. Notice how the virus burns itself out and the count of 'resistant' nodes over time represents an s-curve. Play with the settings: can you arrange things so that the virus never dies out, but remains endemic in the population? Is it a function of the size of the population? Is it a function of the 'virus-check-frequency'? Imagine your own interest in archaeology: are there analogous situations where you can see that a 'virus-on-a-network' might work as a suitable metaphor for some aspect of your work? I can imagine where the introduction of a new way of marking Roman bricks – including the consular date – might be considered a kind of 'virus'. Rutilius Lupus was the first to use consular dates on his stamps. The speed with which this innovation spread in the brick industry is sometimes seen as the result of a government dictate. So let's test that.

Move the **number-of-nodes** slider all the way to the right, to 300 individuals. Move the **initial-outbreak-size** slider to 1. Hit the **setup** button, and then the **go** button. What happens? What are the shapes of the curves compared with when you ran the model from its default starting position? *What does this result mean?* In this case, I don't think that the 'resistant' category is meaningful in the way it would be for an actual disease; instead, it can be used as a kind of indicator of the underlying dynamics going on. The s-curve that we see when starting from a number of infected individuals is not present when we start from a single individual; the time to model completion is much longer; and as we run this in multiple runs we can see that *which* node makes a difference – that starting conditions matter. A poorly connected node infects the network much slower than a well-connected node – but a poorly connected node connected to a well-connected *other* node is a different situation again.

What the model gives us right now is a kind of hypothetical baseline for the behaviour of the dynamics that we're interested in. The task then is to run these dynamics on an *archaeological network*. The archaeological network does not literally need to be a network visible in the archaeological materials. It can be a hypothesized network, but in this case your interests are back-to-front in that you would be trying to use some kind of archaeological dynamic to test the impact of your hypothesized network.

Loading Archaeological Network Data into NetLogo

Let us load an actual archaeological network into the NetLogo environment (or at least a network that we can pretend is archaeological). NetLogo comes with code samples within its model library. (It also comes with tutorials that will enable you to teach yourself the ins and outs of building models, which use the textbook by Wilensky and Rand (2015) and the supporting website at http://intro-to-abm.com).

Look for 'network import example'. We're going to build a simple economic model of trading in Roman pots on top of this code example (we are following and then extending a toy model originally devised by Tom Brughmans (2016) as part of his teaching and shared on his blog, archaeologicalnetworks.wordpress.com). When this code example loads up, you are presented with the basic NetLogo interface with a single button. If you right-click on this button, you can select 'edit' and see that the underlying code is a single command, **import-network**. Switch to code panel (clicking on 'code', the rightmost tab in the interface) and you'll see that **import-network** looks like this:

```
to import-network
  clear-all
  set-default-shape turtles "circle"
  import-attributes
  layout-circle (sort turtles) (max-pxcor - 1)
  import-links
  reset-ticks
end
```

This command first clears the interface and resets all variables. It selects a default shape for representing all the agents (which are turtles, demonstrating NetLogo's descent from the Logo programming language). The next command, **import-attributes**, loads our node-list (archaeological sites with associated information, perhaps), and then **layout-circle** distributes the nodes equally around the interface. The connections between our nodes is loaded by **import-links**, and then the model's clock is reset.

Go back to the interface panel and click on the **import-network** button. A network of directed links with the strength of those links is displayed! The weighting of those links could represent the volume of trade from one node to another. It could represent perhaps the degree of similarity of assemblages of the material culture at the two sites. What would you like it to represent? Whatever you choose, you need to keep careful *paradata*, the information on *why* and *how* you make your choices (the **info** panel in NetLogo is an easy place to do this; hit the 'edit' button there and you can record your thoughts as you go). You can find the **attributes.txt** file in the NetLogo -> models -> code examples directory on your computer. By default, it looks like table A.1. The first column is the node's 'who' number or its identification; the second is the displayed size of the node (and we can understand 'size' to represent all kinds of different information in context); and the final column is the displayed colour for the node. You can open this file in a text editor. Feel free to add some more nodes or change up some of the attributes.

Table A.1. Contents of the file 'attributes.txt'.

1	1.2	red
2	1.0	blue
3	1.5	yellow
4	2.0	green
5	1.8	orange
6	1.4	red
7	2.0	blue
8	1.5	yellow
9	1.0	green
10	1.2	orange

The next file to consider is the **links.txt** file, which is in the same NetLogo -> models -> code examples directory on your computer. The default contains three columns again, arranged source, target and weight (see table A.2).

Table A.2. Contents of the file 'links.txt'.

1	4	0.8
2	3	1
2	5	3
2	7	2.5
2	8	1.3
2	10	2.2
3	9	2.3
5	6	2.8
6	5	1.2
6	9	0.3
7	2	1.1
8	1	2.6
9	8	2.1
10	7	0.9

Thus, node 1 is connected to node 4 with a strength of 0.8. This is a *directed* link. Node 4 *is not* connected to node 1. That is to say, perhaps node 1 exported 0.8 tonnes of goods to node 4, but node 4 exported nothing to node 1. Node 1's relationship to node 4 is different than node 4's relationship to node 1. It might be in our archaeological network that we cannot actually say anything about the *directionality* of the link, that we only know that node 1 and node 4 were connected. In that case, and using this data, we would have to add another row to this file, as in table A.3.

Table A.3. Adding more data to 'links.txt' to denote directionality of the link.

1	4	0.8
4	1	0.8

If you added more nodes to the **attributes.txt** file, you must add those same nodes to the **links.txt** file and specify some connections and the strength of those connections. Save your work. Back in NetLogo, if you then click on the **import-network** button in your NetLogo interface window, your new data appears on the screen!

Remember those other commands that are part of the **import-network** command? They work like this:

```
to import-attributes
  ;; This opens the file, so we can use it.
  file-open "attributes.txt"
  ;; Read in all the data in the file data on the line is in
this order:
  ;; node-id attribute1 attribute2
  while [not file-at-end?]
  [
    ;; this reads a single line into a three-item list
    let items read-from-string (word "[" file-read-line "]")
    create-turtles 1 [
      set node-id item 0 items
      set size item 1 items
      set color item 2 items
    ]
  ]
  file-close
end
```

In NetLogo, any line that begins with a semicolon (;) is a comment. This code example is well-commented throughout, explaining what each line of code accomplishes. The **import-links** command works in a similar fashion to **import-attributes**, iterating over the list of data in the imported files, creating links between the pairs of nodes.

Simulating a Very Simple Pottery Trade on This Default Network

Let's now get something happening on this network. We're going to add a very simple trading mechanic (a reimplementation of Tom Brughmans's 2016 trading model tutorial) on to a network. We are going to assume that our network represents sites that are connected in some kind of trading relationship. We are going to ignore for the moment the weighting between the sites as recorded in the **links.txt** file. In simulations, it's always best to start simple and build in just enough complexity as you go, making sure you understand how the model is behaving at each stage. In the model that we are building, we are going to assume that there is a *trade threshold*, and, in each turn, all of the factors that influence the decision to trade are going to be represented by whether a random number between 0 and 1 is higher than that threshold. That threshold, and whether or not the collection of individual pottery sellers subsumed under the idea of 'site' decides to trade, obviously hides a multitude of social dynamics. This is a very *stupid* model. A far more complex iteration of this basic idea can be found in Graham and Weingart 2015, which builds from this basic idea to develop a laboratory for testing different ideas about trade in the Roman world. Stupid models are nevertheless useful.

The next idea to consider is *how* trade will be represented. Here, we are going to create a fixed number of 'pots' in this world, distribute them randomly across the network, and then trade will be represented by the site sending one pot to one of its neighbours over the link connecting them. One pot leaves, one pot arrives. Before we go any further, what do you think will happen? How will this model behave? The complete code is in appendix B, 'Pot Trade Model Code', but below I walk through how we build it:

1. On the model interface tab, where it says 'button', click there and select 'slider'. Then, click the 'add' button and click anywhere on the empty space below the **import-network** button. This opens up a dialogue allowing you to create a new variable that can be set using a slider interface. In the text box where it says 'global variable', write **trade-threshold**. In the 'maximum' box put '1' and in the 'increment' put '0.1' as the value. Then click ok. You now have a trade threshold value that can be moved from 0 to 1 in increments of 0.1.

2. Make another slider, but call it **num-pots** and make its maximum value 100, and allow it to increment by 1.

3. Make a new button (click on where you selected the slider, change it to button, and then click on add). In the code window that opens, type **go**. Tick off the box that says 'forever'.

Now, you don't have a **go** procedure yet, so the error alert will appear across the top of the NetLogo interface. Don't worry; we'll fix that in a moment. But now would be a good time to save your work. Go to file -> save and save it somewhere sensible on your machine. **Warning!** You are not saving it in the models directory where you found the code sample when we began. This means that when you run this model that you're building and hit the **import-network** button, NetLogo will not find **attributes.txt** or **links.txt**. You can solve this by copying those files and placing them in the same directory where you saved your model, or you can put the full path (location) of the files in the code itself—for example, on my Mac it's this:

```
file-open "/Applications/NetLogo 6.0.4/models/Code
Examples/attributes.txt"
```

Save your work often!

4. Go to the code tab in NetLogo. We're going to give each turtle a **pots** variable by declaring that 'pots' belongs to turtles. We'll also give each turtle an I.D. as well:

```
turtles-own [node-id pots]
```

5. The 'pots' variable will store a random value up to the maximum of the **num-pots** slider you created. We're going to add this next bit of code to the existing **import-network** code:

```
to import-network
  clear-all
  set-default-shape turtles "circle"
  import-attributes
  layout-circle (sort turtles) (max-pxcor - 1)
  import-links
  reset-ticks
  ;; new code that we are adding
  ask turtles
    [set pots random (num-pots)]
end
```

By asking the turtles to **set** something, we've created a new attribute for our turtles, a count of the number of pots that they hold. To begin with, it is a random number anywhere from 0 up to the current setting for that global variable **num-pots**. Our next task is to tell the turtles how to trade. We're only going to ask turtles that *have* pots to do this activity (because otherwise we would get an error, asking turtles who have no pots to trade pots). In the code window, right after the **end** that finished the **import-network** routine, we'll start a new routine that we'll call **trade-pots**.

```
to trade-pots
  ask one-of turtles with [pots > 0]
    [ if random-float 1 > trade-threshold
      [set pots pots - 1
        ask one-of in-link-neighbors
          [ set pots pots + 1 ]
      ]
    ]
end
```

The first line addresses what comes after *only* to those turtles that have any pots. The next line has the turtle see if it's time for them to trade (i.e., that the random number they've drawn is higher than the **trade-threshold** we set using our slider over on the interface page). If that condition is true, then the turtle immediately deducts one pot from its inventory and asks one of the other turtles to which it is connected to increase its inventory by one. You can see that that trade-threshold rule covers a lot of very complicated social mechanisms. Would it help to think of this as a kind of tributary empire? If so, what other mechanisms would you want to add to this simple model?

6. Finally, we'll tell the model how to run, and we'll also add a slight modification so that the site with the most pots changes its size in proportion to the number of pots that it has. In the code window, right after the **end** for the **import-network** routine and before the **to trade-pots** line, insert your cursor and hit return a few times, to give you space. It is a convention of NetLogo models that the **go** routine should be laid out before the routines that it calls. Here's what that routine will look like:

```
to go
  let total-pots sum [pots] of turtles
  repeat total-pots
  [ trade-pots]
  ;resize the turtles to demonstrate how many pots they have
```

```
  ask turtles [set size 0.1 + 5 * sqrt (pots / total-pots)]
  tick
end
```

We start by creating a temporary variable called 'total-pots' which sums up the number of pots we have – remember that when we first create this world with the **import-network** button, each site gets a random number of pots up to the maximum specified by our slider **num-pots**. The next line, **repeat total-pots**, means that we are going to run the next bit, the call to our **trade-pots** routine, the exact number of times that there are pots in this world. (What might the effect of this decision be? Is it warranted, given the scenario we're modelling? What other metrics might we use for deciding how many times to trade?) Once all of the trading has finished, NetLogo moves to the next line and has each turtle change its size in proportion to the number of pots it has compared to the total number of pots in the world.

You've done it! You've built a simulation that loads network data and that simulates a social process that we are interested in. This simple model contains a number of assumptions and simplifications about the world. To answer the question of whether or not these assumptions and simplifications are warranted is to engage with the power of simulation for trying to understand, to deform, our knowledge about the past. We are not simulating the past: we are simulating, we are operationalizing, a *story* we tell about the past. What story does this model tell? Go over to the interface tab and, before you run the model, **save your work**. Then, jot down some ideas: what will you see when this model runs?

To run your model, first click on **import-network**, then click on **go**. What happens? Is it what you predicted? How would you extend this model? Some things you could try might be to change the number of pots traded in an exchange or perhaps add a 'money' variable so that when pots go one way, money goes another.

Game of Thrones Meets Pottery World

I have been making an argument for simulation and archaeogaming as an avenue for enchantment in archaeology, for bringing the artificial life of agent models and simulations into dialogue with archaeologists to find a richer, more reflective and reflexive archaeological practice. One way of doing that is to make the leap from these simulations, these games that play themselves, into games that we can play with these digital golems ourselves. Developing a bit of programming facility with NetLogo *does* translate to other kinds of programming languages; my experiments with Andreas Angourakis translating the Artificial Anasazi model (bundled with NetLogo) into a first-person experience in the Unity game engine involved a lot of translating from NetLogo to the C# language. It also highlighted numerous assumptions and other questions of the simulation, which is one reason why we should do these acts of translation.

In the same way that trying to operationalize our stories about the past into code in the first place forces us to think clearly and carefully about our assumptions, translating from one coding language to another highlights the way that code itself occludes some ideas but makes others easier to implement. NetLogo, for instance, did not originally ship with built-in commands (or 'primitives') that could handle network concepts like links and nodes. These had to be built from other more basic blocks. Now that network concepts are built into NetLogo, we can use these easily, but perhaps these new primitives implement particular understandings of network science that work against the task we are trying to model.

All of that is to say I will not walk you through using the Unity game engine in this book! Instead, we're going to make a playful addition to our pottery model: a 'smite' button to see how *resilient* this world is. Our smite button will function much like R. R. Martin with regard to his characters in *Game of Thrones*: just when things start looking up for a character, he kills them off. A crucial difference is we are not going to **ask one-of turtles [die]** because that would cause the simulation to crash. (Try it for yourself: create a new button, put **ask one-of turtles [die]** as the code within it. Then, click **import-network** and **go** . . . then hit your new smite button. It might work a few times, but then you'll smite a turtle just as it was executing its instructions, and you'll crash your simulation. Dismiss the error message; you can then **import-network** again and start over.)

Instead, we're going to ask the *links* to die, and we're going to slightly reorganize the code so that it won't crash when the link disappears. Our modified **to trade** routine looks like this:

```
to trade-pots
  let target one-of turtles with [pots > 0 and count out-link-
neighbors > 0]
    ;ask one-of turtles with [pots > 0 ]
    if target != nobody [ask target
      [ if random-float 1 > trade-threshold
```

```
        [set pots pots - 1
           ask one-of out-link-neighbors
              [ set pots pots + 1 ] ] ]
    ]
end
```

What we're doing is making sure that when the turtle is running this routine, it absolutely has a link to someone else. We're defining a *target* as an agent with pots *and* links. If we've selected nobody, then we skip this routine and avoid an error message (i.e., if target is not equal to nobody). Having done this, now add a button and put the code **ask one-of links [die]** into it; you can name this button 'smite' or something similar.

Now run your simulation and watch how it reacts to the decay of the network. Sometimes, pots will drain away suddenly to another node; other times, the whole thing just slowly withers. What might this signify for our simulated pottery trade? Instead of smiting these ties between sites, what else could we try? What role are *you* playing in this simulated world?

Let's add the ability to increase links in our model. Make a new button and give it this code:

```
ask one-of turtles [ create-link-to one-of other turtles
    [set strength random-float 3
     set label strength]]
```

This code creates a new link, sets its strength as some number between 0 and 3, and then displays a label showing that strength. How does this affect the running of your model? Do you suddenly see a site's pottery drain away? Why is that happening? Finally, let's use that 'strength' number, the value of the link, as a modulating force on our trade. What if we imagined it as representing the difficulty of trade along that particular route? We might want to create some code that essentially says, 'when trading pots over this route, let a certain fraction be broken and never arrive'. We could implement that like this:

```
to trade-pots
  let target one-of turtles with [pots > 0 and count out-link-
neighbors > 0]
  if target != nobody and random-float 1 > trade-threshold ;;
target represents one site, one turtle at a time that we want
to run our trade routine
  [
```

```
   ask links [set breakage-factor strength]
   ask target
   [
let pots-loss 1 + breakage-factor
set pots max (list 0 (pots - pots-loss));; 1 pot plus the
;; breakage - so we're treating the strength of the link as
;; a kind of friction, a certain kind of wastage on that route.
;; We use max and list so that we don't end up with negative
;; values.
      ask one-of out-link-neighbors
        [set pots pots + 1] ;; no breakage, only the pot arrives
      ]
   ]
end
```

This modified trade routine can be read in English like this:

> First, we make sure we're dealing with a site (a turtle) that has pots
> and has links.
> If we've got such a turtle, and a random number draw is higher
> than the trade threshold, then we're going to continue:
>> We ask the links to transfer their strength value to a global bin
>> called 'breakage-factor'
>> Now ask the turtle that is doing the trade to do the following:
>>> Remove at least one-and-a-bit pots from its inventory
>>> Ask the other site (turtle) to which it's connected to upgrade
>>> its inventory with the one pot that does arrive.
> And end.

If you just pasted the trade-pots code over top of your existing
to-trade routine, you will get an error because we have to set up that
global bin variable, 'breakage-factor'. You do that by adding **breakage-factor** to the 'globals' list at the top of your model code, like so:

```
globals [links-list breakage-factor]
```

Does this make a difference for how the model behaves? Does it
change depending on the number of potential pots that we start with?
Is there a change in behaviour when a certain number of links are
added or removed? Does the code make unwarranted assumptions?
Can you change the code to make it better represent 'trade'? If you're
asking these questions, you are starting to see the power of releasing
digital golems to relive the past. I find it very compelling to watch
these golems go about their tasks, to ask, why do they do that – is it

a function of my programming or is it an emergent consequence of the story that I have encoded? What have I *forgotten* in order to make this work? How is it failing, and where is the productive aspect of that failure?

Golems Who Gossip

In chapter 2, 'Reanimating Networks', I discussed an early model that I made that simulated the diffusion of information along the Antonine Itineraries. That model was built on an early version of NetLogo that did not have the capacity to represent nodes and links. Instead, I painted paths onto the background that the agents wandered over, and I had them follow the paths, bouncing and jostling their ways along. That technical aspect of the model might be suspect and perhaps had undetermined effects on the rate of information diffusion. In this section, we're going to reimplement the key features of that model but on a networked representation of space. Once we get it working, I will point you to a source of data that represents the Roman world as a pattern of nodes and links, and I will leave you to import that data and start seeing for yourself: does Graham 2006a hold up?

This aspect of agent-based modelling is perhaps more terrifying than it is enchanting, for who, in all honesty, wants to have their work critically examined in this way and flirt with the possibility that the work is flawed? I am confident that the overall thrust of that piece will hold up, even if the details change. I would also welcome the opportunity to be wrong because that way, well, won't we have learned something new?

In the Itineraries model, the mechanic modelled was a simple 'Have you heard the message, yes or no?'. The critical bit was the shape of the interactions. We'll build this by starting over with the **network import** code snippet, saved to your workspace with the attributes.txt and links.txt files in the same folder. To build it, I took pieces of code and inspiration from the following examples:

- network import
- communication t-t network example
- link-walking turtles

Take a look at those code snippets and explore what they do. Then we'll begin. The complete code is in appendix C, 'Information Diffusion on a Network'.

We'll start by defining *what* our turtles are, so that different **breeds** have different abilities. We need some turtles to represent **sites** and some to represent the travellers or **walkers** who are moving over the **links** between sites. Eventually, we will use the 'strength' value of those links as a function to modulate the speed with which the walkers walk. With your basic **node-import** code open, change up the first three lines that say **turtles-own links-own globals** to look like this:

```
breed [nodes node] ;; these are our sites
nodes-own [node-id

breed [walkers walker] ;; the turtles who wander around
walkers-own ;; variables that only the walkers own
  [location
  message?
  new-location
  journey-time]

links-own [strength] ;; a better term might be 'distance'
;; or 'ease of travel' (in case of latter, smaller values =
;; easier, right?

globals [links-list travel-factor] ;; travel factor has to
;;be accessible by turtles of either breed
```

The 'breed' command tells NetLogo what the plural and singular are for the new kind of turtle that you've created. Having done that, we can then specify variables that belong only to a particular breed. The next part of our simulation is to put the pieces on the board. We create a new procedure called **setup**:

```
to setup
  import-network
  create-walkers num-walkers [
    set color red
    set shape "person"
    set size 2
    set location one-of nodes ;; tells our new walker its new
home
    move-to location ;; moves the walker there directly
    set message? false ;; ignorance is bliss
    set new-location one-of [link-neighbors] of location
;; gives the walkers a travel goal
    set journey-time 1 ;; initial degree of forward
```

```
;; movement: 1 patch at a time
  ]

  ask one-of walkers [ set message? true ]
  reset-ticks
end
```

In the interface window, create a new button and give it the command **setup.** The **num-walkers** is a variable set by a slider that you make in the interface window. Set that up now, but make sure that the minimum is 2 – that way, one walker will have heard the message and one will have not heard it. **Create-walkers** is a command that tells NetLogo to make new turtles but call them walkers; then each walker will have the following variables or commands performed on it as it is made. In this case, each walker is told that its current location is one of the nodes on the network that we imported, and then the walker is transported to that node. Each walker is then given a destination it will be travelling to by selecting one of the nodes its node is connected to. Each walker is told that its initial speed of travelling will be one step at a time. Finally, one walker is given the message.

Golems are going to walk around this network. When the golem who has the message encounters a golem who does not have the message, the ignorant golem is going to become enlightened. That golem in turn will pass the message on. Soon, all of the golems will have heard the message. It's a direct-touch, direct-message transfer. Is that a reasonable assumption? Given everything you have learned in this section, do you see how you could give a golem a likelihood that they will ignore the message? Garble the message? Sometimes forget to pass it on? What would those situations imply or do for the model? Would it be a better model if we did include these situations? How do you measure *better*?

Our **go** routine will look like this:

```
to go
  ask walkers [
    move          ;; walkers walk
    communicate ;; they talk to anyone else who happens to be
present
    recolor       ;; change their color if they've
;; encountered someone with the message
    check-if-arrived ;; see if they've arrived at their
;; new destination
  ]
```

```
  if ((count walkers with [message?]) / (count walkers)) * 100
= 100 [stop] ;; ending condition
  tick
end
```

In each tick of the clock, walkers will move and gossip; they will change their colour so we know they've heard the message, and they will check to see if they've arrived at their destination. We will also check to see if 100 per cent of the golems on the board have heard the message, in which case the simulation will stop. Then the clock will tick. Create a new button in the interface, give it the command **go**, and tick off the 'forever' button.

Let's build the **move** routine. We want the walkers to walk over the links, and we will want the information in that link to be used to make the journey harder or easier, longer or quicker. We're going to do that by getting each link to pass its information to a global variable which our walkers will access. Here's an interesting problem though – since we are modulating how far a walker steps in a given tick, it is entirely possible that our walker will overshoot its destination, getting trapped in a cycle of back-and-forth jumping. This is what happens when we tell the walker **fd journey-time**. So we'll let the walker slow down sometimes:

```
to move
  face new-location ;; make sure walker is facing its
;; destination at all times
  ifelse random-float 1 > 0.5
       [fd 1][fd journey-time]
end
```

The **ifelse** command is our correction to overshooting the target. If they flip a coin heads, they slow down to one step at a time. Otherwise, they travel at the speed suggested by the information in the link. But how do we get the information from the link to the walker? That happens when we tell the walker to **choose-destination**. That happens once the walker runs the **check-if-arrived** procedure:

```
to check-if-arrived
  let arrived one-of nodes-here
    if arrived = new-location
      [set location new-location
        choose-destination]
end
```

Each turn, the walker looks at where they're at, and if it happens to be a node (**nodes-here**), they compare it against the **new-location** variable they used when they were setting off. If it is, they change their **location** accordingly, which frees them up to select a new destination:

```
to choose-destination
;; see what places are connected to this one
;; adjust the travel-factor (distance, ease of travel) to the
value of the new path/link
;; adjust speed so that it is modulated by this new value

  set new-location one-of [link-neighbors] of location
  ask (end1 = [location] of me and end2 = [new-location] of me)
or
(end2 = [location] of me and end1 = [new-location] of me)] [set
travel-factor strength]
  set journey-time (1 / travel-factor)
    end
```

The speed of travel is set when the walker chooses the new destination. So what about those gossiping golems?

```
to communicate
  if any? other walkers-here with [message?]  ;; hello?
    [ set message? true ]  ;; if yes, then now I know the
message too
end

to recolor  ;; walker procedure
  if message?
    [ set color blue ]
end
```

In **communicate**, the walker looks at where it is and checks to see if another walker is present. If there is and that walker has the message (its **message?** variable is set to **true**), then the walker changes *its* message variable to be true as well. Golems who've heard the message turn blue.

The model is now built and, conceptually, is very similar to the original model I built in 2006. Do you see any assumptions that seem intolerable to you? Do you see assumptions for which you could imagine a reasonable archaeological or historical rationale? How would you test alternative assumptions? What do you think will happen as the model runs? Go to the interface tab and hit the **setup** button and then the **go** button.

The default network reaches a 100 per cent golems-who've-heard-the-message state rather quickly. Can you add a 'kill links' button, or a 'build links' button, knowing what you now know about NetLogo? How does the model respond to adding links? The real test of whether or not my Itineraries model holds up is in the results – the time for full message penetration – given different network geographies. Meeks, Scheidel, Weiland and Arcenas (2014) make the underlying network data for their ORBIS representation of the Roman world (http://orbis.stanford.edu) in node and link tables that can be downloaded at http://purl.stanford.edu/mn425tz9757. Download that data and see if you can get it to import into the model we have just built. Don't worry if the display looks crowded; golems only move along links (although there are ways of making the network layout cleanly, as documented in the NetLogo documentation). Can you extract networks that cover Roman Britain? Roman Spain? Roman France? Roman Italy? Do your findings agree with mine?

Notes

The code throughout these appendices builds upon, uses or adapts exemplar code from Brughmans 2016; Wilensky 2018a, 2018b and 2018c.

A digital adaptation of these appendices is available on the Berghahn Digital Archaeology companion website at http://berghahnbooks.com/digitalarchaeology.

Appendix B
Pot Trade Model Code

```
;; Written in NetLogo 6.0.4
;; We implement Tom Brughmans's (2016) simple pot trade model on
;; top of a network created by the code snippet 'network import
;; example'
;; Here we have also implemented a 'breakage' feature that uses
;; the 'strength' value of the network as an indication of the
;; difficulty of trading pots over a particular route. You might
;; interpret that value as bumpiness of the road, or likelihood
;; of cargoes being lost, etc.

;;---- Things to do in the interface window —
;; in the interface, create a slider with minimum 0, maximum 1
;; and set its value to 0.5. Call it trade-threshold
;; in the interface, create a slider with minimum 1, maximum
100
;; and set its value at 50. Call it num-pots

;; you can create a 'kill' button by right-clicking in the
;; interface, selecting button, and putting the code below
;; into its code panel (without the ;; of course):

;; ask one-of links [die]

;; you can add links to the network randomly by making a button
;; with the following code (without the ;; of course):

;; ask one-of turtles [ create-link-to one-of other turtles
;;                       [set strength random-float 3
;;                        set label strength]]
```

```
;;- Things to notice -
;; when you run the code, notice how the default network seems
to
;; shunt pots to particular nodes; notice how adding links
;; rejigs the way the 'economy' of this model works


turtles-own [node-id pots]

links-own [strength]

globals [links-list breakage-factor] ;; we add the global
;; variable 'breakage-factor' to enable links and nodes to
;; communicate data

to go
  let total-pots sum [pots] of turtles
  repeat total-pots
   [ trade-pots
    ]

  let poorturtles turtles with [ pots < 0 ]
  if any? poorturtles
  [
  ask poorturtles [set pots 1]
  ]
;; this prevents division errors,
;; but could also represent a kind of cyclical production

    ask turtles [set size 0.1 + 5 * sqrt (pots / total-pots)]
  tick
end


to trade-pots

  let target one-of turtles with [pots > 0 and count out-link-
neighbors > 0]

   if target != nobody and random-float 1 > trade-threshold

;; target represents one site, one turtle at a time that we
want
;; to run our trade routine
```

```
   [
;; converts the strength of the link to a number the turtles can
;; use

   ask links [set breakage-factor strength]
   ask target
    [
      print breakage-factor
      let pots-loss 1 + breakage-factor
      set pots max (list 0 (pots - pots-loss))

;; 1 pot plus the breakage - so we're treating the strength of
;; the link as a kind of friction, a certain kind of wastage on
;; that route

   ask one-of out-link-neighbors
         [set pots pots + 1]
;; no breakage, only the pot arrives
      ]
   ]
end


to import-network
  clear-all
  set-default-shape turtles "circle"
  import-attributes
  layout-circle (sort turtles) (max-pxcor - 1)
  import-links
  reset-ticks

  ;; New code that we are adding to the import network
procedure
   ask turtles [
    set pots random (num-pots)
   ]

end

;; This next procedure reads in a files that contains node-
;; specific
;; attributes
;; including an unique identification number
```

```
to import-attributes

  ;; This opens the file, so we can use it.
  file-open "attributes.txt"

  ;; Read in all the data in the file
  ;; data on the line is in this order:
  ;; node-id attribute1 attribute2
  while [not file-at-end?]
  [
    ;; this reads a single line into a three-item list
    let items read-from-string (word "[" file-read-line "]")
    create-turtles 1 [
      set node-id item 0 items
      set size item 1 items
      set color item 2 items
    ]
  ]
  file-close
end

;; This next procedure reads in a file that contains all the
;; links. The file is simply 3 columns separated by spaces. In
;; this example, the links are directed. The first column
;; contains the node-id of the node originating the link. The
;; second column the node-id of the node on the other end of
the
;; link. The third column is the strength of the link.

to import-links
  ;; This opens the file, so we can use it.
  file-open "links.txt"

;; Read in all the data in the file
  while [not file-at-end?]
  [
    ;; this reads a single line into a three-item list
    let items read-from-string (word "[" file-read-line "]")
    ask get-node (item 0 items)
    [
      create-link-to get-node (item 1 items)
        [ set label item 2 items
          set strength item 2 items] ; MAR24 added this
    ]
  ]
```

```
  file-close
end

;; Helper procedure for looking up a node by node-id.
to-report get-node [id]
  report one-of turtles with [node-id = id]
end
```

Appendix C

Information Diffusion on a Network

```
;; built for NetLogo version 6.04
;; a version of the itineraries model that
;; loads a network dataset. 'Travel difficulty' is represented
by
;; the 'strength' value of the links, puts some agents on it,
;; has them wander around, at differing speeds (or distances)
;; and measures how long it takes for a message to be 'heard'
by
;; everyone
;;----
;; the model is built by combining default code snippets in
;; NetLogo:
;; network import
;; communication t-t network example
;; link walking turtles
;; Thanks to Andreas Angourakis for looking over the code and
;; suggesting improvements

;; in the interface, you'll need to create a slider called

;; num-walkers

;; and make sure that the minimum is set to 2 and the 'value'
(starting position of the slider) is at least 2 or more

;; you can also build some monitors. For instance, right-click
in
;; the interface and select new monitor, then paste this code
;; into it:
```

```
;; ((count walkers with [message?]) / (count walkers)) * 100

;; this will tell you the per cent of the population that has
;; heard the message.
;; you could graph this by making a new plot and giving it the
;; same code
;; right-click, select plot, and in plot update commands paste
;; the same code.

breed [nodes node] ;; these are our sites
nodes-own [node-id]
breed [walkers walker] ;; the turtles who wander around
walkers-own [ ;; variables that only the walkers own
  location
  message?
  new-location
  journey-time]

links-own [strength]

globals [links-list travel-factor] ;; travel factor has to be
;; accessible by turtles of either breed


to setup
  import-network
  create-walkers num-walkers [
    set color red
    set shape "person"
    set size 2
    set location one-of nodes ;; tells our new walker its new
;; home
    move-to location ;; moves the walker there directly
    set message? false ;; ignorance is bliss
    set new-location one-of [link-neighbors] of location ;;
gives
;; the walkers a travel goal
    set journey-time 1 ;; initial degree of forward movement:
one
;; patch at a time
  ]

  ask one-of walkers [ set message? true ]
  reset-ticks
end
```

```
to go
  ;; we ask the walkers:
  ;; go walking,
  ;; talk to anyone else who happens to be present,
  ;; change their color if they've encountered someone with the
message,
  ;; test to see if they've arrived at their new destination
  ;; and then if everyone has the message we stop the
simulation.

  ask walkers [
    move
    communicate
    recolor
    check-if-arrived
  ]
  if ((count walkers with [message?]) / (count walkers)) * 100
= 100 [stop]
end

to move
  face new-location ;; make sure they're heading the correct
;; direction at all times
  ifelse random-float 1 > 0.5 [fd 1][fd journey-time]
;; without the chance of them slowing down to one patch at a
;; time, they sometimes will overshoot the target and get
caught
;; overshooting it back and forth.
end

to check-if-arrived
  let arrived one-of nodes-here
;; see if the node they're at happens to be the one they're
;; looking at

    if arrived = new-location
      [set location new-location
        choose-destination]

  ;; if it is
  ;; update their 'location' variable to where they are now
  ;; and search out a new destination
end

to choose-destination
  set new-location one-of [link-neighbors] of location
```

```
;; see what places are connected to this one
  ask one-of links with [
    (end1 = [location] of myself and end2 = [new-location] of
myself) or
    (end2 = [location] of myself and end1 = [new-location] of
myself)]
    ;; adjust the travel-factor (distance, ease of travel) to the
    ;; value of the new path/link

  [set travel-factor strength]

    ;; adjust speed so that it is modulated by this new value
  set journey-time (1 / travel-factor)
end

to communicate ;; turtle procedure
  if any? other walkers-here with [message?]
  ;; hello? anybody here?
    [ set message? true ]
  ;; if yes, then now I know the message too
end

to recolor ;; walker procedure
  if message?
    [ set color blue ]
end


to import-network
  clear-all
  set-default-shape turtles "circle"
  import-attributes
  layout-circle (sort turtles) (max-pxcor − 1)
  import-links
  reset-ticks

end

;; This procedure reads in a files that contains node-specific
;; attributes
;; including an unique identification number

to import-attributes
  ;; This opens the file, so we can use it.
  file-open "attributes.txt"
```

```
  ;; Read in all the data in the file
  ;; data on the line is in this order:
  ;; node-id attribute1 attribute2
  while [not file-at-end?]
  [
    ;; this reads a single line into a three-item list
    let items read-from-string (word "[" file-read-line "]")
    create-nodes 1 [ ;; note the change
      set node-id item 0 items
      set size item 1 items
      set color item 2 items
    ]
  ]
  file-close
end


;; This procedure reads in a file that contains all the links
;; The file is simply 3 columns separated by spaces. In this
;; example, the links are directed. The first column contains
;; the node-id of the node originating the link. The second
;; column the node-id of the node on the other end of the link.
;; The third column is the strength of the link.

to import-links
  ;; This opens the file, so we can use it.
  file-open "links.txt"
  ;; Read in all the data in the file
  while [not file-at-end?]
  [
    ;; this reads a single line into a three-item list
    let items read-from-string (word "[" file-read-line "]")
    ask get-node (item 0 items)
    [
      create-link-with get-node (item 1 items)

;; nb! Create-link-with is undirected, create-link-to is
;; directed!

      [ set label item 2 items
        set strength item 2 items]
    ]
  ]
  file-close
end
```

```
;; Helper procedure for looking up a node by node-id.
to-report get-node [id]
  report one-of nodes with [node-id = id]
end
```

Appendix D

Golems in the City

```
;; built for NetLogo version 6.04
;; a small demo model that loads a map
;; populates it with golems and gives one of them
;; a message - or a virus, pick your metaphor - and turns
;; them loose.
;; Golems move by selecting a target patch of ground ahead of
;; them within their cone of vision
;; where ground they can walk on is the colour of the path
;; in the maps generated by Oleg Dolya's Medieval Fantasy City
;; Map Generator at
;; https://watabou.itch.io/medieval-fantasy-city-generator

;; (Note that other maps can work, but you will need to be able
;; to identify the color value for any paths you want golems to
;; follow.)

;; Preliminaries and Interface Window setup
;; 1. Generate a map there and select the 'sanguine' colour
;; palette (if you select a different palette, you'll have to
;; figure out its colour value for the pcolor variable in the
;; 'walk' procedure.
;; 2. Save that map to your computer in the same place you have
;; this model.
;; In the INTERFACE:
;; 3. Create a button called '1. Load Map' and give it this
code:

;; ca
;; import-pcolors user-file
```

```
;; 4. Create a button called '2. Setup Golems' and give it this
;; code:

;; setup

;; 5. Create two sliders, one called 'loudness' the other
called
;; 'vision' and set their min value to 1 and max value to about
;; 15.
;; 6. Create a 'go' button. Give it this code:

;; go

;; and tick off the 'forever' box.
;; 7. Create a slider called

;; num-walkers

;; and make sure that the minimum is set to 2 and the 'value'
;; (starting position of the slider) is at least 2 or more
;;----

;; the model is built by combining default code snippets in
;; NetLogo:
;; network import
;; communication t-t network example
;; link-walking turtles

;; you can also build some monitors. For instance, right-click
in
;; the interface and select new monitor
;; then paste this code into it:

;; ((count walkers with [message?]) / (count walkers)) * 100

;; this will tell you the per cent of the population that has
;; heard the message.
;; you could graph this by making a new plot and giving it the
;; same code
;; right-click, select plot, and in plot update commands paste
;; the same code.
;; While the model is running, you could type:

;; pd
```

```
;; in the observer box at the bottom of the interface. This will
;; make the walkers draw on the map
;; where they've been. Maybe there's something particular about a
;; city layout that draws walkers to particular places?
;; How else might you expand this?


;; globals
breed [walkers walker] ;; the turtles who wander around
walkers-own [ ;; variables that only the walkers own
  message?
  direction
]

;; setup
to setup

  create-walkers num-walkers [
    set color blue
    set shape "person"
    set size 15
    setxy random-xcor random-ycor
    if pcolor != 38.9 [die]
;; drastic, but we don't want any walkers in the rivers or on
the
;; walls or inside buildings
    set message? false ;; ignorance is bliss

  ]
  ask one-of walkers [ set message? true ]
  reset-ticks
end

to go
  ask walkers [
    ifelse color = blue [walk][chase]
    communicate
;; they talk to anyone else who happens to be present
    recolor
;; change their color if they've encountered someone with the
;; message

  ]
  if ((count walkers with [message?]) / (count walkers)) * 100
> 95 [stop] ;; ending condition
```

```
    tick
end


to walk
ask walkers[
    rt random 30 - 15
    let target one-of patches in-cone 1.5 120 with [pcolor =
38.9] ;; the color of the path
    if target != nobody [
      face target
      move-to target
    ]
  ]
end

to chase
  ask walkers [
    rt random 30 - 15
    let chasee one-of walkers in-cone vision 120 with [color =
blue]
    if chasee != nobody [
     face chasee
     walk
  ]
  ]
end


to communicate ;; walker procedure

;; shouting!

 if any? other walkers in-radius loudness with [message?]

;; or use this line to mimic 'whispering':
;; if any? other walkers-here with [message?]

;; experiment. What difference to your results does whispering
;; versus shouting make?

    [ set message? true ]
;; if yes, then the walker now knows the message too
end
```

```
to recolor ;; walker procedure
  ifelse message?
    [ set color red ]
    [ set color blue ]
end
```

References

Aarseth, Espen J. 1997. *Cybertext: Perspectives on Ergodic Literature*. Baltimore: Johns Hopkins University Press.

Aarseth, Espen J., Solveig Marie Smedstad and Lise Sunnanå. 2003. 'A Multi-Dimensional Typology of Games'. In *Level Up: Digital Games Research Conference Proceedings*, edited by Marinka Copier and Joost Raessens, 48–53. Utrecht: Netherlands Digital Games Research Association.

Adam, Jean-Pierre. 1994. *Roman Building: Materials and Techniques*. Translated by A. Mathews. London: Routledge.

Adams, Colin, and Ray Laurence, eds. 2001. *Travel and Geography in the Roman Empire*. London: Routledge.

Agar, Michael. 2003. 'My Kingdom for a Function: Modeling Misadventures of the Innumerate'. *Journal of Artificial Societies and Social Simulation* 6(3). Retrieved 14 June 2019 from http://jasss.soc.surrey.ac.uk/6/3/8.html.

Aldenderfer, Mark. 1998. 'Quantitative Methods in Archaeology: A Review of Recent Trends and Developments'. *Journal of Archaeological Research* 6(2): 91–120.

Aldrete, Gregory. 2013. 'Riots'. In *Cambridge Companion to the City of Rome*, edited by Paul Erdkamp, 425–40. Cambridge: Cambridge University Press.

Anderson, Marc. 2019. 'Zombies, Manifest Destiny, and Popular Culture'. Public lecture, work in progress. 1 February, Carleton University.

Arnaud, P. 1988. 'L'origine, la date de rédaction et la diffusion de l'archétype de la Table de Peutinger'. *Bulletin de la société nationale des antiquaires de France* 1988: 302–21. Retrieved 14 June 2019 from https://www.persee.fr/doc/bsnaf_0081-1181_1990_num_1988_1_9424.

'Background'. 2016. Emotive: Storytelling for Cultural Heritage website. https://emotiveproject.eu/index.php/about/background/.

Baker, Kevin T. 2018. 'Model Metropolis'. *Logic Magazine* 6. Retrieved 14 June 2019 from https://logicmag.io/play/model-metropolis/.

Barabàsi, Aleber-László. 2002. *Linked: The New Science of Networks*. Cambridge, MA: Perseus.

Barrett, John. 2001. 'Agency, the Duality of Structure, and the Problem of the Archaeological Record'. In *Archaeological Theory Today*, edited by Ian Hodder, 141–64. Cambridge: Polity Press.

Batty, Michael. 2003. 'Network Geography: Relations, Interactions, Scaling and Spatial Processes in GIS'. Centre for Advanced Spatial Analysis, Working Paper 63. Retrieved 4 November 2019 from https://www.ucl.ac.uk/bartlett/casa/sites/bartlett/files/migrated-files/paper63_0.pdf.

Beisaw, April. 2017. 'An Archaeology Carol . . . or How Ghost Hunting Made Me a Better Archaeologist'. *The Geek Anthropologist*. Retrieved 4 November 2019 from thegeekanthropologist.com/2017/12/29/an-archaeology-carol.

Bennett, Jane. 2001. *The Enchantment of Modern Life: Attachments, Crossings, and Ethics*. Princeton: Princeton University Press.

———. 2010. *Vibrant Matter: A Political Ecology of Things*. Durham, NC: Duke University Press.

Bogost, Ian. 2007. *Persuasive Games: The Expressive Power of Videogames*. Cambridge, MA: MIT Press.

Brodersen, Kai. 2001. 'The Presentation of Geographical Knowledge for Travel and Transport in the Roman World: *itineraria non tantum adnotata sed etiam picta*'. In *Travel and Geography in the Roman Empire*, edited by Colin Adams and Ray Laurence, 7–21. London: Routledge.

Broussard, Meredith. 2018. *Artificial Unintelligence: How Computers Misunderstand the World*. Cambridge, MA: MIT Press.

Brughmans, Tom. 2012. 'Facebooking the Past: A Critical Social Network Analysis Approach for Archaeology'. In *Thinking beyond the Tool: Archaeological Computing and the Interpretative Process*, edited by Angeliki Chrysanthi, Patricia Murrieta Flores and Constantinos Papadopoulos. Oxford: Archaeopress – British Archaeological Reports 203.

———. 2016. 'Network Science with Netlogo Tutorial'. Retrieved 4 November 2019 from https://archaeologicalnetworks.files.wordpress.com/2013/11/netlogo_networks_tutorial_v2.pdf.

Brughmans, Tom, Iza Romanowska and Shawn Graham. 2018. *Forvm: Trade Empires of Rome*. The Game Crafter. http://forvm.ca.

Caspari, Gino, and Pablo Crespo. 2019. 'Convolutional Neural Networks for Archaeological Site Detection: Finding 'Princely' Tombs'. *Journal of Archaeological Science* 110 (October): 104998. Retrieved 4 November 2019 from https://doi.org/10.1016/j.jas.2019.104998.

Capelli, Rosanna, and Fabrizio Pesando. 1991. 'Gli itinerary romani: repertorio bibliografico'. In *Via Publicae Romanae: X Mostra europea del Turismo, artigianato e delle tradizioni culturali, Roma, Castel Sant' Angelo, 11–25 aprile 1991*, edited by Rosanna Capelli, 41–44. Rome: Leondardo-De Luca.

Caraher, William. 2014. 'Teaching, Learning and Resistance'. *The Archaeology of the Mediterranean World*. Retrieved 14 June 2019 from http://mediterraneanworld.wordpress.com/2014/03/31/teaching-learning-and-resistance/.

———. 2015. 'Slow Archaeology'. *North Dakota Quarterly* 80(2): 43–52.

———. 2016. 'Slow Archaeology: Technology, Efficiency, and Archaeological Work'. In *Mobilizing the Past for a Digital Future*, edited by Erin Walker Averett, Jody Michael Gordon, Derek B. Counts, 421–42. Grand Forks: Digital Press at the University of North Dakota. Retrieved 4 November 2019

from https://digitalpressatund.files.wordpress.com/2016/09/4_1_caraher
.pdf.

———. 2019. 'Slow Archaeology, Punk Archaeology, and the 'Archaeology of
Care'. *European Journal of Archaeology* 22, Special Issue 3 (digital archaeologies): 372–85. Retrieved 4 November 2019 from https://doi.org/10.1017/
eaa.2019.15.

Cherry, John F. 1977. 'Investigating the Political Geography of an Early State
by Multidimensional Scaling of Linear B Tablet Data'. In *Mycenaean Geography: Proceedings of the Cambridge Colloquium, September 1976*, edited
by John Bintliff, 76–82. Cambridge: British Association for Mycenaean
Studies, Cambridge University Library Press.

Chalk, Andy. 2018. 'Poundmaker Cree Nation Leader Criticizes Cree Portrayal
in Civilization 6'. *PC Gamer*. Retrieved 4 November 2019 from https://
www.pcgamer.com/poundmaker-cree-nation-leader-criticizes-cree-por
trayal-in-civilization-6/.

Cilliers, Paul. 1998. *Complexity and Postmodernism: Understanding Complex Systems*. London: Routledge.

Chan, Tiffany. 2017. The Author Function: Imitating Grant Allen with Queer
Writing Machines. Retrieved 4 November 2019 from https://github.com/
eltiffster/authorFunction.

Cohen, Simchi. 2015. 'A Living Man, a Clay Man: Violence, the Zombie,
and the Messianic in H. Leivick's *The Golem*'. *Cultural Critique* 90: 1–21.
Retrieved 4 November 2019 from https://doi.org/10.5749/culturalcriti
que.90.2015.0001.

Collingwood, Robin George. 2005. *The Philosophy of Enchantment: Studies in
Folktale, Cultural Criticism, and Anthropology*. Edited by David Boucher,
Wendy James and Philip Smallwood. Oxford: Oxford University Press.

Conan Doyle, Arthur. 1890. *The Sign of the Four*. London: Spencer Blackett.

Copplestone, Tara. 2016. 'But That's Not Accurate: The Differing Perceptions
of Accuracy in Cultural-Heritage Videogames between Creators, Consum-
ers and Critics'. *Rethinking History: The Journal of Theory and Practice* 21(3):
415–38. Retrieved 4 November 2019 from http://dx.doi.org/10.1080/136
42529.2017.1256615.

———. 2017. 'Designing and Developing a Playful Past in Video Games'. In
The Interactive Past: Archaeology, Heritage, and Video Games, edited by An-
gus A. A. Mol, Csilla E. Ariese-Vandemeulebroucke, Krijn H. J. Boom and
Aris Politopoulos, 85–98. Leiden: Sidestone Press.

Copplestone, Tara, and Luke Botham. 2014. *Buried*. Retrieved 4 November
2019 from http://www.heritagejam.org/exhibition/2014/7/11/buried-an-
ergodic-literature-game-tara-copplestone-and-luke-botham.

Costopoulos, Andre, and Mark Lake, eds. 2010. *Simulating Change: Archaeology
into the Twenty-First Century*. Salt Lake City: University of Utah Press.

Cox, Angela. 2014. 'Teaching Games as Text: The Problem. Part 3 of 4'. *Play
the Past*. Retrieved 14 June 2019 from http://www.playthepast.org/?p=
4605.

Crawford, Kate, and Vladan Joler. 2018. *Anatomy of an AI System: The Amazon Echo as an Anatomical Map of Human Labor, Data and Planetary Resources.* Retrieved 4 November 2019 from http://anatomyof.ai.

Croxall, Brian, and Quinn Warnick. 2015. 'Failure'. *Digital Pedagogy in the Humanities Concepts, Models, and Experiments.* Retrieved 14 June 2019 from https://digitalpedagogy.mla.hcommons.org/keywords/failure/.

Cuntz, Otto. 1929. *Itineraria Romana.* Vol. 1, *Itineraria Antonini Augusti et Burdigalense.* Reprint 1990. Stuttgart: Teubner.

Dallas, Costis. 2016. 'Jean-Claude Gardin on Archaeological Data, Representation and Knowledge: Implications for Digital Archaeology'. *Journal of Archaeological Method and Theory* 23(1): 305–30. Retrieved 14 June 2019 from https://doi.org/10.1007/s10816-015-9241-3.

Das, Abhishek, Satwik Kottur, Khushi Gupta, Avi Singh, Deshraj Yadav, José Moura, Devi Parikh and Dhruv Batra. 2017. 'Visual Dialog'. In *Proceedings of the IEEE Conference on Computer Vision and Pattern Recognition,* 1080–89. Retrieved 14 June 2019 from https://ieeexplore.ieee.org/document/8099604.

Davies, John K. 2005. 'Linear and Non-Linear Flow Models for the Ancient Economy'. In *The Ancient Economy: Evidence and Models,* edited by J. G. Manning and I. Morris, 127–56. Stanford: Stanford University Press.

Dawson, Ian, and Paul Reilly. 2019. 'Messy Assemblages, Residuality and Recursion within a Phygital Nexus'. *Epoiesen.* Retrieved 14 June 2019 from http://dx.doi.org/10.22215/epoiesen/2019.4.

Dean, Jeffrey, George Gumerman, Joshua Epstein, Robert Axtell, Alan Swedlund, Miles Parker and Steven McCarrol. 2000. 'Understanding Anasazi Culture Change through Agent-Based Modeling'. In *Dynamics in Human and Primate Societies: Agent-Based Modeling of Social and Spatial Processes,* edited by Tim Kohler and George Gumerman, 179–206. Oxford: Oxford University Press.

DeLaine, Janet. 1997. *The Baths of Caracalla: A Study in the Design, Construction, and Economics of Large Scale Building Projects in Imperial Rome.* Supplement, *Journal of Roman Archaeology* 25.

———. 2002. 'Building Activity in Ostia in the Second Century AD'. In *Ostia e Portus nelle loro relazioni con Roma,* edited by Christer Bruun and Anna Gallina-Zevi, 41–102. Rome: Acta Instituti Romanae Finlandiae.

Dennis, L. Meghan. 2016. 'Archaeogaming, Ethics, and Participatory Standards'. *SAA Archaeological Record* 16(5). Retrieved 10 November 2019 from http://onlinedigeditions.com/publication/?i=356358&article_id=26 38934&view=articleBrowser&ver=html5#.

Dexter, Colin. 1991. *The Jewel that Was Ours.* MacMillan: London.

Drummond, Andrew. 1989. 'Early Roman Clientes'. In *Patronage in Ancient Society,* edited by Andrew Wallace-Hadrill, 89–115. London: Routledge.

Díaz-Guardamino, Marta, and Colleen Morgan. 2019. 'Human, Transhuman, Posthuman Digital Archaeologies: An Introduction'. *European Journal of*

Archaeology 22(3): 320–23. Retrieved 4 November 2019 from https://doi.org/10.1017/eaa.2019.26.

Duncan-Jones, Richard. 1990. *Structure and Scale in the Roman Economy*. Cambridge: Cambridge University Press.

Eco, Umberto. 1988. *Foucault's Pendulum*. London: Secker & Warburg.

Emotive: Storytelling for Cultural Heritage Project. Retrieved 10 November 2019 from https://emotiveproject.eu/.

Epstein, Joshua. 1999. 'Agent-Based Computational Models and Generative Social Science'. *Complexity* 4(5): 41–60.

———. 2002. 'Modeling Civil Violence: An Agent-Based Computational Approach'. *Proceedings of the National Academy of Sciences* 99(3): 7243–50.

———. 2006. 'Agent-Based Computational Models and Generative Social Science'. In *Generative Social Science: Studies in Agent-Based Computational Modeling*, edited by Joshua Epstein, 4–46. Princeton: Princeton University Press.

———. 2009. 'Why Model?' *Journal of Artificial Societies and Social Simulation* 11(4). Retrieved 14 June 2019 from http://jasss.soc.surrey.ac.uk/11/4/12.html.

Eve, Stuart. 2011. 'Augmenting a Roman Fort'. *Dead Men's Eyes: Augmented Reality and Heritage*. Retrieved 4 March 2020 from https://www.dead-mens-eyes.org/augmenting-a-roman-fort/.

Eve, Stuart, Kerrie Hoffman, Colleen Morgan, Alexis Pantos, Sam Kinchin-Smith and Shawn Graham. 2014. 'Voices Recognition'. *HeritageJam*. Retrieved 4 November 2019 from http://www.heritagejam.org/jam-day-entries/2014/7/12/voices-recognition-stuart-eve-kerrie-hoffman-colleen-morgan-alexis-pantos-and-sam-kinchin-smith.

Fant, Clayton. 1993. 'Ideology, Gift, and Trade: A Distribution Model for the Roman Imperial Marbles'. In *The Inscribed Economy: Production and Distribution in the Roman Empire in the Light of Instrumentum Domesticum*, edited by William Harris, supplement, *Journal of Roman Archaeology* 6: 145–70 .

Favro, Diane. 1996. *The Urban Image of Augustan Rome*. Cambridge: Cambridge University Press.

Floridi, Luciano. 2003. 'On the Intrinsic Value of Information Objects and the Infosphere'. *Ethics and Information Technology* 4(4): 287–304.

Floridi, Luciano, and Jeff Sanders. 1999. 'Entropy as Evil in Information Ethics'. *Etica & Politica* 1(2). Retrieved 4 March 2020 from www2.units.it/etica/1999_2/floridi/index.html.

———. 2004. 'The Method of Abstraction.' *Yearbook of the Artificial* 2: 177–220.

Forrester, Jay. 1969. *Urban Dynamics*. Cambridge, MA: MIT Press.

Foucault, Michel. 1999. *Aesthetics, Method, and Epistemology*. Vol. 2 of *Essential Works of Foucault, 1954–1984*, edited by James D. Faubion. New York: New Press.

Fredengren, Christina. 2016. 'Unexpected Encounters with Deep Time Enchantment: Bog Bodies, Crannogs and 'Otherworldly' Sites; The Materializing Powers of Disjunctures in Time'. *World Archaeology* 48(4): 482–99.

Garnsey, Peter, and Greg Woolf. 1989. 'Patronage of the Rural Poor in the Roman World'. In *Patronage in Ancient Society*, edited by Andrew Wallace-Hadrill, 153–70. London: Routledge.

Gilbert, Nigel, and Klaus Troitzsch. 2005. *Simulation for the Social Scientist*. 2nd edition. Maidenhead, Berkshire: Open University Press.

Ginn, Franklin, Michelle Bastian, David Farrier and Jeremy Kidwell. 2018. 'Introduction: Unexpected Encounters with Deep Time'. *Environmental Humanities* 10(1): 213–25. Retrieved 14 June 2019 from https://doi .org/10.1215/22011919-4385534.

Godsen, Chris. 2005. 'What Do Objects Want?' *Journal of Archaeological Method and Theory* 12(3): 193–211.

Goodwin, Ross. 2016. 'Adventures in Narrated Reality: New Forms and Interfaces for Written Language, Enabled by Machine Intelligence'. *Artists and Machine Intelligence*. Retrieved 4 November 2019 from https://medium .com/artists-and-machine-intelligence/adventures-in-narrated-reality-6516ff395ba3.

Gould, Peter, and Rodney White. 1974. *Mental Maps*. Harmondsworth: Penguin.

Graham, Shawn. 2006a. *EX FIGLINIS: The Complex Dynamics of the Roman Brick Industry in the TiberValley during the 1st to 3rd Centuries AD*. British Archaeological Reports, International Series 1486. Oxford: John and Erica Hedges Ltd.

———. 2006b. 'Networks, Agent-Based Modeling, and the Antonine Itineraries'. *The Journal of Mediterranean Archaeology* 19(1): 45–64.

———. 2006c. 'The Space Between: Places and Connections in the Tiber Valley'. In *Mercator Placidissimus: The Tiber Valley in Antiquity; New Research in the Upper and Middle River Valley*, edited by Helen Patterson, 671–86. (Proceedings of the Conference held at the British School at Rome, 27–28 February 2004). Rome: Edizioni Qasar.

———. 2009. 'Behaviour Space: Simulating Roman Social Life and Civil Violence'. *Digital Studies / Le Champ Numérique* 1(2). Retrieved 4 November 2019 from http://doi.org/10.16995/dscn.109.

———. 2010. 'My Glorious Failure'. *Play the Past*. Retrieved 14 June 2019 from http:// www.playthepast.org/?p=352.

———. 2013a. 'Counting Bricks and Stacking Wood: Providing the Physical Fabric'. In *The Cambridge Companion to Ancient Rome*, edited by Paul Erdkamp, 278–96. Cambridge University Press.

———. 2013b. 'The Wikiblitz'. In *Writing History in the Digital Age*, edited by Jack Dougherty and Kristen Nawrotzki, 75–85. Ann Arbor: University of Michigan Press. Retrieved 4 November 2019 from http://dx.doi .org/10.3998/dh.12230987.0001.001.

———. 2014. 'Pulling Back the Curtain: Writing History through Video Games'. In *Web Writing. Why and How for Liberal Arts Teaching and Learning*, edited by Jack Dougherty and Tennyson O'Donnell, 149–60. Ann Arbor: University of Michigan Press.

———. 2017a. 'On Games that Play Themselves: Agent Based Models, Archaeogaming, and the Useful Deaths of Digital Romans'. In *The Interactive Past: Archaeology, Heritage, and Video Games*, edited by Angus A. A. Mol, Csilla E. Ariese-Vandemeulebroucke, Krijn H. J. Boom and Aris Politopoulos, 123–31. Leiden: Sidestone.

———. 2017b. 'Slow Archaeology?' *Electric Archaeology*. Retrieved 14 June 2019 from https://electricarchaeology.ca/2017/03/20/slow-archaeology/.

Graham, Shawn, and Scott Weingart. 2015. 'The Equifinality of Archaeological Networks: An Agent-Based Exploratory Lab Approach'. *Journal of Archaeological Method and Theory*. 22(1): 248–74. Retrieved 14 June 2019 from https://doi.org/10.1007/s10816-014-9230-y.

Hamilakis, Yannis. 2014. *Archaeology and the Senses: Human Experience, Memory, and Affect*. Cambridge: Cambridge University Press.

Hanneman, Robert, and Mark Riddle. 2005. 'Introduction to Social Network Methods'. Riverside: University of California, Riverside. Retrieved 4 November 2019 from http://faculty.ucr.edu/~hanneman.

Hao, Karen. 2019. 'Training a Single AI Model Can Emit as Much Carbon as Five Cars in Their Lifetimes'. *MIT Technology Review*. Retrieved 4 November 2019 from https://www.technologyreview.com/s/613630/training-a-single-ai-model-can-emit-as-much-carbon-as-five-cars-in-their-lifetimes/.

Henein Colin, and Tony White. 2004. 'Agent-Based Modelling of Forces in Crowds'. In *International Workshop on Multi-Agent Agent-Based Simulation*, edited by Paul Davidsson, Brian Logan and Keiki Takadama, 173–184. Berlin: Springer. Retrieved 14 June 2019 from http://www.scs.carleton.ca/~arpwhite/documents/AAMAS-HeneinAndWhite-2004.pdf .

Hicks, Mar. 2017. *Programmed Inequality: How Britain Discarded Women Technologists and Lost Its Edge in Computing*. Cambridge, MA: MIT Press.

Hodder, Ian. 2012. *Entangled: An Archaeology of the Relationships between Humans and Things*. Oxford: John Wiley & Sons.

Hodge, Trevor. 1989. *Roman Aqueducts and Water Supply*. London: Duckworth.

Holtorf, Cornelius. 2009. *Archaeology Is a Brand!* Walnut Creek, CA: Left Coast Press. Retrieved 14 June 2019 from https://www.bookdepository.com/Archaeology-is-Brand-Cornelius-Holtorf/9781598741797.

Huffer, Damien, and Shawn Graham. 2017. 'The Insta-Dead: The Rhetoric of the Human Remains Trade on Instagram'. *Internet Archaeology* 45. Retrieved 4 November 2019 from https://doi.org/10.11141/ia.45.5.

Huggett, Jeremy. 2015. 'A Manifesto for an Introspective Digital Archaeology'. *Open Archaeology* 1(1). Retrieved 4 November 2019 from https://doi.org/10.1515/opar-2015-0002.

———. 2018. 'Digital Data Relations'. *Introspective Digital Archaeology*. Retrieved 14 June 2019 from http://introspectivedigitalarchaeology.com/2018/06/28/digital-data-relations/.

Huhns, Michael, and Munindar Singh. 1998. *Readings in Agents*. San Mateo, CA: Morgan Kaufmann.

Ingold, Tim. 1993. 'The Temporality of the Landscape'. *World Archaeology* 25(2): 152–74.

———. 2007. 'Materials against Materiality'. *Archaeological Dialogues* 14(1): 1–16. Retrieved 4 November 2019 from https://doi.org/10.1017/S1380 203807002127.

———. 2011. *Being Alive: Essays on Movement, Knowledge and Description*. London: Routledge.

———. 2013. *Making: Anthropology, Archaeology, Art and Architecture*. London: Routledge.

Jamieson, Dave. 2015. 'The Life and Death of an Amazon Warehouse Temp'. *The Huffington Post*, 21 October. Retrieved 4 March 2020 from https://highline.huffingtonpost.com/articles/en/life-and-death-amazon-temp/.

Janssen, Marco. 2009. 'Understanding Artificial Anasazi'. *Journal of Artificial Societies and Social Simulation* 12(4): 13. Retrieved 14 June 2019 from http://jasss.soc.surrey.ac.uk/12/4/13.html.

Jones, Siân. 2010. 'Negotiating Authentic Objects and Authentic Selves: Beyond the Deconstruction of Authenticity'. *Journal of Material Culture* 15: 181–203.

Joyce, Rosemary, and Ruth Tringham. 2007. 'Feminist Adventures in Hypertext'. *Journal of Archaeological Method and Theory* 14(3): 328–58.

Kapell, Matthew, and Andrew B. R Elliott, eds. 2013. *Playing with the Past: Digital Games and the Simulation of History*. London: Bloomsbury Academic.

Kramer, Iris, Jonathon Hare, Adam Prugel-Bennett and Isabel Sargent. 2017. 'Automated Detection of Archaeology in the New Forest Using Deep Learning with Remote Sensor Data'. *New Forest Knowledge Conference 2017: New Forest Historical Research and Archaeology: Who's Doing It?, Lyndhurst, United Kingdom, 27–28 Oct 2017*. Retrieved 4 November 2019 from https://eprints.soton.ac.uk/416396/.

Kee, Kevin, and Shawn Graham. 2014. 'Teaching History in an Age of Pervasive Computing: The Case for Games in the High School and Undergraduate Classroom'. In *Pastplay: Teaching and Learning History with Technology*, edited by Kevin Kee, 337–66. Ann Arbor: University of Michigan Press.

Kee, Kevin, Shawn Graham, Pat Dunae, John Lutz, Andrew Large, Michel Blondeau and Mike Clare. 2009. 'Towards a Theory of Good History through Gaming'. *The Canadian Historical Review* 90(9): 303–26. Retrieved 14 June 2019 from http://muse.jhu.edu/journals/can/summary/v090/90.2.kee.html.

Kendall, David G. 1971. 'Maps from Marriages: An Application of Non-metric Multidimensional Scaling to Parish Register Data'. In *Mathematics in the Archaeological and Historical Sciences*, edited by Frank Roy Hodson, David G. Kendall and Petre Tautu, 303–18. Edinburgh: Edinburgh University Press.

———. 1977. 'Computer Techniques and the Archival Map Reconstruction of Mycenaean Messenia'. In *Mycenaean Geography: Proceedings of the Cambridge Colloquium, September 1976*, edited by John Bintliff, 83–87. Cambridge: British Association for Mycenaean Studies; Cambridge University Library.

Keshar, Nitish Shirish, Bryan McCann, Lav Varsheny, Caiming Xiong and Richard Socher. 2019. 'CTRL: A Conditional Transformer Language Model for Controllable Generation'. arXiv:1909.05858 [cs.CL].

Lake, Mark W. 2015. 'Explaining the Past with ABM: On Modelling Philosophy'. In *Agent-Based Modeling and Simulation in Archaeology*, edited by Gabriel Wurzer, Kerstin Kowarik and Hans Reschreiter, 3–35. Vienna: Springer.

Laurence, Ray. 1998. 'Land Transport in Roman Italy: Cost, Practice and the Economy'. In *Trade, Traders and the Ancient City*, edited by Helen Parkins and Christopher Smith, 129–48. London: Routledge.

———. 2001. 'The Creation of Geography: An Interpretation of Roman Britain'. In *Travel and Geography in the Roman Empire*, edited by Colin Adams and Ray Laurence, 67–94. London: Routledge.

———. 2002. 'Roman Italy's Urban Revolution'. In *Modalità insediative e strutture agrarie nell'Italia meridionale in età romana*, edited by Elio Lo Cascio and A. Storchi Marino, 591–609. Bari: Edipuglia.

Lawall, Mark L., and Shawn Graham. 2018. 'Netlogo Simulations and the Use of Transport Amphoras in Antiquity'. In *Maritime Networks in the Ancient Mediterranean World*, edited by J. Leidwanger and C. Knappett, 163–83. Cambridge: Cambridge University Press.

Lemercier, Claire, and Claire Zalc. 2019. *Quantitative Methods in the Humanitites: An Introduction*. Translated by Aurthur Goldhammer. Charlottesville: University of Virginia Press.

Levy, Steven. 1984. *Hackers: Heroes of the Computer Revolution*. Garden City, NY: Anchor Press/Doubleday.

———. 2012. 'Can an Algorithm Write a Better News Story than a Human Reporter?' *Wired: GadgetLab*. 4 April 2012. Retrieved 14 June 2019 from http://www.wired.com/gadgetlab/2012/04/can-an-algorithm-write-a-better-news-story-than-a-human-reporter/.

Lewin, Roger. 1993. *Complexity: Life at the Edge of Chaos*. London: Dent.

Ling, Roger. 1990. 'A Stranger in Town: Finding the Way in an Ancient City'. *Greece and Rome* (2nd Series) 37(2): 204–14.

Loyless, Allysa. 2019. 'Visualizing the York Minster as Papercraft'. *Epoiesen*. Retrieved 4 November 2019 from http://dx.doi.org/10.22215/epoiesen/2019.3.

Lynch, Kevin. 1960. *The Image of The City*. Cambridge, MA: MIT Press.

MacDougall, Rob. 2010. 'The Action Figure Curriculum'. *Rob MacDougall*. Retrieved 14 June 2019 from https://web.archive.org/web/20160412074205/http://www.robmacdougall.org/blog/2010/05/the-action-figure-curriculum/.

———. 2014. 'The Killer App: How the Cold War Created Video Games and Vice Versa'. Lecture. Western University. Retrieved 4 November 2019 from https://www.youtube.com/watch?v=_otw7hWq58A.

———. 2019. 'Sympathethic Physics'. *Rob MacDougall*. Retrieved 4 November 2019 from http://www.robmacdougall.org/blog/2019/07/sympathetic-physics/#more-2510.

Mark, David, Christian Freksa, Stephen Hirtle, Robert Lloyd and Barbara Tversky. 1999. 'Cognitive Models of Geographic Space'. *International Journal of Geographical Information Science* 13(8): 747–74.

Marney, John Paul, and Heather Tarbert. 2000. 'Why Do Simulation? Towards a Working Epistemology for Practitioners of the Dark Arts'. *Journal of Artificial Societies and Social Simulation* 3(4): 1–4. Retrieved 4 November 2019 from http://jasss.soc.surrey.ac.uk/3/4/4.html.

Massey, Doreen, John Allen and Steve Pile, eds. 1999. *City Worlds*. Understanding Cities series. London: Routledge.

Merchant, Brian. 2017. 'Life and Death in Apple's Forbidden City'. *The Guardian*, 18 June. Retrieved 4 March 2020 from https://www.theguardian.com/technology/2017/jun/18/foxconn-life-death-forbidden-city-longhua-suicide-apple-iphone-brian-merchant-one-device-extract.

McAlister, Elizabeth. 2012. 'Slaves, Cannibals, and Infected Hyper-Whites: The Race and Religion of Zombies'. *Anthropological Quarterly* 85(2): 457–86.

McCall, Jeremiah. 2012. 'Navigating the Problem Space: The Medium of Simulation Games in the Teaching of History'. *History Teacher* 46(1): 9–28.

———. 2018. 'Path of Honors: Towards a Model for Interactive History Texts with Twine'. *Epoiesen*. Retrieved 4 November 2019 from http://dx.doi.org/10.22215/epoiesen/2017.16.

McKinney, Sierra. 2018. 'Generating Pre-historical Empathy in Classrooms'. M.Sc. dissertation. York: University of York.

Meeks, Elijah, Walter Scheidel, Jonathan Weiland and Scott Arcenas. 2014. ORBIS (v2) Network Edge and Node Tables (software/multimedia). Stanford Digital Repository. Retrieved 14 June 2019 from http://purl.stanford.edu/mn425tz9757.

Milligan, Ian. 2019. *History in the Age of Abundance: How the Web is Transforming Historical Research*. Montreal: McGill-Queens University Press

Mingarelli, Brandon, Chris Tucciarone, Ishpur Bhandal and Zach Lemieux. 2014. 'The Medic's War: Final Assignment for HIST3812'. Unpublished coursework, Carleton University.

Mol, Angus. 2018. 'Path of Honors: First Response'. *Epoiesen*. Retrieved 4 November 2019 from http://dx.doi.org/10.22215/epoiesen/2018.4.

Montello, Daniel, Sara Irina Fabrikant, Marco Ruocco and Richard Middleton. 2003. 'Testing the First Law of Cognitive Geography on Point-Display Spatializations'. In *Spatial Information Theory: Foundations of Geographic Information Science. Proceedings of COSIT '03*, edited by Walter Kuhn, Michael F. Worboys and Sabine Timpf, 335–51. Berlin: Springer.

Morgan, Colleen. 2009. 'Fake Dead People'. *Colleen Morgan* (blog). Retrieved 4 November 2019 from https://colleen-morgan.com/2009/01/12/fake-dead-people/.

———. 2019. 'Avatars, Monsters, and Machines: A Cyborg Archaeology'. *European Journal of Archaeology* 22(3): 324–37. Retrieved 4 November 2019 from https://doi.org/10.1017/eaa.2019.22.

Moshenska, Gabriel. 2014. 'The Archaeology of (Flash) Memory'. *Post-Medieval Archaeology* 48(1): 255–59.

Nowviskie, Bethany. 2014. 'Ludic Algorithms'. In *Pastplay: Teaching and Learning History with Technology*, edited by Kevin Kee, 139–74. Ann Arbor: University of Michigan Press. Retrieved 4 November 2019 from http://dx.doi.org/10.3998/dh.12544152.0001.001.

———. 2016. 'Resistance in the Materials'. In *Debates in the Digital Humanities 2016*, edited by Matthew Gold and Lauren F. Klein. Retrieved 14 June 2019 from http://dhdebates.gc.cuny.edu/debates/text/66.

Otto, Bernd-Christian. 2013. 'Towards Historicizing "Magic" in Antiquity'. *Numen* 60(2/3): 308–47.

Ourednik, André, and Pierre Dessemontet. 2007. 'Interaction Maximization and the Observed Distribution of Urban Populations: An Agent Based Model of Humanity's Metric Condition'. Presented at the 15th European Colloquium on Theoretical and Quantitative Geography (ectqg'07), 7–11 September in Montreux, Switzerland. Retrieved 4 November 2019 from http://ourednik.info/urbanization_mc.

Owens, Trevor. 2012. 'Discovery and Justification Are Different: Notes on Science-ing the Humanities'. *Trevor Owens* (blog). Retrieved 14 June 2019 from http://www.trevorowens.org/2012/11/discovery-and-justification-are-different-notes-on-sciencing-the-humanities/.

Owens, Trevor, and Rebecca Mir. 2012. 'if (!isNative())[return false]: De-Peopling Native Peoples in Sid Meiers Colonization'. *Play the Past*. Retrieved 14 June 2019 from http://www.playthepast.org/?p=2509.

———. 2013. 'Modeling Indigenous Peoples: Unpacking Ideology in Sid Meier's Colonization'. In *Playing with the Past: Digital Games and the Simulation of History*, edited by Matthew Kapell and Andrew B. R. Elliot, 91–106. London: Bloomsbury Academic.

Papagiannis, Helen. 2012. 'Augmented Reality: Future Forward'. Ontario Augmented Reality Network (OARN) Keynote, Toronto, Canada, 5 October.

Parrish, Allison. 2016. 'Programming Is Forgetting: Toward a New Hacker Ethic'. *Open Transcripts*. Retrieved 14 June 2019 from http://opentranscripts.org/transcript/programming-forgetting-new-hacker-ethic/.

Perry, Sara. 2019. 'The Enchantment of the Archaeological Record'. *European Journal of Archaeology* 22(3): 354–71. Retrieved 10 November 2019 from https://doi.org/10.1017/eaa.2019.24.

Perry, Sara, and Colleen Morgan. 2015. 'Materializing Media Archaeologies: The MAD-P Hard Drive Excavation'. *Journal of Contemporary Archaeology* 2(1): 94–104.

Phipps, Keith. 2005. 'Interview: Will Wright'. *The A. V. Club*. Retrieved 14 June 2019 from https://www.avclub.com/will-wright-1798208435.

Poerio, Giulia, Emma Blakey, Thomas Hostler and Theresa Veltri. 2018. 'More Than a Feeling: Autonomous Sensory Meridian Response (ASMR) Is Characterized by Reliable Changes in Affect and Physiology' *PLOSOne*, 13(6): e0196645. Retrieved 10 November 2019 from https://doi.org/10.1371/journal.pone.0196645.

Pratchett, Terry. 1996. *Feet of Clay*. Gollancz: London.

———. 2001. *Thief of Time*. Doubleday: New York.

———. 2004. *Going Postal*. Doubleday: New York.

Quinn, Zoe. 2013. *Depression Quest*. Game. depressionquest.com

Rahimi, Ali, and Ben Recht. 2017. 'Reflections on Random Kitchen Sinks'. *Arg min blog*. Retrieved 4 November 2019 from http://www.argmin.net/2017/12/05/kitchen-sinks/.

Ramsay, Stephen. 2010. 'Algorithms Are Thoughts, Chainsaws Are Tools.' Critical Code Studies Workshop, March 2010. Retrieved 10 July 2015 from https://vimeo.com/9790850.

———. 2014. 'The Hermeneutics of Screwing Around, or What You Do with a Million Books'. In *Pastplay: Teaching and Learning History with Technology*, edited by Kevin Kee, 111–20. Ann Arbor: University of Michigan Press.

Rauch, Jonathan. 2002. 'Seeing around Corners'. *Atlantic* 289(4): 35–46. Retrieved 14 June 2019 from https://www.theatlantic.com/magazine/archive/2002/04/seeing-around-corners/302471/.

Reinhard, Andrew. 2018. *Archaeogaming: An Introduction to Archaeology in and of Video Games*. New York: Berghahn Books.

Richardson, Lorna-Jane. 2018. 'Ethical Challenges in Digital Public Archaeology'. *Journal of Computer Applications in Archaeology* 1(1): 64–73. Retrieved 4 November 2019 from http://doi.org/10.5334/jcaa.13.

Rihll, Tracey, and Alan G. Wilson. 1991. 'Modelling Settlement Structures in Ancient Greece: New Approaches to the Polis'. In *City and Country in the Ancient World*, edited by John Rich and Andrew Wallace-Hadrill, 59–95. London: Routledge.

Risam, Roopika. 2019. *New Digital Worlds : Postcolonial Digital Humanities in Theory, Praxis, and Pedagogy*. Evanston, IL: Northwestern University Press.

Rollinger, Christian. 2015. 'Brot, Spiele . . . und Latrinen? Zur Darstellung römischer Stadträume im Computerspiel'. *THERSITES Journal for Transcultural Presences & Diachronic Identities from Antiquity to Date* 1:1–45. Retrieved 10 November 2019 from https://thersites-journal.de/index.php/thr/article/view/4.

Romanowska, Iza. 2014. 'How to Evaluate a Simulation: A Quick Guide for Non-modellers'. *Simulating Complexity*, 6 October. Retrieved 14 June 2019 from https:// simulatingcomplexity.wordpress.com/2014/10/06/how-to-evaluate-a-simulation-a-quick-guide-for-non-modellers.

———. 2015. 'So You Think You Can Model? A Guide to Building and Evaluating Archaeological Simulation Models of Dispersals'. *Human Biology* 87(3): 169–92.

Roussou, Maria, Sara Perry, Akrivi Katifori, Stavros Vassos, Angeliki Tzougana-tou and Sierra McKinney. 2019. 'Transformation through Provocation? Designing a 'Bot of Conviction' to Challenge Conceptions and Evoke Critical Reflection'. In *CHI 2019: Proceedings of the 2019 CHI Conference on Human Factors in Computing Systems, Glasgow, Scotland, 4–9 May.* Paper No. 627. New York: ACM. Retrieved 14 June 2019 from https://doi.org/10.1145/3290605.3300857.

Roy, Jessica. 2019. 'From Video Game to Day Job: How "SimCity" Inspired a Generation of City Planners'. *LA Times*, 5 March. Retrieved 23 November 2019 from https://www.latimes.com/business/technology/la-fi-tn-simcity-inspired-urban-planners-20190305-story.html.

Rubio, Xavier. Jorge Caro Saiz, Guillem H. Pongiluppi, Guillem Laborda Cabo and David Ramos Garcia. 2017. 'Explaining Archaeological Research with Video Games: The Case of Evolving Planet'. In *The Interactive Past: Archaeology, Heritage, and Video Games*, edited by Angus A. A. Mol, Csilla E. Ariese-Vandemeulebroucke, Krijn H.J. Boom and Aris Politopoulos, 153–66. Leiden: Sidestone Press.

Ruskhoff, Douglas. 2005. 'Renaissance Now! The Gamers' Perspective'. In *Handbook of Computer Game Studies*, edited by Joost Raessens and Jeffrey Goldstein, 415–22. Cambridge, MA: MIT Press.

Ryan, James. 2019. 'Curating Simulated Storyworlds'. Ph.D. thesis. University of California, Santa Cruz.

Saller, Richard. 1989. 'Patronage and Friendship in Early Imperial Rome: Drawing the Distinction'. In *Patronage in Ancient Society*, edited by Andrew Wallace-Hadrill, 49–62. London: Routledge.

Salway, Benet. 2001. 'Travel, *itineraria* and *tabellaria*'. In *Travel and Geography in the Roman Empire*, edited by Colin Adams and Ray Laurence, 22–66. London: Routledge.

Sample, Mark. 2011. 'Rebooting Counterfactual History with JFK Reloaded'. *Play the Past*. Retrieved 14 June 2019 from http://www.playthepast.org/?p=1392.

———. 2012. 'Videogames in Critical Contexts'. HNRS 353-002 (Spring 2012), George Mason University. Retrieved 14 June 2019 from http://samplereality.com/gmu/hnrs353/.

———. 2015. 'Your Mistake was a Vital Connection'. *Sample Reality*. Retrieved 14 June 2019 from https://www.samplereality.com/2015/09/05/your-mistake-was-a-vital-strategy/.

———. 2019. 'Things Are Broken More Than Once and Won't Be Fixed'. *Sample Reality*. Retrieved 4 November 2019 from http://www.samplereality.com/2019/10/16/things-are-broken-more-than-once-and-wont-be-fixed/.

Samuels, Lisa, Jerome McGann. 1999. 'Deformance and Interpretation'. *New Literary History* 30(1): 25–56. Retrieved 10 November 2019 from https://doi.org/10.1353/nlh.1999.0010.

Sauter, Disa, Frank Eisner, Andrew Calder and Sophie Scott. 2010. 'Perceptual Cues in Nonverbal Vocal Expressions of Emotion'. *Quarterly Journal of*

Experimental Psychology 63: 2251–72. Retrieved 10 November 2019 from https://doi.org/10.1080/17470211003721642.

Sayers, Jentery. 2018. 'Paper Computers'. Paper Computers: English 508, University of Victoria, 2018. Retrieved 14 June 2019 from https://jentery.github.io/508v4/.

Scheidel, Walter, and Elijah Meeks. 2012. *ORBIS: The Stanford Geospatial Network Model of the Roman World*. Retrieved 14 June 2019 from http://orbis.stanford.edu.

Schooler, Larry. 2004. 'Playing with Urban Life: How SimCity Influences Planning Culture'. *Technology & Cities* 6. Retrieved 10 November 2019 from https://www.academia.edu/1979187/Playing_with_urban_life_How_SimCity_influences_planning_culture.

Shane, Janelle. 2018. 'The Visual Chatbot'. *Aiweirdness*. Retrieved 14 June 2019 from http:// aiweirdness.com/post/175110257767/the-visual-chatbot.

Sherlock, Alexandra. 2013. 'Larger Than Life: Digital Resurrection and the Re-Enchantment of Society'. *Information Society* 29(3): 164–76. Retrieved 4 November 2019 from https://doi.org/10.1080/01972243.2013.777302.

Sicart, Miguel. 2009. *The Ethics of Computer Games*. Cambridge, MA: MIT Press.

Smith, Gavin. 2018. 'Data Doxa: The Affective Consequences of Data Practices'. *Big Data and Society* 5(1): 1–15. Retrieved 14 June 2019 from https://dx.doi.org/10.1177/2053951717751551.

Staiff, Russell. 2014. *Re-Imagining Heritage Interpretation: Enchanting the Past-Future*. Farnham, UK: Ashgate.

Stonedahl, Forrest, and Uri Wilensky. 2008. 'NetLogo Virus on a Network Model'. *NetLogo*. Center for Connected Learning and Computer-Based Modeling, Northwestern University, Evanston, IL. Retrieved from http:// ccl.northwestern.edu/netlogo/models/VirusonaNetwork.

Storey, Glenn R. 2001. 'Regionaries-Type Insulae 1: Architectural/Residential Units at Ostia'. *American Journal of Archaeology* 105(3): 389–401.

———. 2002. 'Regionaries-Type Insulae 2: Architectural/Residential Units at Rome'. *American Journal of Archaeology* 106(3): 411–34.

Strubell, Emma, Ananya Ganesh and Andrew McCallum. 2019. 'Energy and Policy Considerations for Deep Learning in NLP'. arXiv preprint arXiv:1906.02243, Cornell University. Retrieved from https://arxiv.org/abs/1906.02243.

Tringham, Ruth. 2015a. 'Creating Narratives of the Past as Recombinant Histories'. In *Subjects and Narratives in Archaeology*, edited by Ruth M. Van Dyke and Reinhard Bernbeck, 27–54. Denver: University Press of Colorado.

———. 2015b. 'Dido and the Basket: Fragments towards a Non-linear History'. In *Object Stories: Artifacts and Archaeologists*, edited by Steve Brown, Anne Clarke and Ursula Frederick, 161–68. Walnut Creek, CA: Left Coast Press.

———. 2019. 'Giving Voices (without Words) to Prehistoric People: Glimpses into an Archaeologist's Imagination'. *European Journal of Archaeology* 22(3): 338–53. Retrieved 10 November 2019 from https://doi.org/10.1017/eaa.2019.20.

Turner, Phil. 2007. 'The Intentional Basis of Presence'. In *Proceedings of the 10th Annual International Workshop on Presence, PRESENCE 2007*, edited by Laura Moreno, 127–34. Barcelona: Barcelona Starlab.

Tzouganatou, Angeliki. 2018. 'Can Heritage Bots Thrive? Toward Future Engagement in Cultural Heritage'. *Advances in Archaeological Practice* 6(4): 377–83. Retrieved 14 June 2019 from https://doi.org/10.1017/ aap.2018.32.

Underwood, Ted. 2018. 'Why an Age of Machine Learning Needs the Humanities'. *Public Books*. Retrieved 14 June 2019 from https://www.publicbooks .org/why-an-age-of-machine-learning-needs-the-humanities/.

Urrichio, William. 2005. 'Simulation, History, and Computer Games'. In *Handbook of Computer Game Studies*, edited by J. Raessens and Jeffrey Goldstein, 327–38. Cambridge, MA: MIT Press.

Urry, John. 2000. *Sociology beyond Societies: Mobilities for the Twenty-First Century*. London: Routledge.

Vig, Jesse. 2019. 'OpenAI GPT-2: Understanding Language Generation through Visualization: How the Super-Sized Language Model Is Able to Finish Your Thoughts'. *Towards Data Science*. Retrieved 4 November 2019 from https://towardsdatascience.com/openai-gpt-2-understanding-langu age-generation-through-visualization-8252f683b2f8.

Veigg, Janet. 1997. 'Ars Combinatoria'. *Art Journal* 56(3): 20–29. Retrieved 4 November 2019 from https://doi.org/10.1080/00043249.1997.10791829.

Verboven, Koenraad. 2002. *The Economy of Friends: Economic Aspects of Amicitia and Patronage in the Late Republic*. Brussels: Latomus.

Wallace-Hadrill, Andrew. 1989. 'Patronage in Roman Society: From Republic to Empire'. In *Patronage in Ancient Society*, edited by Andrew Wallace-Hadrill, 63–87. London: Routledge.

Watterson, Alice. 2015. 'Beyond Digital Dwelling: Rethinking Interpretive Visualisation in Archaeology'. *Open Archaeology* 1: 119–30. Retrieved 10 November 2019 from https://doi.org/10.1515/opar-2015-0006.

Weingart, Scott. 2011. 'Demystifying Networks, Parts I & II'. *Journal of Digital Humanities* 1(1). Retrieved 14 June 2019 from http://journalofdigitalhu manities.org/1-1/demystifying-networks-by-scott-weingart/.

———. 2014. 'Digital History, Saturn's Rings, and the Battle of Trafalgar'. *The Scottbot Irregular*. Retrieved 14 June 2019 from http://www.scottbot.net/ HIAL/?p=41109.

Wevers, Melvin, and Thomas Smits. 2018. 'Seeing History: Analyzing Large-Scale Historical Visual Datasets Using Deep Neural Networks'. *Digital Humanities Benelux Amsterdam*. Retrieved 14 June 2019 from http://2018 .dhbenelux.org/wp-content/uploads/sites/8/2018/05/Wevers_Smits_See ing_History_DHBenelux2018.pdf

———. 2019. 'The Visual Digital Turn: Using Neural Networks to Study Historical Images'. *Digital Scholarship in the Humanities*, 18 January. Retrieved 14 June 2019 from https://doi.org/10.1093/llc/fqy085.

Wilensky, Uri. 1999. *NetLogo*. Center for Connected Learning and Computer-Based Modeling, Northwestern University, Evanston, IL. http://ccl.north western.edu/net-logo/.

———. 2018a. 'Communication T-T Example, Netlogo 6.0.4 Models Library, Code Examples'. Center for Connected Learning and Computer-Based Modeling, Northwestern University, Evanston, IL.

———. 2018b. 'Link-Walking Turtles Example, Netlogo 6.0.4 Models Library, Code Examples'. Center for Connected Learning and Computer-Based Modeling, Northwestern University, Evanston, IL.

———. 2018c. 'Network Import Example, Netlogo 6.0.4 Models Library, Code Examples'. Center for Connected Learning and Computer-Based Modeling, Northwestern University, Evanston, IL.

Wilensky, Uri, and William Rand. 2015. *An Introduction to Agent-Based Modeling: Modeling Natural, Social, and Engineered Complex Systems with NetLogo*. Cambridge, MA: MIT Press.

Wilensky, Uri, and Mitchel Resnick. 1999. 'Thinking in Levels: A Dynamic Systems Approach to Making Sense of the World'. *Journal of Science Education and Technology* 8(1): 3–19.

Wilensky, Uri, and Walter Stroup. 1999. HubNet. Center for Connected Learning and Computer-Based Modeling, Northwestern University, Evanston, IL. http://ccl.northwestern.edu/netlogo/hubnet.html.

Wilson, Luc. 2014. 'Algorithms and Urbanisms: SimCity, Lbw2133@Columbia, Spring 2014'. Retrieved 14 June 2019 from http://www.columbia.edu/cu/arch/courses/facsyl/20141/28696_2014_1_Wilson%20Algorithms%20and%20Urbanisms%20SimCity.pdf.

Woolf, Greg. 1992. 'Imperialism, Empire, and the Integration of the Roman Economy'. *World Archaeology* 23: 283–93.

———. 1996. 'Monumental Writing and the Expansion of Roman Society in the Early Empire'. *Journal of Roman Studies* 86: 22–39.

———. 1998. *Becoming Roman: The Origins of Provincial Civilization in Gaul*. Cambridge: Cambridge University Press.

Woolf, Max. 2019. 'Experiments with Making Convincing AI-Generated Fake News'. *Max Woolf's Blog*. Retrieved 4 November 2019 from https://minimaxir.com/2019/09/ctrl-fake-news/.

Wurzer, Gabriel, Kerstin Kowarik and Hans Reschreiter, eds. 2015. *Agent-Based Modeling and Simulation in Archaeology*. Vienna: Springer.

Wylie, Alison. 1989. 'Archaeological Cables and Tacking: The Implications of Practice for Bernstein's Options beyond Objectivism and Relativism'. *Philosophy of the Social Sciences* 19(1): 1–18. Retrieved 14 June 2019 from https://doi.org/10.1177/004839318901900101.

———. 2002. *Thinking from Things: Essays in the Philosophy of Archaeology*. Berkeley: University of California Press.

Index

www.ingramcontent.com/pod-product-compliance
Lightning Source LLC
Chambersburg PA
CBHW070927030426
42336CB00014BA/2568